Railroading Economics

Railroading Economics
The Creation of the Free Market Mythology

Michael Perelman

Monthly Review Press
New York

Library of Congress Cataloging-in-Publication Data

Perelman, Michael.
    Railroading economics: the creation of the free market mythology / Michael Perelman.
        p. cm.
        Includes bibliographical references and index.
        ISBN 1-58367-135-8 (pbk.) — ISBN 1-58367-136-6 (cloth)

1. Economics—History. 2. Economic history. 3. Economics. I. Title.
    HB87.P348 2006
    330.12'2—dc22
        2005036708

Designed by Terry J. Allen

Monthly Review Press
122 West 27th Street
New York, NY 10001

www.monthlyreview.org

10 9 8 7 6 5 4 3 2 1

Contents

Introduction

Setting the Stage

The title of this book, *Railroading Economics*, has multiple meanings. The verb "railroading" refers to the ideological straitjacket of modern economics, which teaches that the market is the solution for all social and economic problems. The adjective "railroading" refers to the experience of economists during the late nineteenth century when the largest industry in the country, railroading, was experiencing terrible upheavals. Many of the leading economists at the time came to grips with the destructive nature of market forces. Competition, which according to conventional economics, is supposed to guide business to make decisions that will benefit everybody, was driving business into bankruptcy and common people into poverty.

This lesson was never allowed to take hold among economists. In fact, the same economists continue to teach their students that markets work in perfect harmony, while they advised policymakers to take quick action to put the brakes on competition. In effect, the railroad economists railroaded economics into perpetuating a free market mythology.

I first explored this subject in *The End of Economics*. This work is a detailed revision of that book.

In this book, I will take issue with conventional economic thinking by using the experience of the railroad economists and other episodes in economic history. I am convinced that an objective analysis of the destructive nature of markets can contribute to setting the economy on the right track.

Confessions of a Lapsed Economist

Let me begin with a frank confession. I am an economist. At least, one major institution has conferred a degree on me that certifies me as an economist.

Despite my credentials, I am a lapsed economist. Yes, I still teach in an economics department, but I can no longer accept the validity of prevailing economic orthodoxy.

I do not claim to be unique in my fall from grace. A small minority of economists always does depart from the orthodox doctrine. A select few of these, as we shall see, sometimes even win the accolades of the economics profession.

Some of those who stray from the path of economic orthodoxy do so for ethical or aesthetic reasons. Others reject key articles of faith because they find technical defects in the analytical machinery of conventional economics. I count myself among this group.

I am by no means the first economist to discover a defect in orthodox economic theory. In the late nineteenth century, a group of economists, who were then considered among the premier practitioners of the discipline in their respective nations, developed a penetrating critique of economic theory. They realized that a modern economy that followed the recommendations of conventional economic theory would court disaster.

These economists did not come by their discovery while hermetically sealed in ivory towers. Instead, they were the sort of economists who worked closely with government and business leaders. Although they were very conservative, they saw market forces tearing industry apart. In order to prevent the economy from disintegrating, they recommended that the great industries of the day be permitted to form trusts, cartels, and monopolies.

Although the vast majority of contemporary economists are unaware of the work of these economists, their ideas still have significant relevance. My intention is to draw attention to and to rehabilitate this largely forgotten economic tradition, in part to call attention to a major defect in conventional economic theory.

The Conservative Rejection of Market Economics

During the late nineteenth and early twentieth centuries, the leading economists in the United States closely followed the railroad industry. Although conventional economic theory would lead one to expect competition to make railroads healthy, these economists realized that competition was wreaking havoc in the railroad industry. By 1893, one-third of the railroads had already fallen into receivership.

Given the experience of the railroads, these economists came to fear the disruptive results of market forces. They became contemptuous of the simplistic economic theories that claimed to justify market forces. In the process, these conservative railroad economists railed against pure market forces with rhetorical flourishes worthy of the Marxian left. Yet these same economists led the way in developing technical explanations of why markets could work perfectly.

While these economists agreed with the Marxists about the deficiencies both of the market and the conventional economic theories of the market, they were not leftists at all. They reached their conclusions by looking at the market from the perspective of business rather than labor.

Rather than calling for a socialist revolution, these economists recommended that large corporations be allowed to protect themselves against excessive competition by forming trusts, cartels, or monopolies. They envisioned something more or less similar to the modern Japanese organization of industry.

The Forgotten Tradition of Railroad Economics

The time has now come to turn the pages of history back to these conservative thinkers of a century ago to rediscover the critical element of their theory, which has since fallen into oblivion.

These early railroad economists centered their critique of economic theory on one particular assumption that was absolutely unwarranted for the railroad industry. Conventional economic theory assumes that investors can easily undo mistaken investments.

Unlike the assumed world of conventional economic theory, the railroads required significant sunk costs. Laying railway track requires an enormous investment. If that investment is misplaced, the railway cannot convert the track into computers or trendy boutiques without cost. That investment is irrevocably lost, except for what the railroad can earn from salvaging it. Salvage values are generally trivial compared to the initial cost of the investment.

As we shall see in Chapter 1, conventional economics teaches that when competition is strong enough, business must set prices equal to the cost of producing one more unit of output. When prices are set in this fashion, the economy supposedly produces an optimal outcome. Unfortunately, this theory works only when investments can move costlessly in and out of industries, that is, when industry has few sunk costs.

Of course, this conventional economic theory made no sense for the railroads, which had enormous investments in fixed capital. The railroad economists realized that the failure to address the complications that sunk costs pose for economic theory made conventional economics absolutely unrealistic for other industries as well as for railroads. For this reason, they rejected the central idea of conventional economics, which holds that strong competition results in ideal outcomes.

We need not blindly follow these economists. In fact, they were not even consistent in following themselves. Despite their strong reservations about the efficiency of market forces and their contempt for simplistic economic theory as a guide to practical economic questions, these same economists wrote economic textbooks extolling the virtues of unfettered markets for reasons that we will discuss later.

The legacy of the railroad economists is mixed. The economics profession continued to follow one tradition of the railroad economists, teaching its students that markets were the most efficient method of organizing a society. At the same time, later economists quickly forgot the valuable insights of the railroad economists concerning the reasons to be leery of markets.

The End of Laissez Faire

In 1926, John Maynard Keynes, perhaps the most influential economist of the twentieth century, wrote an essay entitled "The End of Laissez Faire."[2] About the same time, Keynes, working within the British textile industry, had come to conclusions strikingly similar to the railroad economists in the United States.

Although Keynes rebelled against the conventions of economic thought, he always remained fiercely loyal to the culture of his elite stratum of British society. In this article, Keynes exuded his upbringing, expressing a snobbish contempt for both the deficiencies of a market economy as well as the Bolshevik model that was evolving in the Soviet Union.

Keynes proposed that the values of the well-bred elite would eventually conquer the corporate boardrooms. As a result, the single-minded lust for profits common to the rough-and-tumble world of business was destined to give way to a more public-spirited perspective—at least within the large corporations. Over time, Keynes maintained, the behavior of the large corporations would become indistinguishable from those of universities or other public institutions. In this way, Keynes believed that capitalism could transcend the shortcomings of the market while avoiding the turmoil of a revolution.

Far-fetched as Keynes's vision might sound today, he did not create this theory out of whole cloth. Later, we shall see that many prominent corporate leaders at the time, recognizing the same defects of the market that preoccupied the railroad economists, proclaimed their allegiance to what eventually became known as welfare capitalism—a self-imposed code of public-spirited corporate behavior that flourished in the 1920s, at least, until the Great Depression forced them to abandon any pretense to higher motives.

Emotional Investment in the Imaginary World of Perfect Competition

The railroad economists believed that conventional economics was a restrictive theory, relevant for a special kind of capitalism—the capitalism of perfect competition. We may justly compare this ideal vision of a perfectly competitive capitalism to a unicorn. We all know what it is supposed to look like, although none of us have ever seen it.

Many people express an irrational attachment to this imaginary world of perfect competition. Political and business leaders commonly extol the virtues of this ideal of capitalism with great eloquence, often equating it with morality. Among the general public, many people would willingly go to war—or at least send our young people to war—to protect the sanctity of the capitalist way of life.

Yes, our current economy does bear some passing resemblance to pure capitalism, in the sense that we presently give owners of business a great deal of discretion. Nonetheless, no existing capitalist economy leaves business to its own devices. Instead, government provides enormous supports to keep business from suffering the same fate as the insolvent railroads.

Indeed, much of the dissatisfaction with our present-day economy concerns the numerous departures from the market-based rules. People from all parts of the political spectrum have taken issue with substantial violations of market rules, implicitly assuming that the market, left to itself, would produce a result that would be both fairer and more efficient.

On the right, innumerable commentators vehemently oppose what they consider to be unwarranted government intrusion. They contend that such actions are motivated either by the misguided agendas of the regulators or by the unwarranted influence of special interests. Often they portray the government as socialistic, especially when it comes to the aid of the less fortunate members of society.

Many, but certainly not all people on the left, have made a similar case, although they differ from their more conservative brethren by identifying big business interests, rather than the poor or government bureaucrats, as the major recipients of government largesse. Like the conservatives, they often refer to our present system as socialism, but with an ironic turn of the phrase: they proclaim our existing society as socialism for the rich.

Both critiques of government programs, from the left and the right, single out specific programs as unfair or unjustified. Neither acknowledges that the capitalist system necessarily requires a considerable amount of control.

Business and Laissez Faire

Among those who have their hands on the levers of power, only a distinct minority sincerely believes in the glib slogans of free-wheeling capitalism. Indeed, rant and rail as they might about the abuses of government, more knowledgeable political and business leaders rarely believe their own rhetoric. Their obligatory lip service to the magic of the marketplace is nothing more than a hypocritical attempt to further their own interests.

Certainly, business should have a deep appreciation for the wide range of services that the government performs for them. Not only does the government provide a substantial market for the goods that private business sells, the government also goes to great lengths in an effort to create a "healthy business climate."

The government organizes and regulates financial conditions through central banks, as well as through protective legislation. It creates a legal structure that gives business the upper hand relative to labor. When the economy falters, it increases demand, often by discovering imaginary threats that require more military spending.

In this regard, we will see in later chapters that government and business alike have conspired to thwart market forces throughout most of the history of the United States. Some might mistakenly regard these actions as nothing more than those of an evil cabal. Of course, self-interest was an important motivator, but those who were most attuned to the economic conditions also realized that the failure of the government to intervene could unleash the destructive potential of market forces.

In short, deep down, most political and business leaders are keenly aware that market forces, without any outside guidance, can and often will produce catastrophic results. As a result, they are unwilling to trust the fate of society, or even business itself, to market processes alone.

In this sense, pure capitalism differs from the unicorn. Although unicorns are merely imaginary creatures, no logical reasons preclude their existence. In contrast, as I will show in this book, pure capitalism suffers from such severe internal contradictions that it could never survive on its own—at least in a world with long-lived capital goods.

The Unsteady Support for a Competitive Economy

Business rejection of laissez faire is a long-standing phenomenon in the United States. Faith in competition outside of the economics classroom remained weak in the United States, even after the influence of the railroad economists had waned. During the First World War, the success of wartime planning lent prestige to the belief that the government could control economic conditions. Although the Coolidge administration symbolized a renewed faith in market forces, Coolidge's influential secretary of commerce, Herbert Hoover, was an ever-present advocate of corporate cooperation as an alternative to competition.

The Great Depression, coupled with the success of economic planning during the Second World War, dealt a severe blow to the superstition that competition would guarantee the best of all possible worlds. Although the rise of the Soviet economy eventually made overt support for direct economic planning politically suspect, the avoidance of a serious depression during the first postwar decades left economists overly confident about the ability of the government to control the level of overall economic activity through monetary and fiscal policy, at least until stagnation set in during the late 1960s.

Given the unsatisfactory economic performance of the next decade, the stage was set for a brief revival of faith in competitive forces. Since economic planners took excessive credit for the extraordinary success of the early decades of the postwar period, they had to accept inordinate blame for the economic disappointments of the 1970s.

In its rejection of economic planning, the country naively embraced the free market message of Ronald Reagan. Unfortunately, the magic of the market did not create the general prosperity that the proponents of free markets promised. The mixed economic performance of the Reagan years set the stage for a period of renewed dissatisfaction with the market.

Although the Clinton presidential campaign brilliantly tapped into this sentiment, the Clinton administration failed miserably by refusing to offer a coherent program for reinvigorating the economy. In the wake of this failure of the Clinton administration, disappointment has given way to a combination of cynicism and irrational anger.

In this intellectual and political vacuum, greater claims are now made for market forces than ever before in our history. Supposedly, market forces can resolve all our ills. Privatize the schools. Privatize the libraries. Privatize the roads. Privatize the prisons. Even the military has undergone significant privatization.

With the steady decline in our public sector, profit-minded corporations continually extend their influence. We watch while major corporations are beginning to run more of our hospitals, schools, and even prisons, all the while imposing their values on these institutions.

The yawning gap between rich and poor continues to expand. Not surprisingly, public dissatisfaction runs high. Many of the ills of our society are the logical result of leaving our fate to the workings of markets.

Even so, relatively few people now question markets as such. Many will become incensed at the company that supplies their gas or electric utilities, or the bank that charges too much for a bounced check or the insurance company that denies them health care. Moreover, periodic recessions cause great suffering, especially to the most vulnerable in society. But still, this discontent rarely extends to the tyranny of the market system itself.

Economics, as it is taught in our great universities, is structured in such a way that it cannot address this or other significant problems with markets. I do not pretend to offer some simple crackpot reform that will magically solve all economic problems.

Instead, I intend to expose economics as a pseudo-science that stands in the way of human betterment in the hope that we can develop new practices and better institutions that will allow us to manage our lives in a more satisfactory manner.

I do not believe that the end of economics signals a time of suffering and hardship. No! On the contrary, the end of economics foreshadows a welcome revolution in our lives. Factories will continue to churn out products that will sustain and enrich our lives, but we will radically alter the way in which we decide when or how to invest in new factories, offices, or stores. I also look forward to a time when we will also be able to run these operations in a superior fashion.

I realize that my perspective runs against the grain of the prevailing view about the nature of the economy. I can only ask that you hear me out.

After Economics

The realization that market forces were destructive was central to the work of the early railroad economists. They insisted that in a modern economy, pure market economics just will not work. They accepted that markets may have been appropriate for an earlier age, but they were convinced that a modern, industrialized economy requires a new perspective.

Even though our current economy bears even less resemblance to a world of perfect competition than it did in the heyday of the railroad economists, contemporary economists more than ever stubbornly adhere to the simplistic theory of competition. Because of the powerful hold of their abstract theory, most modern economists lack the business leaders' practical understanding of the destructive nature of pure competition or the theoretical insights of the railroad economists.

Common sense alone reveals the essential problem that economic theory ignores. Just imagine what would become of a firm that develops computer software or a new pharmaceutical if its product were priced at the cost of making another copy of its program! Bankruptcy would be certain. I will explain the logic behind this phenomenon in more detail later.

To prevent such bankruptcy, we grant developers of software or pharmaceuticals protection through copyrights or patents, which limit competition. Because of the longstanding use of these monopolistic arrangements, we readily accept that they are consistent with the principles of free competition. In fact, they are not.

More and more, the existence of sunk costs makes industry resemble a software industry without the protection of copyrights or patents. For example, airline bankruptcies have become almost commonplace. Like the railroads of the nineteenth century or the software developer of the twentieth, an airline commits an enormous investment in an industry where the cost of servicing each additional customer is minimal. As competition drives prices down, the firm becomes unable to meet its financial commitments.

Economic theory as it stands today is irrelevant to understanding this process. Economists may employ scientific tools, such as mathematics and statistics, but they apply them in a context that is questionable at best. Economics purports to be scientific because it grounds its ideology on a rigorous theoretical foundation, but this foundation rests on wildly unrealistic assumptions.

This pretense of rigor is more than a harmless eccentricity. Economics provides an ideological justification for atavistic methods of providing for our economic and social needs. It leads to economic practices that create great harm to both people and the environment.

In questioning the workings of a market economy, I do not deny that markets can and do inspire people to enormous creativity. I am convinced that other forms of incentives also lend themselves to even more creative responses. Nor do I deny the enormous economic achievements of the U.S. economy. I contend that much of this success resulted *in spite of* market forces.

We need to develop a new way of conceiving of the economic process. In calling for an end of economics, I am not suggesting that we should dismiss everything that economists have learned about the economy. Some economic insights are useful. Our goal should be to build up an understanding of the economy in a context that transcends the narrow context of economic theory that characterizes modern economic theory. In doing so, we may lay the groundwork for an economy that transcends our outmoded capitalist way of life.

The Framework of This Book

This book will, for the most part, leave aside the social, cultural, and moral deficiencies of the market. Instead, it will concentrate on the way that market economies frequently careen out of control when competition becomes too strong.

I will describe how, beginning in the late nineteenth century, conservative leaders from government, business, and academia rejected market principles because of the instability that competition engenders. I do not intend to convey the impression that the conservative critique of the market is more legitimate than the radical critique. On the contrary, the conservative critique was a limited, partial critique of the market. It was still a powerful critique, which has two implications.

First, at this moment, the conservatives have succeeded in framing most political and economic debates in the corporate media. In its present form, markets can do no wrong, except when they deliver products that conservatives find objectionable, such as films with too much violence. Absent from this debate is any acknowledgment that markets can self-destruct.

In part, markets have not recently shown the full force of their destructive side because of the controls that conservative interests have succeeded in imposing on markets. So far, the continual paring down of these controls has been attractive to business because it opens up new opportunities for profit. I offer this book as a warning of the folly of excessive trust in market forces.

Second, since this critique came from conservative advocates of a business society, in some circles at least, it may have more legitimacy than it would coming from leftist opponents of capitalism. Since conservative economists were able to see the deficiency in conventional economics so clearly, perhaps they might help modern economists to abandon economics as we know it.

The end of laissez faire will not magically evolve as Keynes had dreamed. It will require hard work. With conventional economics put aside, perhaps we can begin with the job of restructuring economic thought in a way that will contribute to the development of a society that transcends the problems of a market society.

Finally, I confess that I found myself drawn to analyzing the history of markets in the United States from this perspective because this material personally fascinated me. I hope that you enjoy this brief encounter with an obscure side of the U.S. economy as much as I have.

Overview

The bulk of this book recounts the history of the U.S. economy in terms of the development of this conservative critique of the market and its eventual abandonment. I will begin with a brief overview of the nature of conventional economic theory. I will also discuss the training of economists in order to show why most economists today are incapable of recognizing the central theoretical defect of conventional economics, which figured so importantly among the economists of a century ago.

Chapter 1 begins with an analysis of the conventional theory, which economists have cleverly devised to demonstrate the efficiency of markets. We will see that this conventional economic theory, although it purports to be a theory of profit-driven capitalism, lacks an adequate theory for either profit or capital. Instead, it has ignored every feature of capitalism that would allow for a realistic theory of either profits or capital.

One major gap in conventional economic theory is the absence of any theory that addresses the role of long-lived fixed capital. Instead, conventional economic theory treats investment behavior as if the economic problem were similar to a game of poker.

Each agent is dealt a hand. Players will make decisions based on the cards that they might hold. Once the hand is over, the dealer reshuffles the cards and the game begins anew. With long-lived fixed capital goods, agents' decisions today will have unknown ramifications in the future. Because of the risks associated with an uncertain future, rational investors display a reluctance to sink their funds into long-lived fixed capital investments.

Chapter 2 analyzes the implications of the reluctance to invest in long-lived capital goods and the forces that overcome that reluctance. This chapter identifies two such forces: first, the government can take actions to minimize investor risk; second, investors' overly optimistic evaluations of their prospects.

Chapter 3 describes the historical increase in fixed capital, as well as the economic theories that U.S. economists developed to cope with the problem of fixed capital. This chapter first describes the role of irrational expectations in the overinvestment in the U.S. railroad industry.

Based on their analysis of the railroad industry, a good number of prominent economists in the late nineteenth and early twentieth centuries, including some of the most vigorous defenders of capitalism, came to the conclusion that markets were incapable of determining the appropriate level of investment. Even John Bates Clark, the doyen of laissez-faire economists, counted himself among these opponents of competitive capitalism.

These corporatist economists realized that the price system would be especially destructive in industries where firms have large fixed costs relative to the price of their product. Under such conditions, competition will drive prices down below the level at which business can earn a profit, threatening widespread bankruptcy and economic chaos.

Even though these economists taught their students to believe in the efficiency of laissez-faire theory, they never really believed their own theories. They realized that the theory of capitalism is incompatible with the very existence of modern capital. Instead, the development of modern technology and the associated social relations combine to make market-based behavior work to the detriment of capital as well as society as a whole.

These early economists understood that if pure capitalism did exist, it would be inappropriate for a modern economy. Pure capitalism might be capable of organizing an economy of village artisans working with primitive tools, but it could never work in an economy built around sophisticated, modern technologies.

Because these nineteenth century economists recognized this defect in the market economy, they consistently promoted policy recommendations that violated the central tenets of their own economic theories. Specifically, because these economists mistrusted the practical implications of the same competitive forces that they praised in theory, more often than not, they sided with trusts, cartels, and monopolies. These economists believed that these consolidated enterprises would prove to be both efficient and socially responsible.

Chapter 4 concerns the financial side of the railroad industry, when financiers, led by J. P. Morgan, carried out the vision of the railroad economists, reorganizing the railroads. Soon thereafter, they consolidated major industrial sectors for the same reason. We will see that J. P. Morgan, who ruled this world, was no more a friend of the market than the corporatist economists. Instead, Morgan devised corporate reorganizations to increase economic rationality by protecting industry from the ravages of competitive pressures.

Chapter 5 analyzes the brief period between the First World War and the Great Depression. At the time, many business and political leaders advocated a new alternative to the market. They contended that businesses should not merely compete head on. They preferred that businesses rationalize operations by joining together in trade associations to develop standards and determine prices. Herbert Hoover, often incorrectly depicted as an obtuse advocate of laissez faire, personified this approach.

This behavior was supposed to be in the public interest. In fact, some of the great consolidated enterprises adopted a relatively progressive approach toward labor. This strategy, known as welfare capitalism, was an effort to increase productive efficiency.

Chapter 6 discusses finance in the period after the First World War and Morgan's death. So long as Morgan had restrained his greed, business leaders calculated that they had more to gain by letting Morgan reorganize their industry than by attempting to maintain their firms' independence. Eventually, more rapacious financiers began to loot the industries they reorganized, dissipating the potential efficiencies from the new arrangement.

Moreover, financial enterprises vigorously competed with each other to sell stocks and bonds to the willing public. Business, believing itself to be insulated from competitive pressures, took advantage of this situation, and floated significant amounts of stocks and bonds, leaving the financial structure in an increasingly fragile state.

Chapter 7 centers on the Great Depression. It discusses the initial attempts of the welfare capitalists to stem the Depression. For example, they abstained from radical wage cuts until the fall of 1931. It also describes the eventual collapse of welfare capitalism under the growing weight of the Depression.

Chapter 8 describes the growing power of finance and the waning of industry in the postwar U.S. economy.

1

The End of Economics

What Is an Economist?

What is an economist? We could say that an economist is a person who studies economies, but that answer leaves us with an even more difficult question: What is an economy?

We have all seen stores, farms, factories, and banks, as well as workers, employers, and government personnel. They would all seem to be part of an economy, but so too is a nursing mother who is rearing a child of the next generation of workers. Schools, churches, and neighbors also help to shape the way people work. They may affect workers' productivity just as surely as machines do. By the same token, an influence as nebulous as culture in general is a major economic force, even when it is not sold in the form of commodities, such as movies or recorded music. In short, we are hard pressed to find anything that we can exclude from the economy out of hand. This line of reasoning leads to the conclusion that the economy is an all-encompassing subject.

Few economists would feel comfortable describing themselves as experts in the broad field of life in general. If any economists would be foolhardy enough to present themselves in that fashion, they would appear pretentious, if not ridiculous, to the world.

Instead, we economists use the word "economy" in a far more narrow sense, implicitly confining our definition to matters within the business side of life. Luckily, few people will flinch at this use of the term "economy" accepting the term without realizing how vague it really is. Consequently, we can bandy the term "economics" about with an air of breezy confidence, even though nobody can define just what constitutes the business side of life.

The economy is a short-hand expression for a partial view of the world. Sometimes, these partial views—what we may call "abstractions"—serve us well. An abstraction is like a map—a simplification of the terrain that helps us navigate. A map that contained every detail of the land would not be very useful. Such a map might have to be even bigger than the land it is meant to describe.

A simple street map gives us enough information that people can see how to get to their destinations without extraneous detail. Like the street map, abstractions simplify the world around us so that we can feel confident that we can make reasonable decisions. We can refine our definition by adding that economists generally view the world through highly abstract, artificial models of the world that emphasize those parts of our world that are bought and sold.

Now let us return to our initial question: What is an economist? Here is my best definition: An economist is a person trained to look at the world in a particular way.

Abstractions simplify analysis by emphasizing some information and ignoring other supposedly less relevant information. For example, street maps do not usually tell us the color of houses or the mix of vegetation along the way. In the case of a street map, this practice is not controversial.

In economics, by contrast, these simplifications have important implications. For example, economics typically treats everybody alike, even when differences are crucial. In a capitalist economy, the role of the capitalist is not the same as that of a worker. But to ignore that difference is to miss something important about the way the economy works.

Economic models generally serve to teach us a single lesson: that society needs to do very little to improve our lot, except to make sure that government gets out of the way of businesses in their intensive search for profits. These models warn us that almost all reforms, except the elimination of taxation and regulation, are dangerous experiments that put our world at peril.

Alas, our prevailing economic theories reflect an economy that no longer exists, if it ever existed at all. Economists originally developed their models to capture the reality of a simple society with relatively simple methods of production—a world of artisans and craft workers, rather than a world of high technology and rapidly evolving international financial markets. These models may have had a good deal of merit before the American Revolutionary War, when Adam Smith was composing his *Wealth of Nations*.

These models may have helped Smith's contemporaries to understand simple economic ideas, such as supply and demand, but the basic model of the economy has changed little since then. Today, in the context of a modern economy, these same models have little relevance. Instead of revealing essential features of the economy, they actually blind us to important economic forces. I will show in this book why we have reached the point where we must abandon much of our thinking about the economy. In fact, both economics and the economy are at an impasse. Unless we change our ways soon, matters will become even worse.

As long as the prevailing, conventional economic theory obscures new opportunities and new ways of working and of living, it represents a threat. In this spirit, this book calls for an end of economics and the opening to a new, more rational way of organizing our material life.

Sociology of Economics
A Brief History of the Concept of Economics

On a purely theoretical level, the call for an end of economics is not particularly revolutionary. After all, the term "economics" itself is a relatively new term, coined in the late nineteenth century.

Previously, people who theorized about the economy called themselves "political economists." The elimination of the word "political" was not trivial. In fact, it seemed to be a matter of great importance at the time to those who were intent on renaming the subject.

Toward the end of the late nineteenth century, academic political economists were concerned that anybody who voiced a position about the economy could deem herself or himself to be a political economist. This problem seemed especially urgent at the time because the works of Karl Marx were attracting many workers around the world.

As a result, a group of academic political economists, led by Alfred Marshall of Cambridge University, went to great lengths to reconstitute their subject as economics. Marshall was not the first economist to use the term "economics" in the title of a major treatise. Forgotten authors of lesser-known works at the time, such as J. M. Sturtevant (1877) and H. D. Macleod (1878), had preceded him in this respect.[1] However, nobody matched Marshall's obsession with reconstituting the subject as a science.

Marshall resented that anybody could pretend to be competent to carry on a conversation about political economy. This resentment came to a head in 1869. In that year, William Gladstone, by virtue of his position as Prime Minister, appointed Sir John Robert Seeley to the Regius Professorship in Modern History at Cambridge. Seeley, who emphasized the policy role of the chair, was convinced that political economy fell within the scope of his subject.[2] Marshall was offended that a mere historian could aspire to speak about weighty matters of political economy. Renaming the discipline "economics" might help to bar people such as Seeley from meddling in economic controversies. Once political economy took on more scientific pretensions, only those people who had undergone formal training in economics would be deemed to be qualified to participate in debates over economic questions.

Marshall and his wife, writing in their *Economics of Industry*, explained that they thought it better to drop "political" since "political interests generally mean the interest of some part or parts of the nation" rather than the nation as a whole.[3] This stance allowed economists to dismiss anyone who questioned their objectivity as being mistaken or representing some nefarious special interest.

Marshall's interpretation of the notion of political economy is misleading in two respects. To begin with, the term "political economy" had actually been intended to assert a community of interests. Indeed, the term "economy" without the modifier "political" had originally referred to parochial self-interest.

Before people began to write on political economy, an extensive body of writing had developed on the subject of managing the economy of large feudal estates.[4] The early political economists consciously appended the word "political" to suggest a broad extension of the idea of economy. Whereas economy had previously concerned only the rational management of a private household, the early political economists widened the scope of economy to the polis—the community as a whole. Just as the early manuals could instruct estate managers how to get the most production out of their land, political economy was intended to guide national leaders in ruling their dominions.

The Role of Interests in Political Economy

In the age of classical political economy, say from Adam Smith's *Wealth of Nations* (1776) until around 1830, political economists generally ceased to view the economy from the perspective of the crown. Instead, they sided with the rising middle class. Accordingly, the emphasis in political economy shifted.[5] The leading political economists, such as Smith and David Ricardo, called for political changes that would make the economy conform to the norms of the market, what economists called "laissez faire."[6]

Since the rules of laissez faire required sacrifices from both the aristocracy and the poor to accommodate the rising business class, clashing interests within the economy began to play an increasingly important role within classical political economy. The classical political economists condemned the aristocracy, who defended their existing privileges, impeding the freedom of business. They were also critical when the poor demanded improvements in their living conditions.

Although the classical political economists advocated measures that would primarily benefit the well-to-do commercial and manufacturing interests, they still maintained that their recommendations were in the best interest of society. They argued that the interests of the rising business community somehow coincided with the interests of society as a whole.

Not everybody accepted that classical political economy was as disinterested as its practitioners maintained. For example, Karl Marx's *Capital*, published in 1867, forcefully argued that classical political economy callously took the side of employers vis-à-vis labor.[7] Marx brilliantly showed how the analysis of classical political economy, built around the analysis of production, could be turned to demonstrate how employers exploited their workers.

Although most professional economists rejected Marx's contention, they were troubled by the widespread acceptance of his ideas among leaders of the working classes. As a result, many economists felt a need to recast economics as a science of exchange rather than production. Around 1870, the founders of this new brand of theory, William Stanley Jevons, Leon Walras, and Karl Menger, published their respective masterworks.[8] The first two of this trio, who presented their work in abstract mathematical form, were far more influential.

This new emphasis on the mathematical modeling of exchange had several appeals. By stressing the formal mathematics of exchange relationships, economists could take a more scientific posture. Although political economists could hardly pretend to have a monopoly on the analysis of production, no other discipline could claim to be a science of exchange. Moreover, analysis of the economy from the perspective of exchange seemed to be relatively effective in obscuring conflict. Both parties must benefit from voluntary exchange; otherwise the exchange would never have occurred in the first place.

Marshall already displayed an acute concern with unruly labor when he first began to lecture on economics. His rechristening of political economy as economics reaffirmed the change in emphasis from production to exchange. In this new form of economics, capitalists and workers alike no longer appeared as members of distinct classes, but as part of a homogeneous group of individuals. Whether the "individual" is Wal-Mart selling toilet paper or a worker selling labor makes little difference.

Exchange rather than work is central to this story. Workers mostly function as consumers, who enjoy the fruits of a growing economy. This emphasis succeeds in removing all traces of conflict from the happy fable. Each of these "individuals" engages in impersonal exchanges in which both parties benefit. Within this framework, the economy grows and everybody prospers.

Certainly, Marshall clearly understood the stakes in the new terminology. He seems to have been attracted to H. D. Macleod's approach in using the term "economics" in the latter's "What Is Political Economy" (1875) specifically because it succeeded in forcefully linking the science of economics with exchange rather than production, where the appearance of conflict was more likely.[9] Presumably, Marshall expected that his readers would join him in accepting economics as an objective science, capable of representing the interests of society as a whole.

The new terminology had other appeals. Economists had long considered physics to be the premier science. The seemingly more scientific term "economics" was intended to sound scientific—like physics. More important, by claiming to be objective scientists, economists could presume to be above politics. Those who disagreed with the economist's conclusions could be dismissed as being merely political. For example, Joseph Schumpeter wrote, political economy had become, in the eyes of orthodox practitioners of economics, "economic policies that its author advocates [on a nonscientific basis—Author] on the strength of certain unifying (normative) principles."[10]

Now with his successful challenge to the pretensions of political economy, Marshall sought to lay claim for a scientific basis of economics with an eye to winning support for his own preferred policies. This new science of economics was intended to prove that the interests of capitalists as a whole (as distinguished from individual capitalists) are in harmony with the best interests of society.

The community of academic political economists enthusiastically embraced the Marshalls' terminology. For example, in the second edition of his *Theory of Political Economy*, published in the same year as the Marshalls' work, Jevons felt the need to apologize for the title of his book.[11]

Those who continued to describe their work as political economy in later years tended to do so to underline the overtly political objective of their work.[12] In response, professional economists condemned such works as unscientific. Political economy was hereafter written off as the arena of heretics, cranks, and malcontents.

Economics as a Science

Over time, professionalization of economics took on a momentum of its own with less than desirable results. Economists adopted a false air of objectivity and impartiality. They pretended that their scientific analysis allowed them to represent the best interests of society.

The idea that economics could be an objective science is rather ironic to say the least. Although economics is based on the assumption of people acting in their own self-interest, economists, even those with wildly partisan or even mercenary intentions, invariably deny that self-interest could color their own work. Instead, they pride themselves on their own scientific objectivity. As George Stigler, himself a Nobel Prize–winning economist, noted:

...economists do not relish an explanation of their own scientific behavior in ordinary economic terms. To tell an economist that he chooses that type of work and viewpoint which will maximize his income is, he will hotly say, is [sic] a studied insult.[13]

Of course, economics is not a science at all. Chemists or physicists can create controlled experiments to analyze their materials. Economists have little or no opportunity for controlled experiments. Instead, economists merely perform thought experiments on data that they find at hand. These thought experiments can range from the commonplace to the highly abstract.

In the early years of economic theory, these commonplace experiments generally yielded about the same conclusions as common sense. In more recent times economists have discovered more and more ingenious methods for validating their preconceived preferences in economic policy. In recent years, economists have engaged in a headlong rush to develop justifications for expanding the frontier of market relations to new and uncharted areas, such as the purchase and sale of babies or human organs.

The highly abstract model of economics, which girds this theory, depends on a number of unrealistic assumptions. Typically, we have no way of knowing whether or not any particular model provides a guide to economic policy that improves on common sense because of the enormous gap between conditions in the real world and the unworldly assumptions made in constructing the model.

What then has economics accomplished? At times, economists have helped to root out logical errors in our commonsense thinking about the economy. In this sense they do a great service. But for the most part, such contributions are challenges to those who rely on abstract economic models. For example, John Maynard Keynes was able to demonstrate that the common remedy of reducing wages that economists proposed to eliminate unemployment would actually make things worse.[14]

More frequently, economists have propagated errors of their own, which have been codified in disastrous public policies. For example during the Reagan era, a number of influential economists developed models to show huge tax cuts could generate so much extra economic activity that total tax revenues would increase. Conservative politicians grabbed on to this idea, passing tax cuts that created huge budget deficits rather than increased economic activity. I should mention that this outcome did not displease the conservatives because the deficits gave them an excuse for cutting valuable social and regulatory programs.

Economic models also promised the deregulation of electricity would provide benefits for consumers. When electricity prices skyrocketed, some economists explained that the problem was that deregulation had not gone far enough. Undeterred by such disasters, economist continued to pretend that their work was scientific.

Economic Rhetoric

Rather than seeing economics as a science, we would do better to look at economics from an altogether different perspective. Despite its admittedly impressive scientific apparatus, deep down, economics consists of a collection of stories about how the economy works.[15]

In this context, economists measure their success by one of two paths. First of all, they win professional respect by developing ever more sophisticated techniques for telling their stories, such as new mathematical theorems or novel statistical procedures. The realism of the story is of secondary importance. This path puts a premium on technical virtuosity for its own sake.

Although this technical virtuosity resembles science, it is very different. For example, Lawrence Summers, whose career path includes a tenured chair at Harvard, chief economist at the World Bank, secretary of the treasury, and president of Harvard, has charged that elegant statistical demonstrations have never succeeded in convincing the community of economists of anything except the skill of the practitioner.[16]

The second path to professional status depends upon an ability to craft a new story or a variant of an old one. These altered stories must be capable of convincing other economists to revise their understanding of some feature of the economy. To make the new story credible, the economist must at least display a minimum level of technical virtuosity.

Unfortunately, this minimum is forever increasing. Gans and Shepherd claim, "Until the 1970s, editors [of economics journals] regularly rejected articles because they contained technical mathematics."[17] In the 1970s, the technical tide rolled in. Now, very few articles appear without a display of technical of virtuosity.

Ironically, winners of the Nobel Prize in economics have been at the forefront of those who lament the increasing mathematization of economics.[18] For example, Gerard Debreu, who won the Nobel Prize in economics for his work in developing sophisticated mathematical economic theory, calculated that in 1940 less than 3 percent of the referred pages of the *American Economic Review* included rudimentary mathematical expressions; by 1990, nearly 40 percent of the pages included mathematics.[19]

Debreu also noted that the lag between important mathematical discoveries and their application in economics is shrinking. For example, a branch of mathematics called "nonstandard analysis" began at the beginning of the 1960s. It was applied to economics in 1972.[20] Debreu acknowledged "the increasing impenetrability to the overwhelming majority of our Association of the work done by its most mathematical members." He observed:

The spread of mathematicized economic theory was helped even by its esoteric character. Since its messages cannot be deciphered by economists who do not have the proper key, their evaluation is entrusted to those who have access to the code. But the acceptance of the technical expertise also implies acceptance of their values.[21]

This obtuseness even extends to the books assigned to economics students. In this regard, Stigler has noted:

Less than a century ago a treatise on economics began with a sentence such as "Economics is a study of mankind in the ordinary business of life." Today it will often begin, "This unavoidably lengthy treatise is devoted to an examination of an economy in which the second derivatives of the utility function possess a finite number of discontinuities. ...Only elementary mathematical tools such as topology will be employed, incessantly."[22]

Even more caustically, Robert Solow, another Nobel Prize–winning economist, observed:

My impression is that the best and the brightest in the profession proceed as if economics is the physics of society. There is a single universal model of the world. It only needs to be applied. You could drop a modern economist from a time machine—a helicopter, maybe, like the one that drops the money—at any time in any place, along with his or her personal computer; he or she could set up in business without even bothering to ask what time and which place. In a little while, the up-to-date economist will have maximized a familiar-looking present-value integral, made a few familiar log-linear approximations, and run the obligatory familiar regression. The familiar coefficients will be poorly determined, but about one-twentieth of them will be significant at the 5 percent level, and the other nineteen do not have to be published. With a little judicious selection here and there, it will turn out that the data are just barely consistent with your thesis advisor's hypothesis that money is neutral (or non-neutral, take your choice) everywhere and always, model an information asymmetry, any old information asymmetry, don't worry, you'll think of one.[23]

In short, succeeding as an economist requires one to write in such a way that even most economists are incapable of understanding. Despite the occasional public protestations of distinguished economists such as Stigler and Debreu, the process continues unabated. This increasing technical demand imposed on students of economists goes a long way toward explaining the source of the problem with contemporary economics.

The Limits of Storytelling

Within the economics profession, only the most distinguished participants can present their stories outside of a mathematical model. To do otherwise is to confess an absence of technical competence.

Of course, the full complexity of real-life situations cannot be reduced to a mathematical model. As a result, economists have had to simplify their stories. A typical story will highlight some simple relationship in the economy. All other elements of reality fall from view.

The most influential articles consist of purely mathematical models, with maybe a smattering of data that supposedly confirm the story. To make a story more complex would preclude encapsulating it in a mathematical model or applying a statistical technique to test its validity.

Space limitations contribute to the simplicity of economic models. In general, economists package their stories in articles of 10 to 30 pages or a book of 300 pages. Much longer works require too much of a commitment on the part of the audience. As a result, these stories give partial truths at best.

Alas, despite the intricacy of the mathematics, the typical story is downright simple, offering little more than a caricature of reality. Even if it were physically possible to construct a comprehensive story, the complexity of such a story would overwhelm the audience. After all, no individual or even the world's fastest computer is capable of processing all the relevant facts of the economy.

Like fun-house mirrors, these stories necessarily distort reality by highlighting certain features at the expense of the rest. By concentrating our attention on particular elements of economic processes, economic stories can be useful reminders of the importance of certain isolated phenomena. They can just as easily mislead us by emphasizing notions that are at odds with reality.

Robert Lucas is one of the most influential modern practitioners of the craft of turning sophisticated mathematics into models of the economy. He repeatedly reminds his readers that his models are indeed artificial.[24] He cites the poet Wallace Stevens with approval: "It helps to see the actual world/to visualize a fantastic world."[25] Lucas considers the artificiality of his fantastic models as a badge of honor, insisting that looking at the world as it appears to us can be a source of error. Unfortunately, Lucas fails to acknowledge that artificiality by itself is no guarantee of scientific rigor. In the words of Wassily Leontief, an early Nobel Prize–winning economist, "Uncritical enthusiasm for mathematical formulation tends often to conceal the ephemeral substantive content of the argument behind the formidable front of algebraic signs."[26] Similarly, Frank Hahn, himself a highly respected modeler, observed in his presidential address to the Econometric Society:

> ...the achievements of economic theory in the last two decades are both impressive and in many ways beautiful. But it cannot be denied that there is something scandalous in the spectacle of so many people refining the analysis of economic states which they give no reason to suppose will ever, or have ever, come about. ... It is an unsatisfactory and slightly dishonest state of affairs.[27]

Economics and the Real World

In effect, an economist simply assembles a collection of existing stories, hoping to put enough of a twist on it that fellow economists will consider it to be a significant contribution to the professional literature. However, the selection of stories is far from random.

Economists habitually regard those who challenge or even question the prevailing theoretical basis of their literature with suspicion. Young economists soon learn that those who dare to challenge the prevailing wisdom risk subjecting themselves to ridicule and even professional ostracism.

The different schools of economic thought have varying boundaries of acceptable stories. Many will reject out of hand any story that hints that people behave irrationally or that markets do not work well.[28] Others will allow such imperfections in the economy so long as the story suggests a gentle policy that corrects a minor defect without disrupting business as usual.

Few economists feel limited by these restrictions. On the contrary, they become passionate in debating what goes on within the restrictive field of debate. Indeed, the questions that economists pose are not trivial. Can government policies make the economy grow faster? Is monetary or fiscal policy more effective? Cynicism creeps in from another direction. Economists lack a standard by which they can compare their contradictory stories. They realize that no matter where they stand, someone else can just as easily create a different model or pull up another set of data that will confirm a contrary view.

Economists understand that, more often than not, these stories are incomparable because each individual story depends on a special set of severely unrealistic assumptions or a questionable adjustment of a data set. Making adjustments or even a slight change in any one of these assumptions can lead to an entirely different outcome. As a result, even the most diligent student cannot reconcile the myriad of economic stories.

Although proof that the model accurately captures a part of reality is out of the question, most authors do go through the motions of marshalling a few selective facts to suggest that their story might not be incorrect. In any case, data is of secondary importance. In the more prestigious journal literature, articles emphasizing data are generally unacceptable. Instead, the profession relegates empirical articles to less prestigious journals.[29]

Even though economists face ostracism for challenging the status quo, they do respond to the outside world in a limited way. At any point in time, one or another economic school becomes associated with the dominant economic policies of the time. So long as these policies seem to bring about positive results for those in power, the prestige of that school increases. Eventually, the economy falls into a deep recession or depression casting the prevailing school into disrepute.

One of the other schools then rises to prominence until it too suffers the same fate. Then adherents of the previously discredited school will reappear with new models and new stories, showing that their policies were blameless for the earlier misfortunes. Instead, either its policies were not administered correctly or some other force, unrelated to its policies, was the culprit.

The Training of Economists

By and large, the training of economists consists in teaching students the basic tools of economics by working through a central core of stories that illustrate how an economy works. Most introductory economics students resist the lack of reality that their textbooks offer. They rebel against the confines of simple models, often peppering their professors with questions that demonstrate their skepticism about the stories. These questions are frequently intended to challenge the professor to square the abstract assumptions of economic models with the students' own experiences of the economy.

Over time this resistance breaks down. Those who continue to question the assumptions of the model soon abandon the study of economics. Almost all those who remain eventually fall under the sway of the conventions of economic thought, learning to accept a small group of stories based on a common set of assumptions.

Although the stories that graduate students must learn may be simple, I cannot emphasize enough that students must master extraordinarily complex techniques of statistical and mathematical analysis in order to express them in an acceptable form. The very ardor of their training reinforces a peculiar way of thinking unique to economists.

This training demands that economists must devote an enormous amount of time to master the mathematical and statistical techniques that comprise the basic tools of their trade. Little time remains for coming into direct contact with the people, industries, or institutions that economists supposedly study. In this sense, the education of economists resembles the manner in which cults indoctrinate new members.

Graduate students have to concentrate on developing their techniques so that they can create a story of their own (the dissertation) that will satisfy a committee of their teachers. The strenuous demands of this task leave little time or inclination to investigate real economic problems or even to think critically about their subject.

To make matters worse, the committees that approve dissertations are generally conservative bodies. The members themselves have invested a good deal of time and trouble in building their reputations by convincing other economists with their stories. Any new story that undermines their work represents a professional threat. As a result, a student cannot easily challenge the committee's beliefs without running the risk of having the dissertation rejected. Successful appeals of a committee's decisions are all but impossible.

This training is very effective. Prudent students soon realize that they must tell a conventional story that does not trouble their committee. So, what Keynes wrote about the business world certainly holds true for the training of economists: "Worldly wisdom teaches that it is better for reputation to fail conventionally than to succeed unconventionally." [30]

A survey of prestigious economics departments asked graduate students what abilities would place them on the fast track. The most common response was "being smart in the sense of being good at problem solving" (65 percent). Next came excellence in mathematics (57 percent). In contrast, "having a broad knowledge of the economics literature" did not rank very high (10 percent). Nor did "having a thorough knowledge of the economy (3 percent).[31]

Students soon learn that the surest route to professional success is to craft a story that makes a modest innovation, without straying beyond the boundaries of conventional thinking. The system will reward them even if they tell the same story as others, so long as they successfully apply a new mathematical or statistical technique.

After graduation, the conditioning of students generally continues to work its effect. Graduates soon develop a professional persona with a vested interest in not rocking the boat, recognizing that to launch a significant challenge of orthodox beliefs can lead to professional ostracism.

Professional conformity becomes the order of the day, even though the consensus among economists, as we shall see later, is at odds with the rest of the world. Indeed, several surveys have documented a far-reaching consensus among professional economists.[32]

Despite the long-lasting effects of academic indoctrination, many economists do realize that this system serves as a barrier to understanding the economy. Once the set of core stories congeals into a widely accepted picture of reality, economic doctrine serves to dull economists' alertness to other aspects of reality.

Specifically, after a long-standing lack of concern about one of the forgotten elements of reality, economists find themselves ill-prepared for the inevitable time when a crisis catches them off guard. Like the proverbial generals who insist on fighting the last war, economists often excel in offering explanations for the present state of affairs, but they generally fail to help us prepare for future surprises.

In fact, economists themselves express a widespread dissatisfaction with their present system of education and training. The Commission on Graduate Education in Economics, appointed by the president of the American Economic Association, concluded that both students and faculty recognize that the overemphasis on tools and the inattention to creativity and problem solving represent a serious deficiency in graduate economics.[33]

Unfortunately, little can be done until economists themselves reform the way in which they reward technical virtuosity, as well as traditions of graduate education.

The Discreet Charm of the Professional Economist

A process of self-selection probably facilitates the indoctrination of economists. Several studies have found that economics students, both graduate and undergraduate, tend to behave less altruistically than non-economics students.[34]

Whether because of nature or nurture, professional economists often regard their training as a badge of distinction that sets them apart from most other people who have not endured the experience of graduate school. They pride themselves on thinking differently than other people.

Take the issue of fairness. In our ordinary life, we often behave as if fairness were important. Robert Frank has noted: "Travelers on interstate highways leave tips for waitresses they will never see again. … People walk away from profitable transactions whose terms they believe to be 'unfair'."[35]

Accommodation to notions of fairness, while not universal, is widespread. Even profit-minded businesses from time to time have to modify their behavior out of fear that the public will seek retribution if they give the appearance of unfairness.[36] Widely different cultures agree that fairness should be an important consideration in society. For example, one survey found similar notions in fairness among samples of people in the United States and the USSR.[37]

Still, fairness has no place within the core of economics. According to economic theory, the market alone should determine what is fair. Deviations from market-based outcomes represent irrationality.

Economists seem to incorporate these views into their personal life. For example, economics professors appear to be less inclined to donate to charities than professors from other disciplines.[38]

One might think that such unsocial attitudes might work to exclude economists from positions of influence. Already in 1879, Francis Amasa Walker, first president of the American Economic Association, published an article asking why economists seemed to be in bad odor among real people.[39] He identified failings of economics similar to what we have just noted: excessive abstraction and neglect of institutions, customs, and the like.

Despite Walker's skepticism about the long-term influence of economists, today, more than a century later, economists wield far more power than they ever have. How can we explain this state of affairs?

Economic Expertise

We might expect that economists wield great power because of the special insights that their techniques offer. Ironically, although economists are legendary for applying their sophisticated techniques to the most arcane of subjects, those economists who are involved in making important policy decisions rarely make use of anything but the most elementary economics tools.

Consider the testimony of Herbert Stein, who was the chief economic advisor to the Nixon administration. According to Stein, "It may seem a shocking thing to say, but most of the economics that is usable for advising on public policy is at about the level of the introductory undergraduate course."[40] Alain Enthoven, who was chief economist of the Department of Defense during the early 1960s, came to a similar conclusion. He explained to his audience at the annual meetings of the American Economic Association:

> ...the tools of analysis that we use [at the Defense Department] are the simplest, most fundamental concepts of economic theory, combined with the simplest quantitative methods. The requirements for success in this line of work are a thorough understanding of and, if you like, belief in the relevance of such concepts as marginal products and marginal costs. ...
>
> The economic theory that we are using (in the department) is the theory that most of us learned as sophomores. The reason Ph.D.'s are required is that many economists do not believe what they have learned until they have gone through graduate school and acquired a vested interest (in conventional economic theory)...[41]

Again, faith in the conventional stories, rather than expertise, seems to count most.

True, in some quarters economists' techniques command a high value. Wall Street pays fabulous sums to economists to devise formulae to help speculators turn a profit (although more recently, Wall Street has been turning to unemployed physicists and mathematicians for this work). These economists do not specialize in predicting market behavior; instead, they typically find existing inconsistencies within the structure of prices.

The Conservatism of Economics

Graduate study succeeds in conditioning the majority of economists to accept a basic core of stories, however much they may differ on peripheral issues. We can do no better than to turn to the conservative Nobel laureate George Stigler in this regard. In an article entitled "The Politics of Political Economists" he observed:

> The main reason for the conservatism [of economists] surely lies in the effect of the scientific training the economist receives. He is drilled in the problems of *all* economic systems and in the methods by which the price system solves these problems. …
> He cannot unblushingly repeat slogans such as "production for use rather than for profit." He cannot believe that a change in the *form* of social organization will eliminate basic economic problems.[42]

Self-interest does play an important role in shaping economic doctrine. In the 1960s, several factors combined to give a little breathing room to left-leaning economics. Liberal economists had apparently succeeded in figuring out how to avoid depressions. The antiwar and the civil rights movements had done a great deal to demonstrate the need for social change. Since teaching positions were relatively easy to land, the job market was not penalizing students as much as usual for unorthodox ideas.

In recent decades, teaching jobs have become increasingly difficult to obtain. More and more, economists had to turn to private business and the nonprofit sector for employment. Business jumped at the opportunity to help shape economic doctrine:

> The corporate community went on the offensive in the 1970s, trying to transform the intellectual environment to justify lowering wages and taxes. Business poured money into a "conservative labyrinth" of think tanks, funded scores of "free enterprise" chairs, and sponsored numerous university lecture series and individual scholars' research. In the simile used by Heritage Foundation head Edwin Feulner, the design was, like Procter & Gamble's in selling soap, to saturate the intellectual market with studies and "expert" opinion supporting the proper policy conclusions. This was a powerful and conclusion-specific "demand" for intellectual service.[43]

Finding an academic job does not free the young economist from the clutches of the corporate sector, since winning grants is often an important consideration in the promotion process.[44]

The combination of the educational process combined with job pressures has led to a deadening conservatism, much to the delight of conservatives. Listen to what Peter Warren told readers of a Heritage Foundation magazine:

> The creeping rot of multiculturalism, feminism, deconstructionism, and other fashion-ably radical intellectual trends has spread to nearly every branch of study in American universities. But economics appears to have developed an immunity to such diseases. It is one of the few disciplines in which radical Left ideology has failed to take root. Market capitalism—anathema to the bulk of the professorate—flourishes in economics departments, where Keynesians have been unable to prevent the growth of various off-shoots of classical free-market thought. This lack of political correctness is one of the reasons why U.S. economics programs are considered to be among the best in the world, while humanities and most other social sciences attract fewer foreign students.[45]

The idea of an economic consensus might seem absurd. Economists seem to disagree about everything. Anybody who has witnessed an encounter between two economists has seen the sparks fly. Economists generally seem to agree on nothing whatsoever, whether it be free trade, minimum wage laws, comparable worth, or any other popular issue. You may have heard the old saw, "If you lay all the economists in the world, end to end, they will never reach a conclusion."

In truth, these polemics are not what they seem. For example, one survey of economists' beliefs correctly concluded, "perceptions of widespread disagreement are simply wrong."[46] Yes, economists hotly dispute peripheral issues, only because they agree so strongly about their core beliefs. More than anything, these intense arguments are part of a strange bonding ceremony among a unique group of people who share a view of the world that they know to be at odds with the rest of society.

Economists' vehemence in these disputes serves as a warning to the rest of society: If you do not have the credentials to play this game, watch out! Let a hapless non-economist stumble into one of these debates among professional economists and utter a view at variance with the prevailing orthodoxy, and the economists will ruthlessly pounce upon this unfortunate creature for unforgivable naiveté. Few economists would dare to tell a story that would threaten the stories of the majority.

Those who succeed in economic debates manage to tell a slightly different story with a dash of extra mathematics or a clever statistical technique, without offending the majority. Their stories will provide a slight twist that might tweak a few participants, but they will never, never completely deviate from the core.

As Richard Whitley has noted, "Scientists compete for recognition from their colleagues/competitors" by publishing in professional journals. "Claims which are too innovatory and reject much of the conventional wisdom are unlikely to be published or recognized as useful contributions to knowledge."[47]

So-called Revolutions in Economics

Not surprisingly, intellectual revolutions are rare among economists, probably rarer than in any other discipline. Occasionally, a professional economist who has already achieved considerable eminence suggests a break with the herd. Typically. the profession will receive their criticism with polite silence and continue unfazed.

As a result, we have seen only a few modest uprisings rather than revolutionary movements in the mainstream economics literature. In truth, when economists themselves refer to revolutionary change, they usually mean nothing more than to observe that someone has merely suggested shifting the emphasis from one side of a relationship to another. For example, when the Great Depression began, most economists thought that lowering wages would eliminate unemployment. John Maynard Keynes diverted economists' attention from wages as a cost of production to wages as a source of demand. Given Keynes's perspective, what business would save in wages it would lose in demand. Consequently, lowering wages restricts demand, creating pressure for further wage decreases.

Keynes also contended that high interest rates would not necessarily increase savings because the interest rates would stifle economic growth, leaving a smaller pool of earnings from which people could save. Again, he merely shifted the emphasis. Instead of viewing interest rates as an incentive to save out of a given level of income, he altered the perspective. From Keynes's perspective, we should consider interest rates in terms of their impact on growth.

Modest as his innovations might seem, Keynes probably came closest to a successful economic revolution. He forced the majority economists to modify a few elements of the orthodoxy for a while, but only temporarily.

The Keynesian counterrevolution rapidly developed on two fronts. To begin with, less than a decade after Keynes published his major book, economists had already succeeded in recasting his work in mathematical form in an attempt to show that it was consistent with the very theories that he set out to attack. In the process, they managed to wring much of the heretical tone from Keynes's work. Today, a student guided by the professional literature can safely read Keynes without becoming tainted with improper ideas.

More important, most policy-oriented economists, especially in the United States, incorrectly interpreted Keynes to mean that government spending was the key to prosperity. When the economy began to flounder in the early 1970s, the opinion of mainstream economics abruptly reversed its course, abandoning the belief in the efficacy of government and assuming that laissez faire would ensure universal affluence. Today, Keynesian economics is largely ignored. Robert Lucas, a conservative, Nobel Prize–winning economist, chortled:

> One cannot find good under-forty economists who identify themselves or their work as "Keynesian." Indeed, people even take offence if referred to as Keynesians. At research seminars, people don't take Keynesian theorizing seriously anymore; the audience starts to whisper and giggle at one another.[48]

The fate of other would-be revolutionaries is also instructive. Thorstein Veblen attempted a more thoroughgoing critique of economics, but except for a small group of dedicated disciples, most economists dismissed his work and he remains little studied today. Today, a handful of economists attempt to follow Veblen's trail, but students who adopt this line of thinking find themselves disadvantaged professionally to say the least.

Joseph Schumpeter suggested a less complete break with the past. His uprising created less resistance because he took care never to make his break with conventional economics explicit. Although many prominent economists now give lip service to his work, Schumpeter's influence also remains limited.

In short, the core of economic theory has not evolved at all in the last century, despite the enormous changes in the economy. Nonetheless, from time to time, when the economy breaks down, such as during the Great Depression of the 1930s, events shatter economists' faith in their dogma.

At such times, economists begin to see the world more realistically. Later, when the economy appears less threatening, the economics profession reverts back to its prior faith in markets.

These temporary relapses are very instructive. Much of this book concerns a lesser known incident around the turn of the last century. We shall see that Schumpeter's celebrated ideas were really echoes of the forgotten economists of this period.

A Child's Guide to Price Theory

I have already explained why we should regard economics an ideology designed to defend existing practices rather than as a science. Despite the tremendous advances in economic techniques, the core of economic theory has remained unchanged over the last century. Above all, economic theory teaches that we should rejoice that markets set prices at a level that equates supply and demand. According to the "science" of economics, if prices are free to work in this fashion, the world will run smoothly and any attempt to interfere with this mechanism will cause harm.

Remember that economists generally accept the convention that everything begins with the process of exchange. A typical economics story about investment might read like this: Consumers want more lemonade than is presently for sale on the market. This demand will drive up the price of lemonade.

Some of the many sellers of Kool-Aid, as well as people who are not presently selling beverages, realizing that they can make a healthy profit selling lemonade, will make the necessary investment to enter the lemonade business. In this way, the supply of lemonade will increase until competition causes the price to fall enough that sellers of lemonade cannot earn any more than the normal rate of profit.

This last point is particularly striking. Economists have never come up with an explanation about what a normal rate of profit is or how it is determined. Instead, they fall back upon this term, "normal rate of profit," which sounds so obvious that nobody ever worries about what it might be.

Over and above the nebulous concept of the normal rate of profit, the theory implicit in this story depends upon a set of very special assumptions, which economists call "perfect competition." In a world of perfect competition, each market has a large number of sellers and buyers, none of which is large enough to have any appreciable effect on prices. In perfect competition, people can easily enter a market or leave a market in pursuit of higher profits.

Indeed, the situations that most conform to the assumptions of perfect competition bear little resemblance to a modern market economy. One of my favorite examples of a situation akin to perfect competition comes from Charles Babbage's wonderful account of the unusual, labor-intensive enterprises that surrounded the establishments for slaughtering horses at Montfaucon, near Paris, in the nineteenth century. The unusual conditions here illustrate a corner of an earlier economy where conditions resembling perfect competition existed.

1. The hair is first cut off from the mane and tail. It amounts usually to about a quarter of a pound, which, at 5d/lb, is worth 1.25d.

2. The skin is then taken off, and sold fresh to the tanners. It usually weighs about 60 lb., and produces 9s to 12s.

3. The blood may be used as manure, or by sugar refiners or as food for animals. …A horse produces about 20 lb. of dried blood, worth about 1s.9d.

4. The shoes are removed from the dead horses. …The average produce of the shoes and shoe-nails of a horse is about 2 1/2d.

5. The hoofs are sold partly to turners and combmakers, partly to manufacturers of sal ammonia and Prussian blue, who pay for them about 1s 5d.

6. The fat is very carefully collected and melted down. In lamps it gives more heat than oil, and is therefore demanded for enamelers and glass toy makers. It is also used for greasing harness, shoe leather, &c; for soap and for making gas; it is worth about 6d per lb. A horse on an average yields 8 lb. of fat, worth about 4s, but well fed horses sometimes produce nearly 60 lb.

7. The best pieces of the flesh are eaten by the workmen; the rest is employed as food for cats, dogs, pigs, and poultry. It is likewise used as manure, and in the manufacture of Prussian blue. A horse has from 300 to 400 lb. of flesh, which sells for from 1l. 8s. to 1l. 17s.

8. The tendons are separated from the muscles: the smaller are sold fresh, to the glue makers in the neighbourhood; the larger are dried, and sent off in greater quantities for the same purpose. A horse yields about 1 lb. of dried tendons, worth about 3d.

9. The bones are sold to cutlers, fan makers, and manufacturers of sal ammoniac and ivory black. A horse yields about 90 lbs., which sell for 2s.

10. The smaller intestines are wrought into coarse strings for lathes; the larger are sold as manure.

11. Even the maggots, which are produced in great numbers in the refuse, are not lost. Small pieces of the horse flesh are piled up, about half a foot high; and being covered slightly with straw to protect them from the sun, soon allure the flies, which deposit their eggs in them. In a few days the putrid flesh is converted into a living mass of maggots. These are sold by measure; some are used for bait in fishing, but the greater part as food for fowls, and especially for pheasants. One horse yields maggots which sell for about 1s. 5d.

12. The rats which frequent these establishments are innumerable, and they have been turned to profit by the proprietors. The fresh carcass of a horse is placed at night in a room, which has a number of openings near the floor. The rats are attracted into it, and the openings near the floor are closed. 16,000 rats were killed in one room in four weeks, without any perceptible diminution of their number. The furriers purchase the rat skins at about 3s. the hundred.[49]

Just as in the example of the lemonade stands, people in the slaughterhouses could work with these waste products without any significant investment in fixed capital. Most everything in this marketplace depends upon current conditions. Time is irrelevant. In this environment, just as in an imaginary world of perfect competition, competitive forces can universally drive prices down to the level where sellers recover their cost of production, including a small markup representing a "normal" rate of profit. Incidentally, economists never explain how this normal rate is set.

Economists have a special definition of the cost of production. It is the extra cost incurred by producing one more unit of output, together with a small markup to allow for the "normal" rate of profit. They refer to this cost as the marginal cost. Notice that the definition of marginal costs excludes the tables and glasses that the lemonade stand uses since they remain unchanged, whether or not another person buys some lemonade.

This idea that with perfect competition the cost of all commodities will equal marginal costs is the foundation of conventional economics. Many people over the years have pointed out how restrictive and unrealistic the notion of perfect competition is. Nonetheless, the devotees of naive price theory have remained impervious to all criticism.

Marginal Costs and Economic Psychology

The notion of marginal cost is the lynchpin of price theory. In the case of our lemonade stand, the marginal cost seems relatively easy to define, but it is still quite slippery because of the changing nature of sunk costs. For children deciding to set up the stand, marginal costs would equal the cost of the ingredients and labor (which could be what they consider their time to be worth or the amount they pay for hired labor) plus an allowance for a normal rate of profit. Once they have laid out the money for the ingredients, the marginal cost changes since the ingredients are sunk. If the ingredients spoil by the end of the day, the marginal cost changes again. The marginal cost would fall back to the labor costs alone since the ingredients would have no value tomorrow.

Now suppose that these entrepreneurs are children who borrow a card table and some glasses from their parents. Ignoring the possibility of breakage, their parents' property does not enter into their capital costs. At the end of the day, the children can return these "capital goods" no worse for wear when they close up shop.

Selling an extra glass of lemonade does no harm either to the table or the glass, ignoring the possibility of breakage. So as long as the children can get something more than the marginal cost of another glass of lemonade, which equals the cost of purchasing new ingredients, they will earn some extra profit from selling one more glass, regardless of how much the parents originally paid for the card table and glasses. In fact, even if the children had to buy their glasses and tables on their own, these expenses still would not enter into the calculation of marginal costs—except for an allowance of wear and tear or breakage.

Now let us acknowledge an important complication to the concept of marginal costs. Suppose that the lemons are nearing the end of their shelf life. By the end of the day, they will spoil. To make matters worse, business is slow. Assuming that the young entrepreneur had stocked enough lemons for a busy day, to set a price equal to the marginal cost would lead to losses from spoilage. The shortening of the lifetime of the lemons combined with the weakening of the business removes much of the value of the lemons from marginal costs of production.

The stand operator should get what value she can out of the lemons, regardless of their original purchase price. Given this situation, the child would increase profits—or more precisely, minimize losses—by selling the product below the previously defined marginal cost in an attempt to get something for the soon-to-be-worthless lemons.

The price of the lemonade would still have to reflect the value of the sugar. After all, unlike the aging lemons, sugar is not particularly perishable. It has a value that can carry over to tomorrow. As a result, the firm has no reason to feel pressure to dump the sugar at a loss.

Economically speaking, the aging lemons with a limited durability now resemble the durable table more than the sugar. Using either the lemons or the table does nothing to diminish the value of the enterprise's stock. In contrast, serving the sugar today reduces the future supply of sugar.

The child's miscalculations about the lemons reveal a layer of complexity omitted from most treatments of price theory: the complications created by uncertainty. The child might attempt to avoid the risk of spoilage by purchasing the ingredients on consignment, rather than laying out a fixed amount for the lemons and the sugar, but then someone else would have to take on the risk that the lemons might rot.

The problem of uncertainty is pervasive in the economy. Some economists seek to finesse the complications of uncertainty mathematically by assuming that the young entrepreneur can somehow calculate the odds of being caught with spoiling lemons. In that case, the child could add something to the price of lemonade to compensate for the risk of spoilage. This extra profit could be equivalent to an insurance policy against spoilage.

In truth, nobody can calculate future odds. Even in this simple case where uncertainty is at a minimum, the lemons might be rotten inside despite a healthy external appearance. As a result, investment depends on psychological as well as business conditions.

Decreasing Returns

The example of a small lemonade stand might seem out of place in a discussion of economic theory. In fact, it is not because conventional economic theory assumes constant or decreasing returns to scale.

Return to scale is a central concept in economics. It measures how much unit costs go up or down when production takes place in larger units. For example, constant returns to scale in the lemonade industry means that any firm using the best available technology will have the same costs regardless of its size. If a major corporation took over all the lemonade stands in a city, its cost of preparing a glass of lemonade would be no different from the child's lemonade stand. Decreasing returns to scale would imply that the corporate operation would be less efficient than the child's stand.

In the days before economics became formalized, decreasing returns to scale made a lot of sense. Since the majority of the workers were engaged in agriculture, many economic ideas came from agriculture. Economists observed that the application of more seed or more weeding usually increased production. But they also saw that doubling the amount of seed or weeding did not double the farm's output. This phenomenon suggested that agriculture suffered under decreasing returns. In terms of modern economics, as farmers worked the land more intensively marginal costs were increasing because of decreasing returns to labor. Following the agricultural tradition, economists continued to think in terms of constant or decreasing returns to scale, even after modern industry began to take hold.

Yes, economists noted increasing returns to scale. Adam Smith, often seen as the father of modern economics, made the point that a larger operation would have certain advantages. For example, individuals who attempted to assemble cars on their own would be at a disadvantage compared to a business that had a large enough scale to set up an assembly line, where people did not have to waste time and energy retrieving different tools and materials.[50] The remarkable Charles Babbage, who wrote about the slaughterhouses and anticipated a modern computer, recognized that a larger operation would have an additional advantage. At any moment, most of the tools that an individual assembler used would lie idle. A large enough business could purchase tools or machinery in the right proportion so that they would be working all the time.[51]

Yet, economists continued to build models on the assumption of constant or decreasing returns to scale. This assumption has a convenient mathematical property that makes it attractive to modern economists. In the absence of increasing returns to scale, large-scale industry will not have any technical advantage over small-scale industry. This condition is crucial for the assumed existence of perfect competition, which presumes that the coexistence of many small firms leads to the greatest possible economic efficiency.

While decreasing returns to scale was consistent with an economic theory based on perfect competition, it was inconsistent with the realities of modern industry, where bigger firms had obvious cost advantages. Astute economists recognized this contradiction, but when it came to choosing between reality and their economic theory, they rejected reality.

Alfred Marshall even mentioned increasing returns in his influential textbook, but then he enveloped it in a mist of hazy prose. Marshall then went on teaching his theory as if the subject never arose.[52] In Joan Robinson's words, "Marshall had a foxy way of saving his conscience by mentioning exceptions [to the world of perfect competition], but doing so in such a way that his pupils would continue to believe in the rule."[53]

The Unrealistic World of Conventional Price Theory

Remember that conventional price theory assumes that unbridled competition brings prices down to marginal costs and that this process leads to the best of all possible outcomes. The first part of this contention is correct, given the assumption that competitive forces are allowed to hold sway. The second part is absolutely incorrect. If ever prices fell to the range of marginal costs, the economy would collapse. This fact is key to my suggestion that we are approaching the end of economics.

What is wrong with the conventional perspective? In our previous discussion of the economics of the lemonade stands, we saw that traditional price theory takes no account of the risks associated with fixed capital, such as the glasses or tables. After all, under conditions of perfect competition, conventional price theory correctly assumes prices will be determined by marginal cost alone. Neither fixed costs nor sunk costs have any role to play in this theory. Unfortunately, to the extent that conventional price theory is correct—that prices will tend to approximate marginal costs—perfect competition, in the presence of substantial fixed costs, will spell disaster for business.

Just consider how competition would occur in a railroad industry where 1,000 parallel lines exist. Of course, no sane person would want to invest in the thousandth railroad line, or even the second one. Just keep in mind that the cost of hauling one extra ton of freight on a railroad is insignificant.

Suppose that each line charges just enough to pay off the loans to its creditors and earn a little profit besides. Let us say that the going rate is $10 per ton of freight. Finally, suppose that each company is running half empty.

This state of affairs will not last long. Sooner or later one company will realize that if it drops its price down to $9.90, it will lose only one percent of the money it earns on its existing traffic, but since each shipper will want to take advantage of the cheapest rates it might double its shipments and run at full capacity. This extra business would outweigh the minor loss from the reduced price.

In effect, the railroad will treat the use of its excess capacity of freight cars as a free good, except for wear, tear, and maintenance costs. After all, empty boxcars will not earn them any profits. By lowering the price, the railroad hopes to put its equipment to use, even if the revenues are small compared to the original cost of the fixed capital.

As a result, profits for the railroad that lowers its rates will soar—but only so long as all the other railroads accept this new situation. Of course, they will not. Eventually, some other railroad will drop its rates below $9.90 and these price cuts will continue to escalate. Sooner or later, rates will fall close to the marginal cost. In the process, all the railroads with outstanding debt will be unable to meet their credit obligations and fall into bankruptcy. In fact, something very similar occurred in the railroad industry in the nineteenth century and more recently with U.S. airlines.

In short, I accept that conventional price theory provides an accurate description of what would happen if two unlikely conditions occurred. First, firms would be able to calculate their marginal costs. Secondly, the economy would become very competitive.

The first condition might be coming to pass in the sense that marginal costs are rapidly diminishing for many production industries. As marginal costs shrink toward insignificance, many multiproduct firms are unwilling to incur the expense of trying to create an exact measure of their marginal costs. After all, absolute precision in keeping track of costs is impossible.

Even moderate accuracy might not seem to be worth the expense. For example, accountants for a furniture factory were reported to classify sandpaper as an indirect expense rather than to incur the cost of tracing how use is distributed among specific types of furniture.[54]

Rather than attempting to base their prices on marginal costs, firms seem to use rules of thumb to set prices. For example, a number of people who have studied corporate pricing practice have observed that firms set prices at a level sufficient to earn a target rate of profit.[55]

Unfortunately, the increasing relative importance of fixed costs means that the second condition—unbridled competition—would lead to utter chaos. Indeed, no major industrial economy is willing to give full rein to competition since allowing prices to converge toward marginal costs would prove to be a disaster.

We do find some competitive sectors. Agriculture is a typical example, but vigorous competition is the exception for most highly industrialized sectors. A great deal of empirical evidence suggests that competition typically is not strong enough to force prices to converge to marginal costs.[56] As Rotemberg and Summers note: "Airlines charge high prices for seats in half empty planes. Hotels with vacant rooms charge much more than the cost of cleaning a room for a night's stay."[57]

Competition may occasionally break out in a specific industry. When competition does become strong, the results for business are disastrous. Airlines are a modern case in point, but such examples are the exception rather than the rule.

The lack of contact with the actual workings of the economy, coupled with the enormous effort invested in learning the arcane techniques of economic models, has blinded economists to the increasing irrelevance of their theory to a world in which fixed costs become increasingly important. Instead, most economists blithely insist on applying conventional price theory, which presumes that marginal costs will some-how determine prices even though the evidence for marginal cost pricing in a modern industrial context is slim to nonexistent.

Few economists consider the risks involved in marginal cost pricing. As a result, conventional economics is a dangerous guide to framing economic policy.

Sunk Costs

I have already made note of the economic similarity between the perishable fruits and long-lived durable capital goods. These two classes of goods share one important characteristic. The owners of both face a use-it-or-lose-it situation. In effect, we can think of the durable capital good as providing a sequence of services similar to a periodic delivery of soon-to-be-rotten lemons.

Each day that a fixed capital good lies unused, the owner suffers a lost opportunity similar to the person who lets unused lemons rot. Using it will not add to marginal costs except to the extent that the utilization might require some maintenance effort to keep it in good repair. So long as the owner can get anything exceeding the marginal cost of utilization, she will have an incentive to do so. As a result, the marginal costs do not include existing fixed capital, except for maintenance.

The decision to purchase capital goods is a different matter. Just as the purchase of a lemon is part of the anticipated marginal cost of production, so too is the *purchase* of the table. For example, assume that, for some reason, the table at the lemonade stand is too small to handle more than 100 servings per day. The marginal cost of the 101st serving somehow must take account of the prospective extra expense of renting a new table for the day. The rental would probably not make sense for a single serving of lemonade, but if the proprietor believes that the new table would accommodate many more expected sales, then the rental might be profitable.

So, once business expands almost to the point where sales cannot increase without an additional table, the child must then make a guess about the future of the business. If the child believes that only 101 glasses will be sold, then she might decide that the profit from serving a single glass will cover the cost of renting a second table. If she anticipates that sales will reach 110 glasses, then each sale must return at least 10 percent of the cost of the second table.

Alternatively, the child may purchase a new table outright. In that case, the business will be investing in a capital good that may be expected to last for years. Before doing so, the child must estimate whether the extra profit from increasing the capacity of the lemonade stand over the economic lifetime of the table will cover the cost of purchasing the table. She must go further than just considering the expense of the table. She must also take into account the inability to use the money, which is tied up in the table, as well as the potential resale value of the table. At this point, the table is still part of the expected future marginal costs.

This example suggests the importance of uncertainty in the investment decision. It also points out the fluidity of the notion of marginal costs.

Once the child purchases the table, the cost is sunk. Once the child takes possession of the table what the child had previously anticipated about the economic future of the enterprise becomes irrelevant. After the child purchases the table, it is no different from the one borrowed from the parents. Neither table represents an ongoing cost.

Of course, if the table can be profitably used elsewhere, the owner would reason that the table should earn at least as much profit in the lemonade business as it would in its alternative employment. In the language of economics, the table might be a sunk cost, but it need not be a fixed cost since it can be turned to other uses.[58]

So, if capital goods could easily shift from one use to another, decisions based on incorrect expectations would not penalize investors very much. Unfortunately, the market price for most used capital goods is very small. So the sunk cost problem looms large in the real world.

Fixed Costs

We have seen that the original cost of durable capital goods is irrelevant to the marginal cost. Strictly speaking, the firm does not treat the expense of fixed capital as a cost. Instead, it counts the depreciation of the fixed capital as a fixed cost.

Here again, we see the arbitrary nature of seemingly solid measures of costs. After all, depreciation is not really a cost at all. It is a fictional cost devised as a rule of thumb to pressure the firm to earn back what it originally spent on the capital good.

This approach is inconsistent with the logic of conventional price theory, which holds that a firm should make all decisions based only on its current and expected future circumstances. All past actions are irrelevant in terms of conventional price theory. Nonetheless, the accounting approach has some merit. In the long run, if the firm cannot recover its past outlays, it will not be able to make the future investments in fixed capital that are required to stay in business.

Firms face other types of fixed costs besides depreciation. They have contractual obligations to lay out future funds, including the repayment of money borrowed in the past. Of course, we have to be careful not to double count the cost of fixed capital, as well as the funds to repay money borrowed to purchase the same capital goods.

Rent is also generally a fixed cost. For example, the lemonade stand might have a lease. The lessee has the obligation to pay the rent no matter how slow the sales are.

Consequently, this rent is a fixed rather than a marginal cost. As such, it does not affect price under purely competitive conditions since prices will tend to converge to marginal costs. But the obligation to pay interest or rents means that if prices fall to marginal costs, then the business will suffer losses.

Unfortunately for the realism of conventional price theory, the distinction between fixed and marginal cost is not cut and dried. For example, a parent might consider the glasses at the lemonade stand to be closer to marginal than fixed costs. After all, sooner or later, one of the glasses is bound to break. The child would be more inclined to see them as fixed costs, confident that all would safely find their way back to the kitchen. Despite such complications, the fact remains that strong competitive pressures will induce a firm to tend to set prices approximately equal to marginal costs—at least what the firm perceives its marginal costs to be.

Since difficulties in measurement, such as the furniture factories experienced, will tend to make firms overestimate fixed costs and underestimate marginal costs, competition may even tend to drive prices below marginal costs. In any case, no matter what may be the intricacies of marginal cost calculations, no firm that relies heavily on long-lived, durable capital goods will earn a profit when prices approach marginal costs.

Liquidity

We have seen that, in one sense, the difference between long-lived capital goods and the soon-to-rot lemons is merely one of degree. The lemons may have an economic lifetime measured by a few days or weeks. Large fixed-capital investments generally take years before they are even ready to come on line. In either case, the firm must either tie up its funds in the purchase of capital goods or it must take on a commitment to repay the money that it borrows to buy the fixed capital. The commitment of funds for fixed capital entails taking a risk. In the words of John Hicks, a Nobel Prize-winning economist, "an entrepreneur by investing in fixed capital gives hostages to the future."[59]

In another sense, lemons differ significantly from long-lived fixed-capital goods. In the story of the lemonade stand, the operator might be able to have a rough idea about how much lemonade people might want to drink today, but how can managers know the demand for their product, say, five years hence? Even if managers could know future product demand, how could they predict what sort of investments its competitors will have in the future? How can they be sure that their investment will not be technologically obsolete soon after it is ready for production?

Economists say that fixed capital lacks liquidity. This expression, "liquidity," suggests the ease with which an asset can be turned into money. Money is, of course, generally the most liquid of assets because it is already money. In rare times, however, when people feel certain a good will appreciate in value or that money will depreciate in value, some goods may achieve an even greater liquidity than money. For example, if high levels of inflation are severely undermining the value of a currency and people confidently expect this process to continue, some good, often real estate or gold, may be seen as a more secure store of value than money.

We can liquidate an asset in two ways: We can either sell it or convert it to money over time by using it to earn a profit over the lifetime of the asset. The owner of a durable capital good generally sells it only as a last resort, because used capital goods sell at a steep discount.[60]

The problem facing the owner of a capital good is more extreme than that of the owner of a car, because capital goods are usually so specialized that relatively few of any specific capital good are sold. As a result, matching buyers and sellers requires a good deal of effort. Because of this complication, people who broker such sales earn healthy commissions.

The resale price of capital goods also depends on expectations of future value. If nobody expects that the good will have much economic value in the future, then buyers will be unwilling to pay much for it. If business is expected to pick up in the future, the good might have some resale value, but then the person who sells it loses the opportunity to reenter the market when and if business becomes brisk again.

If the capital good produces a storable commodity, the owner could use it to produce inventories to be sold later. Unfortunately, if many producers pursue this strategy, the buildup of inventories may eventually glut the market and prices will become even less favorable than they are today.

Another possibility exists in the case of the lemonade stand. The family probably can absorb some of the losses in the form of a lemon meringue pie. In contrast, the owner of specialized industrial equipment cannot get much personal use out of such objects.

Conclusion

Modern economic theory generally evades wrestling with the thorny subject of the accumulation of long-lived fixed capital, even though many economists identify economic progress with the accumulation of long-lived fixed capital. Instead, economic theory unrealistically assumes that long-lived capital goods do not exist or that the economy can somehow transmute capital goods from one form to another.

In the next chapter, we will see that the same forces that make long-lived capital goods difficult to integrate into economic theory also make investors reluctant to invest their funds in long-lived fixed-capital goods.

2

Economic Theory and
the Historical Increase of Fixed Capital

The Reluctance to Invest in Fixed Capital

Although we might regard the increase in fixed capital as an inevitable consequence of doing business, in one sense, it is relatively surprising considering the risk of committing funds to earn profits in the future without any certain knowledge of what is to come. Recall Hicks's notion of investment giving "hostages to the future."[1]

Here we come to the crucial problem in investment theory: the problem of information. To clarify this point, let us return to our earlier example of the lemonade stand. If the owner had some way of knowing the future with certainty, she would have an easy time choosing between purchasing an extra table to expand capacity and continuing with only one table. She would merely have to compare the future sales that a new table would permit with the extra costs associated with increasing capacity. If the revenues exceeded the costs by a sufficient amount, the investment would proceed. With perfect information, she could rank all possible investments, always choosing the one that promised the highest rate of return.

In the real world with imperfect information, things are not so simple. No investor has precise information about the future. Once the proprietor of the lemonade stand committed to investing in the new table, the funds sunk on the project are gone forever. The investor can only hope to recover that money by earning a profit on the table in the future or by reselling the used table, most likely at a substantial loss.

The risk always exists that either competition or a slacking off of demand will drive prices down to marginal costs or even lower. Should this occur, the investment would fail to return enough profits to cover the original cost of the table, which has now become part of the fixed costs of production.

Rational investors are painfully aware of the risks associated with sinking funds into fixed capital. Because of these risks, investors are reluctant to part with their money unless they can expect to make far more profits than they could earn through safe alternatives, say by investing in something that seems to be as secure as a government bond. For example, most firms appear to be unwilling to invest in a project unless they expect it to pay three or four times as much as the firm has to pay for the money it would borrow to make the investment.[2]

Irrationality and the Expansion of Fixed Capital

A rational investor should expect very high—often unrealistically high—profits from any investment. Yet, despite the risks and the likelihood that investments will pay much less than the expected profits, substantial investments still occur.

Many disappointed investors, who find that they have committed funds to fixed capital investments in foolish ventures, might take some comfort in the knowledge that they are not alone in their folly. Sir Isaac Newton may even offer them some consolation. After losing considerable money speculating on the stock of the South Sea Company, he reportedly said that he could calculate the motions of heavenly bodies, but not those of the madness of crowds.[3]

Newton was actually investing in a speculative venture rather than putting his money into fixed capital, but that distinction is not altogether relevant. Ultimately, all investment is speculation. Let us turn to the supposed founder of modern economic theory, Adam Smith, for guidance in this regard. According to Smith:

> The establishment of any new manufacture, of any new branch of commerce...is always a speculation, from which the projector promises himself extraordinary profits. These profits are sometimes very great, and sometimes, more frequently, perhaps, they are quite otherwise; but in general they bear no regular proportion to those of other old trades in the neighborhood.[4]

Most of us have seen some location in a town where one restaurant after another fails. Each new venture opens up with some fanfare, seemingly confident that it will succeed where its numerous predecessors have faltered. Why then are so many investors willing to speculate when the failure rate is so high? Here again we can turn to Adam Smith for some insight into this riddle. He observed:

> The over-weening conceit which the greater part of men have of their own abilities, is an antient evil remarked by the philosophers and moralists of all ages. Their

absurd presumption in their own good fortune, has been less taken notice of it. It is, however, if possible, still more universal. ...The chance of gain is by every man more or less over-valued, and the chance of loss is by most men under-valued.[5]

So Smith attributed the frequency of unsuccessful investments to a common character defect, which led causes most people to overestimate their own likelihood of success. He was not alone in his recognition of the tendency to overestimate good fortune. His contemporary, Samuel Johnson, a famous writer of the period, also displayed an acute awareness of this all-too-human failing. Boswell, Johnson's equally famous biographer, recounts a wonderful example of Johnson's insight. Thrale, the great brewer who had recently deceased, had appointed Johnson one of his executors. In that capacity it became his duty to sell the business. When the sale was about to go on, Boswell reported:

Johnson appeared bustling about, with an inkhorn and pen in his button-hole, like an exciseman, and on being asked what he really considered to be the value of the property which was to be disposed of, answered—"We are not here to sell a parcel of vats and boilers, but the *potentiality* of growing rich beyond the dreams of avarice."[6]

Modern behavioral economics has recently rediscovered this phenomenon and modern psychologists have confirmed Smith's observation.[7]

Keynes and "Animal Spirits"

The intensity of Johnson's "dreams of avarice" is not constant. At times, people are more hesitant to invest. This hesitancy can be contagious. As Avanish Dixit noted, "If one firm observes that no other firm has invested, it infers that their [*sic*] evaluations were insufficiently favorable, and adjusts its own evaluation downward. When all firms do this, they may all decide to wait."[8]

When enough firms choose to wait, the economy falls into a depression creating serious hardships for much of society. Eventually, things become so bad that even a small bit of good fortune can seem to be so propitious that people take it as a harbinger of better times. In this way, a trivial occurrence can encourage a slight increase in investment, which can create a contagion of optimism, eventually setting off a boom, which will eventually create a new cycle of disappointment.

Keynes made such fluctuations of investor psychology, what he called "animal spirits," into the centerpiece of his *General Theory of Employment, Interest and Money*. For Keynes,

Generally speaking, in making a decision we have before us a large number of alternatives, none of which is demonstrably more 'rational' than the others. ...To avoid
being put in the position of Buridan's ass [which died of starvation from being
unable to choose between two equivalent bales of hay] we fall back...on habit,
instinct, preference, desire, will, etc.[9]

In much the same spirit as Smith, Keynes wrote:

Most, probably, of our decisions to do something positive, the full consequences of
which will be drawn out over many days to come, can only be taken as the result of
animal spirits—of a spontaneous urge to action rather than inaction.
  ...individual initiative will only be adequate when reasonable calculation is sup-
plemented and supported by animal spirits, so that the thought of ultimate loss
which often overtakes pioneers, as experience undoubtedly tells us and them, is put
aside as a healthy man puts aside the expectation of death.[10]

Keynes believed that "much of the material progress of the nineteenth century
might have been impossible without the artificial stimulus to capital accumulation
afforded by... successive periods of boom."[11]

As a result, despite the reasons for reluctance to invest in fixed capital and despite
the frequency of misplaced investments, our society has witnessed a remarkable
increase in the quantity of fixed capital, symbolized by the huge manufacturing com-
plexes of the advanced industrial economies.

More on Irrationality and Investment

Since market economies depend upon investment, economic growth ultimately
requires a certain degree of individual irrationality. Of course, irrationality by itself is
insufficient to ensure prosperity. Such investment that does occur must also be more
or less appropriate for the economy to prosper.

Unfortunately, those who do make investments are not always the people who are best
suited to choose how our society should channel its resources. The business press is full
of evidence of herdlike behavior as an excessive number of investors swarm in pursuit of
the fabled profits that surround the latest technology fads. For example, consider the disk
drive industry:

From 1977 to 1984, venture capital firms invested almost $400 million in 43 differ-
ent manufacturers of Winchester disk drives...including 21 startup or early stage

investments. ....During the middle part of 1983, the capital markets assigned a value in excess of $5 billion to 12 publicly traded, venture capital basked hard disk drive manufacturers. ...However, by 1984, the value assigned to those same 12 manufacturers had declined...to only $1.4 billion.[12]

Even more dramatically, the bursting of the dot-com bubble wiped out almost $5 trillion in the U.S. stock market. Much of these losses were only paper losses, but even so the value of many hundreds of millions of dollars' worth of investment disappeared.

Again, we can turn to Adam Smith, who had anticipated this phenomenon more than two centuries ago:

> Bankruptcies are most frequent in the most hazardous trades. ...The presumptuous hope of success seems to act here as upon all other occasions, and to entice so many adventurers into those hazardous trades, that their competition reduces the profit below what is sufficient to compensate the risk.[13]

How many relatively new capital goods soon find their way to scrap heaps or languish unused? To take a common example, how often do we see relatively new fixtures in a failed restaurant torn out when new owners confidently choose a new decor?

These misplaced investments prevent society from taking full advantage of its available resources. In Adam Smith's words, "Every injudicious and unsuccessful project...tends...to diminish the funds destined for the maintenance of productive labour."[14]

What about the possibility of alternative uses for failed investments? Sometimes, capital goods are so specific to a particular project that they are little value to any other business. Sometimes, other firms can turn this fixed capital to good use, but such redeployment invariably requires modifications or other expenses that typically substantially reduce the value of the capital goods. In either event, at least some of the resources sunk in the investment are wasted.

Of course, not all great risk takers squander society's resources on foolhardy adventures. Some risk takers are visionaries who divine a great potential that others fail to recognize. Others are just lucky. Occasionally society reaps great rewards from the works of such people, but alas, such visionaries are in a distinct minority among those who make investments.

Economists generally have little to contribute to the subject of poor investments. Sometimes, we can easily identify an individual investment as bad or inappropriate long after it has gone sour. At other times, even investments that appear to be inappropriate at the moment may actually be productive in paving the way for future investments. Recall the old saying about pioneers being the ones with the arrows in their backs.

Psychology of the Business Cycle

Keynes's belief that irrationality may be necessary for economic progress runs head-long into a cherished belief of conventional economic theory, namely, that markets are efficient because prices supposedly provide accurate signals that allow econom-ic agents to make rational decisions. Of course, prices must be relatively stable for people to be able to extract much information from these signals. If prices are con-tinually jumping around, nobody can know what to make of them. For this reason, many economists believe that what makes inflation so destructive when it reaches heights of several hundred percent per year is the manner in which it obscures the informational value of the price system.

The idea that prices are informational implicitly makes another strong assump-tion, namely, that prices can guide rational behavior because they reflect the actions of others in the economy who are also behaving more or less rationally. When an excess of fools lay their hands on too much money, they attempt to bid resources away from one another by raising prices. In the process, prices become increasingly disconnected from underlying values.

The degree of foolishness, however, is not fixed. It varies over the course of the business cycles with the level of animal spirits. For example, as an economy moves out of the depression stage, confidence gradually takes hold.

After an economy has been flourishing for a while, firms begin to take their pros-perity for granted. At such times, firms are relatively unconcerned with modernizing existing plant and equipment. Instead, they concentrate on expanding capacity, both in existing and in emerging industries.[15]

This new investment stimulates demand, which produces economic growth, which reinforces confidence, which then results in even more investment. Eventually, confidence gives way to overconfidence. The basic population of fools wins many new recruits. A get-rich-quick, speculative psychology becomes rampant. As the boom wears on, firms will tend to invest in more and more unrealistic ven-tures, which are symptomatic of unsustainable bubbles. In a relatively short time, wild speculative excesses become commonplace.

In the process, the structure of prices becomes increasingly disorderly. For example, during the telecom boom of the 1990s the soaring demand for fiber-optic capacity caused a run-up in the demand for high-tech equipment, such as switching gear and office space in the vicinity of the hubs of high-tech activity. This demand kept prices arti-ficially high.

These suppliers of direct and indirect inputs for the telecom bubble were follow-ing supposedly rational price signals, but many of them later discovered that the basis for their investments was imaginary. Prices were not conveying accurate information; instead, they were misleading investors.

All the while, this temporary economic success masks speculative excesses. At the same time, firms also tend to take on more and more unnecessary costs while the economy is expanding. Executives get jets for their personal use; lower level managers get more personnel. Inevitably, along with the other contradictions of the market, the undermining of the informational value of the price system takes a serious toll on economic efficiency by luring unwary investors into making unproductive investments and by steering them away from more potentially productive activities. As a result, below the glowing surface of the economy, efficiency suffers.[16]

True, firms are installing new plant and equipment, which are more efficient than the older vintages; however, the older plant and equipment presumably continues to deteriorate, dragging efficiency down. Except in relatively new industries or industries experiencing extremely rapid growth, the additional new investment each year represents a small share of total capacity. As a result, typically, the aging of the existing capital stock more than compensates for the installation of new capital goods.[17] Consequently, after a boom continues for a while, the rate of productivity growth diminishes or even turns negative, even though the official productivity measures may still be increasing.

As the boom progresses, the economy continues to become more vulnerable, even to minor shocks. A few highly visible speculative ventures will eventually fail, setting off a panic. Confidence will disappear and the economy will then sink into a slump.[18] When the momentum of this process becomes too extreme, the economy will experience a disaster, such as the Great Depression. During such times, the empty buildings and scrapped machines stand as stark testimony for the irrationality of the existing system of organizing investments.

The seeming inevitability of recurrent depressions led Keynes to believe that despite great hopes the typical investor is unsuccessful. As he once observed, "If we exclude the exploitation of natural resources and monopolies, it is probable that the actual average results of investments, even during periods of progress and prosperity, have disappointed the hopes which prompted them."[19]

Keynes was not alone in his conviction that most investment is unsuccessful. We have already seen that this idea is implicit in the work of Adam Smith.

Of course, Keynes understood very well that although the vast majority of investments fare poorly, many investors have succeeded royally. Some of these fortunate few were brilliant enough to discern an opportunity that now looks obvious in hindsight. More were just lucky. Still more profited from advantages that the government bestowed upon them rather than from the free play of market forces, as Keynes suggested when he associated success with monopolies.

Accounting and the Quest for Rational Decision Making

Business people do not normally consider themselves to be acting irrationally. Nor do they expect to suffer losses. On the contrary, many pride themselves on their good business sense. Even those of a more speculative bent generally exhibit great confidence in the soundness of their projects.

In a more naive age, many economists believed that bankers had the specialized expertise to distinguish between the visionary and the fool. Supposedly, bankers would use this knowledge to channel funds to the most productive investments. As we learned in the wake of the savings and loan scandals of the 1980s and the failed loans to less developed countries during the 1970s and 1980s, bankers are just as fallible as the rest of us. In the dot-com era of the late 1990s, bankers were more than willing to channel funds to projects that they knew to be less than solid because they could collect huge fees while passing much of the risk on to other unsuspecting investors. At the same time, the bankers shielded themselves from the disastrous consequences of these investments by shunting the risk onto others, often insurance companies and public pension funds.[20]

What about accounting as an anchor for business rationality? Certainly, the widespread adoption of seemingly solid accounting practices contributed to the illusion of a sound basis for business action. Even as astute an observer as Max Weber associated accounting practices with rationality.[21]

This attitude toward accounting is not surprising. Indeed, the erratic movements of markets disappear in the accountant's ledgers, which exude a misleading image of straightforward calculations of profit and loss.

Unfortunately, accounting is anything but an exact science. It will remain an imperfect instrument for making business decisions because of two related challenges that defy any attempt to reduce management to a matter of objective measurement.

First, accounts are necessarily backward-looking. Accountants must necessarily base their calculations on historical costs, even though they can make allowances for changes that have occurred since the original purchase.

Ideally, an investor would want accounts that could provide exact information about the future rather than what happened in the past, but alas, accountants, just like the rest of us, lack the capability of predicting the future. Since account books are based on historical information, they will be better guides if the business venture is a relatively short-lived affair. After all, tomorrow is more likely to resemble today than sometime in the far-off future will.

Second, the methods that accountants use to make these adjustments are necessarily based on inexact conventions rather than precise measurements. Finally, as the dot-com bubble proved, accountants can easily mislead even supposedly sophisticated investors. Accounting firms even accommodated failing corporations by providing fraudulent information rather than risk losing lucrative contracts.

The treatment of capital in conventional economic theory had its origins in the long-obsolete accounting principles of early merchants.[22] When early merchants first developed their accounting practices, accounting was relatively easy. The merchants presumably understood the nature of their business. They had some overhead costs, but overhead was generally moderate. They knew more or less what their products cost them. In addition, they generally did not have to worry about far-off future events since they anticipated that their stock would turn over relatively rapidly. So long as changes in their business climate were within some normal bounds, knowledgeable merchants had a fair idea of what their customers wanted.

True, great profits could be made by those who were most adept at keeping ahead of the market. For the more conventionally inclined, modest profits were probable. All they had to do was to keep score. In that environment, accounting probably offered a reasonable picture of the world.

The economic environment of the early merchants' shops conditioned later accounting practices, especially their treatment of fixed capital. Even as late as the time of Adam Smith more than two centuries ago, fixed capital requirements were relatively modest.

The bulk of production expenses at the time consisted of direct labor costs and the costs of materials.[23] In fact, in late-eighteenth-century England, more money was spent on horseshoeing than was invested in capital in the entire textile industry, even though textile production was the core sector of the industrial revolution.[24]

The early-eighteenth-century British accountants did not seem to be far off the mark when they accepted the common practice of attributing all overhead costs— even the cost of capital goods—to what they considered to be unproductive labor. Since overhead activities do not directly contribute to the transformation of raw materials into finished products in the merchant's world, until relatively recently accountants presumed that they did not add to the value of the finished products in general.[25]

In a world where long-lived capital goods have become more important, accountants' services are far less dependable. Since accountants have never been able to discover a satisfactory method of handling long-lived capital goods, accounting provides a frail foundation for business rationality in a developed economy where long-lived fixed capital assumes great importance.

A great gulf separates the world as an economist sees it from the world as seen by an accountant. This gulf becomes wider the more fixed capital enters into the picture. The economist attempts to analyze how people organize their behavior in order to maximize their future satisfaction. For business leaders, profits are the basic indicator of satisfaction. The accountant's perspective is backward looking. Given what the firm has laid out in the past, the accountant tries to calculate how much profit the firm has already made.

Ronald Coase, who like Hicks won a Nobel Prize in economics, once noted that an accountant would say that the cost of a machine is the depreciation of the machine. The economist would say that "the cost of using the machine is the highest receipts that could be obtained by the employment of the machine in some alternative use." If no alternative exists, the cost of the machine is zero.[26]

Ideally, Coase is correct. Unfortunately, no economist can hope to calculate the highest receipts that could be obtained. To do so would require knowledge of the future of all industries that could possibly use the machine. As a result, economists generally either accept the accountant's calculations in violation of their own principles or they assume away the problem of long-lived capital goods.

Economists rarely consider this defect in economics because they avoid any serious consideration of time in their models. Instead, in dealing with investment decisions, the models typically pretend that investors are able to accurately foresee the future.

The Role of Recessions in Market Economies

Since irrationality is a major driving force within a market economy, recurrent crises serve as a necessary corrective force. During depressions firms have little choice but to attempt to undo some of the mistakes that they made during the previous boom.

During depressions, an entirely different psychology is at work. Animal spirits are at low ebb. Few firms willingly invest in new productive capacity. Instead, competitive pressures, as well as the need to make payments on outstanding debt, force firms to prune costs. During depressions, firms concentrate their investment in modernizing their existing plant and equipment.

The cold bath of recessions and depressions forces the price system to become more coherent and warns investors to become more realistic. As a result, in the colorful language of Joseph Schumpeter, business cycles are not "like tonsils, separable things that might be treated by themselves, but are, like the beat of the heart, of the essence of the organism that displays them."[27]

At the time of the Great Depression, many economists understood that depressions were an integral part of a market society.[28] In more recent times, this view has fallen out of fashion. Modern economic theory attempts to explain why economies inevitably move toward a stable equilibrium. In the process, economists generally evade the question of irrationality. Irrationality generally plays no role in most economic models. When irrationality does appear, economists treat it as an anomaly, which interferes with the otherwise smooth functioning of the economy.

So most contemporary economists imagine that the economy somehow smoothly sails along, avoiding both depressions and recessions. In the wake of each economic downturn, modern economists look back with disdain upon past speculative follies, without acknowledging that some of the problem is inherent in the market system itself. Instead, modern economics implicitly assumes that more rational investment behavior might somehow have prevented the disruptive, speculative excesses, without acknowledging that speculative behavior was crucial for new investment, which made the previous boom possible.

The unrealistic nature of economic theory contributes to the belief in the possibility of a depression-free economy. Within this imaginary context, people and firms would effortlessly grope toward equilibrium, except for some disturbing influence, such as irrational investors or the government.

The Paradox of Rationality

Let us return to the idea of Smith and Keynes that most investments are likely to fail. Nobody went further in this respect than Karl Marx. Marx repeatedly noted that new technology destroys capital values so rapidly that virtually no factory covers its initial investment costs.[29] In one letter to Engels, he wrote:

> More than 20 years ago I made the assertion that in our present society no instrument of production exists which can last 60 to 100 years, no factory, no building, etc., which by the end of its existence has covered the cost of its production. I still think that one way and another this is perfectly true.[30]

Consider an industry where technology is advancing at a rapid pace. Marx cited Charles Babbage's example of frames for making patent-net—a light woven cloth. The early frames had first sold for 1,200 pounds only to fall to 60 pounds within a few years.[31]

The microcomputer revolution, which has caused the prices of computers to plummet at breathtaking speed, offers a more recent example of this phenomenon. We may think of this situation as a part of the paradox of market rationality: If investors are too rational, the economy will collapse.

Recall Keynes's image of Buridan's ass, which starves to death from being overwhelmed with the difficulty of making a decision. For Keynes, irrational animal spirits rather than rationality drive investment forward. For Smith, these animal spirits are doubly irrational, since most investors overestimate their chances. Keynes added that if enough investors are confident enough the economy might enjoy a boom sufficient to temporarily allow a good number of these irrational investments to earn a profit.

Here we encounter another layer of paradox. If too many investors are too rational, too visionary, in the sense of making investments capable of revolutionizing methods of production, the intensity of the resulting sequence of price revolutions can overwhelm the market, creating as much havoc as an excess of irrationality. Under such conditions, prices can provide as little information as they would under the influence of a wave of price-distorting speculation.

Remember that the informational content of prices should depend on a degree of stability, or at least predictability. Extraordinary price revolutions can unsettle all previous calculations.

Investors could sink funds in a project based on existing prices only to find out that an entirely new set of prices would be in effect once the investment were ready to produce goods for the market. The new prices might wipe out a substantial proportion of their investment in a short period of time, ensuring that the firm suffers devastating losses.

Once firms realize that the risks associated with such near-term price revolutions are substantial, they may fall back on a different type of rationality, choosing to refrain from investing altogether. After all, why should anyone undertake a substantial investment when a subsequent investment might wipe out the value of the initial investment before it can repay itself?

The microcomputer industry is littered with the corpses of failed companies, most of which were founded with the expectation of becoming the next IBM. We might also interpret the example of the Winchester disk drive industry, discussed above, in terms of the rapid devalorization of the capital stock, rather than as a failure of rationality. Taking note of this possibility reminds us that what might sound like absurd irrationality, as in the description of the disk drive industry as reported in the business press, might actually be the result of an excess of rationality.

In any case, once an industry experiences very rapid technical change, firms would not want to invest without some prior assurance that their equipment will not become obsolete soon after it is installed.[32] If this reaction should occur, investment might be paralyzed. Consequently economic growth could be greater if the rate of introduction of new technology were restricted.[33]

Sawyers asserts that such conditions actually did exist in the British maritime industry: "There were times, between the wars, when marine engineering was changing in such a rapid yet uncertain way that firms in the highly competitive shipping industry delayed investment in the replacement of old high-cost engines by the low-cost engines."[34]

So while economists build their models on the assumption that markets are rational, irrationality plays a fundamental role in the real economy. No investor can know the future, which depends in part upon the decisions of other investors. Each investor tries to guess future market conditions by guessing the behavior of other investors. These guesses occur within waves of optimism and pessimism.

This sort of arrangement leads to herdlike behavior. If the herd of investors becomes too pessimistic, the economy becomes paralyzed like Buridan's ass. If investors become very optimistic, they can generate speculative bubbles. At the same time, within the speculative bubbles revolutionary innovations can develop, which can wipe out massive capital values. The rapid destruction of values, either by the bursting of bubbles or by technological revolutions, can unsettle the economy enough to create serious recessions or depressions. The dot-com bubble of the 1990s illustrates that both kinds of value destruction can occur simultaneously. Almost invariably economists avoid such complications by neglecting the role of long-lived fixed capital in their analysis.

This layering of paradoxes of rationality indicates that capitalism is a very complex system built upon a multitude of contradictions. Economists make a grave error in building their models on the assumption that everybody is rational and that economies almost inevitably move toward a stable equilibrium. In fact, just the opposite is the case. What prevents the economy from running off the rails every few decades is a combination of government regulation and anticompetitive behavior on the part of business.

Investment and Economic Progress

Our understanding of the paradox of rationality helps us to understand what we might call the paradox of investment. Although most investments turn out to be disappointments, except when they prosper by virtue of government protection from market forces, the overall process of investment has made possible enormous improvements in the standard of living.

For example, at the time of the Norman Conquest of England, a woolen tunic would be a peasant's most valuable possession. Upon death, relatives were likely to squabble over this meager scrap of inheritance.[35] Today, people even of modest incomes in the advanced countries enjoy luxuries that would have been unimaginable in ancient society.

This paradox of investment resolves itself quite easily when we view investments in the context of an economy as a whole rather than from the perspective of an individual investor. Imagine that you invest in a revolutionary technology. If your investment is successful, it will probably hurt your competitors by reducing the value of their existing investments. To remain competitive, they may have to respond by making their own new investments in their business, which may tend to devalue your latest investment. If this process becomes too intense, it can set off a destabilizing, downward spiral of capital values.

Your same investment also has a contrary effect. Your employees will learn from their experience with the new technology, in the process upgrading their abilities. Your competitors will also acquire new knowledge from studying your investment. Even people from other industries often reap benefits from such investments. As a result, your investment, even if it might turn out to be a personal disaster, can make your employees and your competitors, and even others outside of your industry, more capable.

The loss of capital values is a temporary phenomenon, in the sense that the loss today will not directly injure the economy tomorrow, except to the extent that capital is sunk in fixed investment without value in alternative uses. In contrast, the increase in social capabilities is a permanent gain, so long as people continue to exercise their capabilities.

Such capabilities are extremely important. We have seen many examples of rapid recoveries of war-torn economies. Despite enormous capital losses, the capabilities that survive the battles allow economies to surpass their previous economic heights with amazing speed. However, when competitive forces continually batter down capital values for an extended period of time, the economy will indeed suffer.

This chapter has shown one reason why capitalist markets do have an inherent tendency toward extended downturns. In the late nineteenth century and again following the stock market crash of 1929, the economy fell into prolonged depressions—neither of which were ended by market forces. Beginning in the late 1890s, business organized anticompetitive arrangements to thwart the downward tendencies of the economy, pulling the economy out of its slump. The Second World War ended the Great Depression that began in 1929.

In the next chapter, we will explore the first of these two depressions. The chapter demonstrates the weakness of both conventional economics and the capitalist economy.

3

Railroads and the Increase in Fixed Capital

The Historical Increase in Fixed Capital

Despite the innumerable risks associated with investment, much investment has nonetheless occurred. Even during the worst of times, some firms still make investments in fixed capital. More important, much of that investment has proven to be productive, even though the original investors may have suffered losses.

Over time, fixed capital has become a substantially more important factor in the structure of production. We might well regard the essential feature of the first two centuries of the industrial revolution to be a tendency toward an increasing dependence on ever more specialized productive capital goods that have few alternative uses.

The tendency for fixed, specialized capital goods to become important has not been a steady process. Instead, the accumulation of capital spurted ahead during booms when animal spirits were buoyant and lagged during recessions when animal spirits sagged. During economic contractions, business concentrates on increasing efficiency rather than adding capacity.

Every few decades economies experience great booms that economists associate with the rise of a new core industry, such as railroads, cars, or computers. These new industries are so influential that they stimulate great demand for whole networks of suppliers and open up vast new opportunities for whole ranges of new businesses. In the development of the early United States, the new core industries of canals and then railroads were crucial because these transportation services allowed industry to serve the great expanse of the country.

These transportation industries began to issue stock in the 1830s. Many investors welcomed the opportunity to put their money in these ventures. Often these companies paid very handsome dividends, far in excess of what they could afford, because they failed to make any provision for the renewal of their fixed capital stock. Even so, initially the volume of stocks was relatively small. As late as 1856, the total value of railroad, bank, and canal stocks was about $825,000—the equivalent of about $16 million at then-current prices.[1]

In these companies, management was relatively free from any interference by the investors. So long as the shareholders expected to make a profit on their assets, they took little interest in day-to-day management matters. In addition, a good number of the investors lived abroad. Finally, firms took care to disperse stock-holding among many individuals. For example, the Western Railroad in Massachusetts reported 2,331 individual share-owners in 1838; in 1853, the New York Central Railroad had 2,445, and the Pennsylvania Railroad over 2,600.[2] Given the primitive communication systems of the time, these stockholders would have had great difficulty in forming a coalition effective enough to challenge management practices.

Just after the Civil War in the United States, the structure of the economy began to shift because of a dramatic acceleration in capital accumulation. Although all temporal subdivisions of an economy are somewhat artificial, identifying the Civil War as a watershed in the historical evolution of the role of fixed capital in the United States does make a good deal of sense.

During the war, the military created levels of demand that were previously unknown, setting off an unprecedented economic boom. Because the war drained off so much labor and grain prices were so high, farmers invested heavily in labor-saving devices, such as reapers.[3] No doubt, other businesses followed a similar course. This spurt in prosperity ushered in a great railway boom.

Railroad Speculation

By the late nineteenth century, railroads became the preeminent form of big business. For example, in the 1850s, the largest nonrailroad employer in the United States, Pepperell Mills at Biddeford, Maine, had only 800 workers. Its expenses exceeded $300,000 in only one year in the 1850s. In 1855, the Erie Railroad's expenses were $2.8 million; the Pennsylvania's were $2.1 million.[4] Investment in a railroad also represented a heretofore unimaginable commitment of fixed capital.

Railroads involved enormous investments in laying track, providing locomotive power, as well as cars. These heavy investments required many years of profitable service before they could be expected to repay their expenses. At the same time, the marginal costs of carrying an extra ton of freight for this capital-intensive industry were relatively trivial. Given this cost structure, one might imagine a pervasive reluctance to invest in railways. Competition that drove prices toward marginal costs would mean that railroads would not be able to earn enough to meet their obligations to their bondholders.

In light of this natural disinclination to invest in railroads, local and state government, as well as Washington, went to great lengths to subsidize railroad investment. The enormous stretches of land that the federal government awarded to the transcontinental railroads to help defray the cost of fixed capital represent the most well-known subsidy, but in fact, local subsidies were even more important during the early years of railroading.[5]

These subsidies were modest compared to the overinvestment that occurred in their wake. Railroading seems to have caused many investors to fall into a hysterical enthusiasm.

Although the technology was relatively new, railroads already had a history of speculative excesses. In the 1840s, a similar mania in railroad investment swept across England. By October 1845, investors in Britain were seeking Parliamentary approval for approximately 1,200 railroad projects for 10,000 miles of track costing 300 million pounds. In that same month, James Wilson wrote an article in the *Economist* warning that current plans to invest were wildly excessive. He compared the magnitude of the planned investment to the annual savings of Britain, which he estimated at 60 million pounds per year. By that time, Parliament had already approved projects costing about 74 million pounds over the next five years.[6]

Not surprisingly, this article caused considerable alarm, leading to the subsequent abandonment of numerous projects. In the process, the railway mania of 1845 gave way to an equally overreactive railway panic. Approximately 30 million pounds of share capital evaporated within three short weeks, while the shares of the ten leading railway companies fell 78 million pounds between 1845 and 1847.[7] Even so, many investors went unchastened. About 32 million pounds, or 70 percent of Britain's total fixed capital formation, went into further railway construction between 1846 and 1848.[8]

Overinvestment in railroads was no less extreme in the United States. Investment in railroads exceeded aggregate investment in manufacturing for every decade from 1850 to 1890. It was more than twice as large as aggregate investment in manufacturing from 1850 to 1880.[9] Until 1904, the book value of capital in the railroad industry exceeded the aggregate capital invested in the entire industrial sector.[10]

Charles Francis Adams, Jr., great-grandson of President John Adams, and grandson of John Quincy Adams and perhaps the most influential writer in the United States on the subject of railroads, observed that after the railroad mania of 1844, "Free trade in railroads was then pronounced a failure."[11] The distinguished British economist John Stuart Mill independently had reached a similar conclusion a few decades before, shortly after the British railway panic.[12] Unfortunately, their pronouncements had little effect on either economists or investors at the time.

The inability of most economists to understand the nature of the problem presented by the railroad mania paralleled an even larger failure that is a central topic of this
book: Economists were ill-equipped to come to grips with the nature of fixed capital.

Accounting for Profits in the Railroad Industry

In part, we can attribute at least some of this enthusiasm for railroads to the common
accounting error we discussed in the last chapter. The merchant-oriented accounting
profession was ill-suited to offer guidance concerning the problems of fixed capital,
which were so pressing for the railroads.

According to the standard accounting practices of the time, railroads ignored depreciation of fixed capital goods altogether. They charged all replacement and repairs as
current expenses, presuming that asset maintenance alone would permanently maintain
capital goods.[13] For example, the Annual Report of the Pennsylvania Railroad in 1855
contended that by charging repairs and renewals to operating expenses, the property
accounts could continue to reflect true value of capital assets. It noted, "The practice of
the Company in relation to its running equipment is to preserve the number of cars and
locomotives charged to construction account, in complete efficiency; thus, if a car or
locomotive is destroyed, or has become old and worthless, a new one is substituted in
its place, and its cost charged to the expense account."[14]

In other words, following the logic of their account books, many railroads did not recognize the need to set aside funds to replace depreciated capital goods in the future or to
cover rising maintenance costs.[15] Instead, the accountants would treat the purchase of a
locomotive as lump-sum cost when the firm bought it. In subsequent years, the accountants would record repairs and maintenance as costs, but the locomotive itself would then
be treated as if it cost nothing until the time came to replace it with a new one.[16]

This method of accounting made railroads appear to be a wonderfully attractive
investment since the capital stock was already in place. Because a railroad costs relatively little to maintain, especially in the early years of its operation, the accountants reported most of its revenue as profits during the early years.[17] This practice allowed them to
pay huge dividends out of capital to the delight of shareholders without realizing that
eventually maintenance costs would increase and new investments become necessary.

These spectacular windfalls for short-term speculators at the expense of the long-
term health of the business were not entirely accidental. In the words of a history of
accounting thought, "Railroad asset valuation policies had two conflicting purposes: to
attract investors…while at the same time accumulating funds to replace equipment."[18]

Since railroads seemed to be such an attractive investment, investors, hungry to soak
up railroad paper, funded far more rail lines than the economy could absorb at one time.

The inevitable shakeout devastated the railroads. Many fell into bankruptcy, revealing financial incompetence as well as scandalous behavior, along with inadequate accounting practices. In the wake of these revelations, some lines did adopt cost-based depreciation, but in many cases they abandoned it when they found that their depreciation provisions were inadequate to replace their fixed assets.[19]

Although accounting illusions may have fueled the frenzy of railroad speculation during the boom years of the 1840s and prepared the way for the subsequent bust, investors in the railroads soon learned that the problems in the industry ran far deeper than questionable accounting practices. The railroad booms emerged out of an excessively buoyant view of the future prospects for the industry.

After all, accountants can do little to protect investors from their own short-sightedness. An accountant's job is to coordinate the values of past and present business actions so that a firm can get a handle on its current profitability. In contrast, the problems that businesspeople face depend more on future outcomes than on the past.

The lessons of the first railroad boom were short-lived. After the Civil War, a brand-new railroad boom developed. At the time, the rapidly industrializing U.S. economy attracted huge amounts of European (particularly British) capital. Soon British investors sent Scottish- and English-chartered accountants to visit the United States to evaluate the American properties and to check for fraud. In the process, they eventually transplanted new British accounting practices, which included a crude form of capital budgeting,[20] but better accounting procedures were not enough to bring rationality into railroading.

The Delayed Reflection of Fixed Capital in Economic Theory

We have seen that the effect of the expansion in the scale of investment was to increase substantially the importance of fixed costs in advanced economies. Although any realistic economic theory must take account of these fixed costs, conventional price theory is incapable of doing so.

Just as the accountants took their cue from the world of the merchant, the early economists adopted the perspective of merchants, who were uninvolved in the production process, and for whom fixed capital was relatively unimportant. Despite the veritable explosion of industrial activity in the United States, dislodging outdated mercantile ideas was no easy matter. In the case of the United States, this intellectual inertia was not at all accidental. Churches ran almost all the colleges, with the major exception of the University of Pennsylvania. In his study of the teaching of political economy in the United States, Michael O'Connor took note of the dominance of "the clerical school of political economy."[21] The clergy who ran the schools were not financially independent. They counted on merchants to donate enough money to keep their colleges solvent. In return, the merchants insisted that students be indoctrinated in the wisdom of laissez-faire theory.

Since the primary concern in teaching economics was to offer instruction that would meet with the approval of the merchants, more often than not the president of the college took personal responsibility for teaching the economics courses.[22] As a result, the experience of merchants inspired much of early economic theory.

Henry Carey was one of the first major economists to break with the merchant conception of economics. Although Carey began as a typical exponent of the prevailing merchant-oriented brand of economic theory, his views abruptly changed to a more productionist perspective after he experienced bankruptcy. Thereafter, he became every bit as much a vigorous protectionist as he had been a doctrinaire free-trader before.

In developing his protectionist theories, Carey maintained that the erosion of value due to an increase in fixed capital values lay at the heart of the capitalist process. For Carey,

> ...value...is simply *our estimate of the resistance to be overcome, before we can enter upon the possession of the thing desired.* That resistance diminishes with every increase in the power of man to command the always gratuitous services of nature.

> With every increase in this direction, there is a diminution in the value of all accumulated machinery, because of the steady diminution in *the cost of reproduction*, as nature is more and more forced in the service of man.

> The cost of production has ceased to be the measure of value, the cost at which they can be reproduced having fallen.[23]

Carey's theory of progressively falling values dovetailed with another popularly held idea at the time: Industry in the United States with its high wages could not effectively compete against the low-wage labor employed in the rest of the world. Over time, with enough protection, improved industrial methods would allow labor in the United States to outcompete the workers in the rest of the world, who were contemptuously referred to as pauper labor. But for the time being, protection was essential.

Carey was very influential in Europe.[24] Within the United States, a growing number of political leaders took him quite seriously. He even inspired, if not wrote, the first Republican Party platform on trade.[25] Nonetheless, the merchant-oriented universities dismissed Carey's theories. To remedy the neglect of Carey's teachings, Joseph Wharton, the great Pennsylvania iron manufacturer, founded the Wharton School of Business at the University of Pennsylvania to expose students to Carey's views.[26]

The Initial Theoretical Retreat from Laissez-Faire Theory

Conventional economics paints a beautiful picture. It teaches that the economy will be relatively stable because buyers and sellers quickly respond to each other's actions.

Despite this comforting idea, the theory was flawed by neglect of the role of fixed capital. As Hans Thorelli realized, taking fixed capital into account, "The logical outcome of 'survival of the fittest' thinking was monopoly, while static analysis of classical economics envisaged a timeless equilibrium of perfect competition."[27] What Thorelli meant was that competition would drive firm after firm out of business. The last firm standing would have the industry to itself. Once that happened potential new competitors would have difficulty dislodging it.

By the late nineteenth century, events confirmed the fallacy of conventional economic theory. Although the 1880s were the most rapid decade of economic growth in the post–Civil War period, measured by per capita growth of reproducible tangible wealth, amount of savings, investment funds, and growth of per capita income, the economy was running amok.[28] In addition, industry was rapidly introducing powerful new technologies. Between 1869 and1889, the average factory doubled in size and capital invested per manufacturing worker grew from $700 to $2,000.[29]

Judging by these numbers, you might expect great prosperity during this period. In fact, hardship was widespread. Wages fell. More surprisingly, most of the business community suffered from this technological revolution.

The adoption of new technology by a competitor forced owners of outdated plant and equipment to adopt one of three options. First, they could passively withdraw from production. Second, they could adopt improved technologies, which would decrease prices. Or third, they could attempt to meet the competition by dropping their prices while continuing to use their existing plant and equipment.

Apparently, relatively few took the first option. As a result, prices plummeted. For example, the Bessemer process reduced the price of steel rails by 88 percent from the early 1870s to the late 1880s; electrolytic refining reduced aluminum prices by 96 percent; synthetic blue dye production costs fell by 95 percent from the 1870s to 1886.[30]

On a macroeconomic level, the general price index fell from a high of 129 in 1864 to a low of 71 in 1894, where it remained until 1896. The wholesale price of pig iron fell by about two-thirds and refined petroleum by over 90 percent.[31]

In this deflationary environment, installed capital generally depreciated well before firms could amortize their investments. Because firms had to abandon equipment before it had paid for itself, profits fell. Fourteen of the twenty-five years between 1873 and 1897 were years of depression or recession.

During the Great Depression of the twentieth century, while a generation of economists was shedding its trust in market forces, Joseph Schumpeter reminded his readers of the magnitude of this earlier period of hardship:

> As far as mere figures go, some aspects…of the depression were quite as dark in 1873 and in 1877 as they were in 1929 to 1933. …[I]f we…believe in the figure of three million "tramps" (in the Winter of 1873 to 1874) then this…would indicate that relative unemployment was actually worse than it was during the recent world crisis.[32]

Just as was the case in the twentieth century, the economic crises of the late nineteenth century spawned extensive dissatisfaction with the market as a universal regulator of economic activity. Many, if not most, prominent economists had difficulty maintaining their devotion to market principles at the time. Many leading business figures also joined in this rejection of the market. Those who broke with the prevailing economic orthodoxy in the United States dismissed the merchant-oriented heritage of laissez-faire economics as mere "commercial theory."[33]

Unlike the reaction to the Great Depression of the 1930s, none of these leading academic economists at the time became advocates of socialism. Even so, within the bounds of respectable economics, the breadth and depth of this earlier change of opinion was just as profound as the one that occurred in the midst of the twentieth century depression.

Certainly, the nineteenth-century economists whom we shall discuss took positions that were considerably more heretical than those that Keynes proposed during the 1930s. Unlike most heretics, who are relegated to the institutional wilderness for railing against established powers, these heretics supported the actions of some of the richest and most powerful industrialists and financiers in the nation. Not surprisingly, their heresies did not prevent them from enjoying their comfortable positions in government and academia.

David A. Wells was a prime example of this tendency. Wells is all but forgotten today. Some modern economists may still recognize his name, but only because Harvard students still vie for the coveted David A. Wells Prize. Even so, Wells was a major figure in the United States at the time.

Wells's career extended beyond economics, ranging from developing improvements in textile technologies to writing scientific books and working in the publishing industry, but Wells owed his fame to his work as an economist. Despite his seemingly unimportant title of special commissioner of revenue, he was by far the most important economist within the U.S. government. He was also responsible for bringing eminent economists such as Francis A. Walker into government service.

For most of the second half of the nineteenth century, presidents and other high offi-cials prized Wells's ability to further their preferred economic policies. His biographer wrote, "Some of the most trustworthy contemporary observers insisted that no one man contributed as much to the election of Grant as Special Commissioner Wells."[34]

Besides his influential role in shaping economic policy, Wells produced a verita-ble stream of books and articles that were effective in molding public opinion on eco-nomic matters. Wells's *Recent Economic Changes* (1889) was "probably the most cited book of the period 1890–1910."[35] Hans Thorelli called this book "by far the most popular work along somewhat heterodox lines."[36] Its influence lasted into the 1920s. In 1927, four decades after its appearance, Herbert Hoover, then secretary of com-merce, created a Commission on Recent Economic Changes, chaired by Hoover him-self. The commission clearly connected its own work with Wells's heritage, noting in its second paragraph, "Forty years ago David A. Wells wrote his *Recent Economic Changes*, showing that the quarter century that ended in 1889 was a period of 'pro-found economic changes.' "[37]

Henry Carey, David Wells, and Destructive Market Forces

Wells began as a devout disciple of Henry Carey.[38] He expressed his devotion to Carey in a letter written on May 1, 1858:

> I am at present...engaged in writing a series of scientific school books. ...In writing
> them, I have kept steadily in view the principles of political economy as I have learned
> from you and have endeavored to shape my teachings into consonance with them.[39]

Both Carey and Wells were attempting to correct deficiencies in the market, but after 1867 Wells parted company with Carey on the issue of free trade. Carey emphasized the competitive threat from abroad, fearing that excessive foreign competition could under-mine domestic manufacturing. Carey was confident that protection alone would be suf-ficient to allow market forces to bring about an ideal world.

Carey overlooked the destabilizing nature of domestic competition. He had not anticipated the dramatic destruction of capital values resulting from competitive forces. This neglect is ironic since declining values were central to his theory. Instead, he asserted that new technology, developed within the context of a prosperous, self-sufficient economy, would serve to broaden prosperity by means of a continuous process of cheapening capital goods.

For Carey, the falling cost of reproducing capital goods was an indication of prosper-ity. Carey saw only the positive side of this phenomenon. He was content that the more the price of capital goods fell the greater both the wage share and rents would be. In this way, he associated the cheapening of capital goods with an augmentation of the value of both labor and natural resources, allowing both workers and farmers to enjoy a good life.

Carey gave no indication that he recognized that continual declines in the reproduction costs of capital goods caused corresponding capital losses for owners of existing capital goods. Nor did he anticipate that the employers would try to recoup some of these losses by cutting wages.

As a result, Carey never seemed to realize that domestic competition could disrupt the economy. Only foreign competition presented a danger from his perspective. Once business concentrated on serving local markets within a protected economy all would be well.

Wells, writing later than Carey, abruptly abandoned his earlier faith in protectionism, becoming convinced that manufacturing in the United States had become so powerful that it had little to fear from international competition. Indeed, he believed that the strength of modern manufacturing in the United States had reached such proportions that internal competitive forces threatened the very existence of the domestic manufacturing system.

The Economy of High Wages

Wells's break with Carey was not just about protectionism. Carey believed that protection would allow industry in the United States to reach a point at which it could outcompete foreign industry. Wells may have merely concluded that the United States had already passed that point.

Wells differed with Carey on wages. For Carey, pauper labor abroad represented a fundamental threat to industry in the United States. For Wells, high wages were not an obstacle to development. In fact, high wages in the United States were an appropriate reward for high productivity. He wrote:

> High wages, then, are the normal result of low cost, and low cost is the normal result in turn of intelligence, conjoined with good machinery, applied to great resources for production.[40]

Wells noted that wages in England's cotton industry were 30 to 50 percent higher than in France, Belgium, and Germany. He observed that an English cotton operative received more wages in a week than a Russian in a month. Yet the Continent demanded protection against English labor.[41]

Later research bore out Wells's contention. Gregory Clark published an extensive survey of this relationship between high wages and British competitiveness in an article entitled "Why Isn't the Whole World Developed? Lessons from the Cotton Mills."[42] Although British wages were less than those earned in the United States, they were high relative to the rest of the world. According to Clark, compared with Manchester, hourly wages on the Continent ranged from less than 25 percent to as high in Prussia to 47 percent in Rouen.[43]

In 1911, 140 years after the first cotton mills and despite an enormous wage cost disadvantage, 40 percent of all factory spindles were in England. Another 22 percent were in the United States and Canada. Low-wage countries had only 39 percent of all spindles worldwide.[44]

Clark also reported that in 1910 one New England cotton textile worker was equivalent to 1.5 British or 2.3 German workers. Compared to lower-wage economies, the difference was phenomenal. New England textile operatives tended six times as much machinery per shift as workers in the Greek, Japanese, Indian, or Chinese textile industries.[45]

Within a short time after Wells observed that high wages did not represent a threat to domestic industry, others took his thought one step further. They proclaimed that high wages actually provided an advantage to industry in the United States. For example, in the late nineteenth century, the United States secretary of state commissioned Joseph Schoenhof to inquire into the effects of high wages on the competitiveness of business in the United States. Schoenhof reported:

> the employer of labor is...benefited by the inevitable results of a high rate of wages.
> ...[T]he first object of the employer is to economize its employment.
> Manufacturers introducing a change in manufactures have a machine built to accomplish what in other countries would be left to hand labor to bring about. Machinery, used to the limit of its life in Europe, is cast aside in America if only partially worn.[46]

The Cornell economist Jeremiah Jenks, whom we will discuss later in this chapter, asserted:

> No sooner has the capitalist fairly adopted one improved machine, than it must be thrown away for a still later and better invention, which must be purchased at a dear cost, if the manufacturer would not see himself eclipsed by his rival.[47]

This pattern of rapid capital renewal made the manufacturing capacity in United States the envy of the world. By the turn of the century, exports from the United States were inundating Europe, much the same as Japanese exports are displacing U.S. production today. Just as people in the United States today try to discover the secret of

Japanese ascendancy in popular books, English readers pored over alarmist books with titles such as *The American Invaders* (1901), *The Americanization of the World* (1901), or *The American Invasion* (1902).[48]

David Wells and the Theory of Creative Destruction

Wells reversed his former master's analysis of competition. Where Carey deplored foreign competition, Wells viewed it in a positive light. For the mature Wells, foreign competition was benign because it posed little threat to the advanced technology of the United States. In contrast to Carey, who viewed the domestic economy as a system of harmonies, Wells warned that domestic competition was rife with danger. Unlike Carey, who saw shrinking capital values as a sign of progress, Wells worried that the combination of violent competition coupled with rapid technological advances was destroying capital values too rapidly. This process was driving the economy into chaos.

In order to avert disaster, Wells called for an even more dramatic break with the market than Carey had ever considered. He reasoned that the combination of the extraordinary rate of investment in modern technologies, together with an inadequate rate of exit on the part of inefficient producers, made overproduction the inevitable consequence of modern industry. These conditions destroyed business's ability to earn adequate profits. Wells cited a German professor, Wilhelm Lexis, in this regard:

> It was formerly a general assumption that, when price no longer equaled the cost of production and a fair profit on capital, production would be restricted or suspended; and that the less favored producers would be crowded out, and by the relief thus afforded to the market normal prices would be restored. But this doctrine is no longer applicable to modern methods of production. Those engaged in great industrial enterprises, whether they form joint-stock companies or are simply wealthy individuals, are invested with such economic powers that none of them can be easily pushed to the wall, inasmuch as they can continue to work under conditions that would not permit a small producer to exist. Examples are familiar of joint-stock companies that have made no profit and paid no dividends for years, and yet continue active operation. The shareholders are content if the plant is kept up and the working capital preserved intact, and even when this is not done, they prefer to submit to assessments, or issue preference shares and take them up themselves rather than go into liquidation, with the chance of losing their whole capital.[49]

[N]o other means of avoiding such results [overproduction] than that the great producers should come to some understanding among themselves as to the prices they will ask; which in turn naturally implies agreements as to the extent to which they will produce.[50]

In short, Wells realized that competitive forces would not allow producers to recover their investments in fixed capital. As a result, the market would self-destruct. He recommended that industry be allowed to organize itself into trusts, monopolies, and cartels. Nothing could be further from the teachings of Adam Smith and the merchants!

David Wells realized that overproduction was not the only threat to capitalism; rapid technical progress also destroys capital values. Although Wells failed to link this phenomenon to Carey's insight about falling reproduction costs, in other respects he went far beyond Carey. Wells wrote of "the relentless impartiality with which the destructive influences of material progress coincidentally affect capital [property] as well as labor."[51] He concluded:

> It seems to be in the nature of a natural law that no advanced stage of civilization can be attained, except at the expense of destroying in a greater or less degree the value of the instrumentalities by which all previous attainments have been affected.[52]

For Wells, anticipating Joseph Schumpeter's widely acclaimed idea of creative destruction (1950), the measure of the technical success of any invention was the extent to which it could destroy capital values.[53] He offered the example of "[t]he notable destruction or great impairment in the value of ships consequent upon the opening of the [Suez] Canal."[54] He asserted that each generation of ships becomes obsolete within a decade. Generalizing from the shipping industry, he concluded, "nothing marks more clearly the rate of material progress than the rapidity with which that which is old and has been considered wealth is destroyed by the results of new inventions and discoveries."[55]

In slighting Carey, Wells claimed no originality for his work. Instead, he credited his idea to a friend:

> by an economic law, which Mr. [Edward] Atkinson, of Boston, more than others, has recognized and formulated, all material progress is effected through the destruction of capital by invention and discovery, and the rapidity of such destruction is the best indicator of the rapidity of progress.[56]

Wells may have had a good reason for not linking his theory with that of Carey. For Wells, Carey's theory might have some long-run relevance, but Wells was writing in the midst of the immediate threat of a crisis of overproduction. At the time, falling capital values compounded the problems created by the tendency of competition to drive prices toward marginal costs, threatening rather than reinforcing prosperity.

Wells's analysis was not lost on the generation of influential economists who were most actively confronting the nature of the economics of railroads. During the second half of the nineteenth century, railroading was the most dynamic industry in the United States. It attracted economists who were accustomed to being close to the seat of power.

Boom and Bust Again in the Railroad Industry

Given that investment in fixed capital can repay itself only in the unknowable future, railroad investment ultimately came down to a question of psychology. In the end, investor psychology was far more unstable and difficult to refine than accounting practices.

In the case of railroad industry, the psychology of investors proved time and again to be disastrously overoptimistic. Railroad investment advanced at a breakneck pace. Far too many railroads competed for the existing traffic. Much like the telecom industry in the 1990s, everybody assumed that increased demand in the future would make the investments profitable in the near future. Instead railroads went bankrupt with remarkable regularity. When investors eventually did realize how dire the prospects for their industry were, their optimism quickly turned to gloom—until, of course, the next round of euphoria sprouted.

Excessive optimism of investors was only part of the problem. Cynical railroad corporations would start "blackmail" lines parallel to existing roads, as a tactical maneuver to threaten their rivals. They were fully aware that this investment could not earn a profit hauling freight. They calculated that existing railroads would buy up their investment rather than risk becoming caught up in a destructive rate war. Finally, many of the railroads' largest customers, such as Rockefeller and Carnegie, successfully demanded large rebates on their freight bills.[57]

In the end, the railroads offered a stunning indictment of market forces. Industry leaders did a poor job of managing their investments. Rates were both unstable and unreasonable. They were too high on the isolated feeder routes that linked sparsely populated agricultural regions to the main trunk lines. On other routes, especially along once profitable trunk lines, rates were too low to earn a profit when shippers could choose between alternative routes. Consider Alfred Chandler's description of the railroad industry in the late nineteenth century once the problems in the industry became apparent:

Railroad competition presented an entirely new business phenomenon. Never before had a very small number of very large enterprises competed for the same business. And never before had competitors been saddled with such high fixed costs. In the 1880s fixed costs...averaged two-thirds of total cost. The relentless pressure of such costs quickly convinced railroad managers that uncontrolled competition of through traffic would be "ruinous." As long as a road had cars available to carry freight, the temptation to attract traffic by reducing rates was always there. Any rate that covered more than the variable costs of transporting a shipment brought extra income. [A weak road that succumbed to bankruptcy would have competitive advantage.—Author] It no longer had to pay the fixed charges on its debt. Since American railroads were financed largely through bonds, these charges were high. To both the railroad managers and investors, the logic of such competition would be bankruptcy for all.[58]

This upwelling of competition created havoc among the railroads. Reported revenue per ton mile fell from 1.88 cents in 1870 to 1.22 cents in 1880, even though rates remained high on many feeder routes. By 1890, rates had reached 0.94 cents. By 1900 rates had fallen to 0.73.[59] Ultimately, half of all the track constructed in the United States before 1900 fell into receivership, despite the best efforts of the foreign accountants.[60] As a result, a wave of bankruptcies engulfed the industry, opening up an opportunity for a new type of financial agent, personified by J. P. Morgan, whom we will discuss later.

The economic impact of the railroad industry was far from inconsequential. J. S. Foreman-Peck estimated that the unregulated, free enterprise system of railway investment in Britain probably raised construction costs by 50 percent and lowered national income per head by at least 0.75 percent in static terms around 1906.[61] In the United States, where conditions were more extreme, the effect must have been considerably greater.

Charles Francis Adams, Jr., and Railroad Economics

Despite the dramatic lessons of the railroad industry, academic representatives of conventional economic theory taught at the time, just as they continue to teach today, that although competitive pressures may create difficulties for particular individuals or industries, society as a whole will benefit from the free play of market forces. Supposedly one of the great benefits of capitalism is that it succeeds in directing investment where it can be used most productively. Conventional economic theory offers "proof" of this conclusion, but these proofs assume away the influence of sunk costs.

Railroad economists came to an entirely different conclusion. They realized that railroading bore no resemblance to the conditions of perfect competition. Because of the enormous amounts of fixed capital required, firms could not easily enter and exit the railroad industry. In addition, where two firms did enter the same market, the preponderance of fixed capital meant that competition would force prices to gravitate toward marginal costs, guaranteeing bankruptcy according to the rules of perfect competition.

Perfect competition also assumes perfect knowledge on the part of investors. In reality, financial manipulators effectively controlled many railroads in the late nineteenth century. These speculators had no interest in having their firms aim at profit maximization. Instead, they were intent at driving stock prices up or down to their own financial advantage. The rest of the railroad investors were at the mercy of these unscrupulous rogues.

Charles Francis Adams, Jr., as the descendent of two presidents, was too much of a patrician to care much for such shenanigans. In fact, he had little use for businessmen in general. Late in life, he recalled:

> I have known, and known tolerably well a good many "successful" men—"big" financially—men famous during the last half-century; and a less interesting crowd I do not care to encounter. Not one that I have ever known...is...associated in my mind with the idea of humor, thought or refinement. A set of mere money-getters and traders, they were essentially unattractive and uninteresting.[62]

As a young man, Adams was disinclined to earn his fortune at business. Despite his famous family and his training at the Harvard Law School, he never landed a bona fide client as a lawyer.[63] Instead, he staked his future as a public figure concerned with railroads. He wrote to the ubiquitous David Wells, "I want a war with the [railroad] Rings" (14 January 1869).[64] The railroads' promoters were notoriously corrupt, bilking and fleecing investors with abandon.

Adams chose as his prime target the notorious Erie Railroad. His choice was fortuitous. The Erie had a checkered history, replete with horrendous cost overruns and the flagrant manipulation of ignorant investors. The Erie had first won its charter in 1832. At the time, it had $1 million worth of stock subscribed for an estimated construction cost of $3 million. By the time it had issued its first report, the estimated cost had doubled to $6 million. By 1842, the estimate soared to $12.5 million. Insolvent, it passed into receivership. In 1845, New York State surrendered its claim to the $3 million it previously had lent the project. The company floated another $3 million worth of stock and borrowed an additional $3 million. By 1851, the road finally opened. By 1859, the organization could no longer meet the interest payment on its mortgages. It was reorganized once again in 1861. The original project, initially estimated to cost $3 million, actually cost $50 million to complete.[65]

The directors of the railroad realized that manipulating the stock was far more profitable than concentrating their energies on the mundane task of improving the railroad operations. Within four short years, by financial sleight of hand, they recapitalized the Erie Railroad from $17 million to $78 million. In one case, Daniel Drew and the other directors purchased a worthless road, the Buffalo, Bradford, and Pittsburgh, for $250,000, then issued $2 million worth of bonds in the name of the company. Then they leased the road to the Erie for 499 years. The Erie then assumed the bonds, leaving Drew and his associates with a handsome profit.[66]

While the manipulators manipulated, investors in the railroads naively staked their fortunes on the rigged market. In this vein, Adams observed, "Gambling is now a business where formerly it was a disreputable excitement. Cheating at cards was always disgraceful; transactions of a similar character…are not so regarded."[67] Eventually, the Erie became the scene for an epic struggle for control among the great financial manipulators of the day—Cornelius Vanderbilt and Daniel Drew, Jay Gould and Jim Fisk. These scoundrels openly flouted the public interest, purchasing judges and politicians, without any pretense of serving any public good.

Although Adams found business figures personally uninteresting, his Olympian descriptions of these colorful crooks make a wonderful read. The lessons of the Erie Railroad were soon forgotten. Each time a stock market bubble burst, the public learns about a new generation of scoundrels perpetuating new frauds. A few regulations are enacted, then weakened, and finally ignored. Lacking a historical perspective, both the public and the pundits expressed shock that a "few bad apples" have not "played by the rules," even though this behavior is part and parcel of a market economy.

While working on his study of the Erie, Adams had lobbied for the creation of the Massachusetts Board of Railroad Commissioners. The state returned the favor and appointed him to the commission, where he became the dominant figure in that organization.[68]

Adams eventually abandoned his earlier disdain for business affairs. He parlayed his administrative position as a railroad commissioner into work for the railroads as the Chairman of the Board of Arbitration for the Eastern Trunk Lines Association, which set rates for railroads in the region.[69]

The railroad magnates intended this board to put an end to destructive competition, but it never succeeded. Instead, by the late 1880s, a series of disastrous price wars had ruined the association.

The Conundrum of Railroad Economics

Building upon his intimate knowledge of the railroad industry, Adams concluded that the underlying assumptions of conventional economic theory made no sense at all for understanding railroads. How could a market be rational when, at least in Adams's eyes, investors in the railroads suffered from pervasive irrationality? He observed that "the private individuals who constructed the railroads…built roads everywhere, apparently in perfect confidence that the country would so develop as to support all the roads that could be built."[70]

Moreover, varying degrees of competition among railroads produced a disorderly structure of prices from place to place. He wrote:

> …while the result of…ordinary competition was to reduce and equalize prices, that of railroad competition was to produce local inequalities and to arbitrarily raise and depress prices. The teachings of political economy were at fault. The variation was so great that it was evident that some important factor in the problem had been overlooked.[71]

Adams boldly challenged conventional economics to explain the functioning of the railroad industry. For Adams,

> …the railroad had developed one distinctive problem, and a problem which actively presses for solution. …[It] has become apparent that the recognized laws of trade operate but imperfectly at best in regulating the use made of these modern thoroughfares by those who both own and monopolize them.[72]

Adams's practical analysis of railroad affairs led him to reject market solutions, reaching the "conclusion which is at the basis of the whole transportation problem: *competition and the cheapest possible transportation are wholly incompatible*" (emphasis in original).[73]

At the time, many observers incorrectly assumed that railroads were somehow different from other economic activities. After all, as Alfred Chandler once noted, "The great railway systems were by the 1890's the largest business enterprises not only in the United States but also in the world."[74] Instead, the railroads blazed the trail for a new generation of industry. As Chandler observed in continuing his thought on the subject, "The railroad was…in every way the pioneer in modern business administration."

Adams may have been the first to break with the tradition that had treated the railroads as an exceptional case.[75] Instead, he was convinced that the experience of the railroad industry heralded the future destiny of the economy as a whole. He explained:

> The traditions of political economy…notwithstanding, there are functions of modern life, the number of which is also continually increasing, which necessar-

ily partake in their essence of the character of monopolies. ...Now it is found that, whenever this characteristic exists, the effect of competition is not to regulate cost or equalize production, but under a greater or less degree of friction to bring about combination and a closer monopoly. This law is invariable. It knows no exceptions.[76]

Hadley and the Generalization of the Railroad Problem

During the 1880s, while many conventional academic economists busied themselves with the arcane theory of perfect competition, some economists began to follow Adams's lead in proposing that the railroad business was not as exceptional as it initially appeared to be. Adams's friend, Arthur Twining Hadley, was the first economist to apply the experience of the railroads to the economy in general in his book *Railroad Transportation*, first published in 1885.[77] Hadley's distinguished career included the presidency of both the American Economic Association (1898–1899) and Yale University (1899–1921); he also taught economics as well as Greek, logic, and German and Roman law. Later, he also served as head of the Connecticut Public Utilities Commission. There, Hadley observed how the existence of large sunk costs makes conventional economics irrelevant:

> A railroad differs from many other [small-scale] business enterprises, in the existence of a large permanent investment, which can be used for one narrowly defined purpose, and for no other. The capital, once invested, must remain. It is worth little for any other purpose.[78]

Hadley noted that the growing importance of fixed capital was causing many other industries to resemble the railroads. Hadley's generalization of the railroad experience was timely because of the enormous increase in the scale of manufacturing throughout the antebellum period.

In fact, the average factory in the United States, measured by wage earners per establishment, grew more rapidly during the 1870s and 1880s than during any subsequent decade through the 1920s. The average factory doubled in size between 1869 and 1889. In comparison, it increased by only a quarter between 1899 and 1929.[79] Capital endowment per worker also doubled during the 1880s.[80]

Economists had reason to expect that the growth in manufacturing would make the economy more stable. Agriculture, a notoriously irregular industry because of the vagaries of the weather, was representing an increasingly small share of the national economy, while services, which tend to be stable, were rising in importance.[81]

Unfortunately, the growing role of fixed capital in industry brought instability in its wake, just as it had in the railroad industry.[82]

The increasing severity of the business cycle created a challenge for economists. Either economists had to show how the market could bring stability to the economy or they had to consider alternatives to the market. Hadley was the first major establishment economist to confront this challenge.

Hadley began by emphasizing the role of fixed capital. Given the revolutionary changes afoot in industrial technology, we should not be surprised by that approach. However, since large, fixed-capital investments invalidate the assumptions of conventional economics, Hadley was far ahead of his time. Only recently have a few modern economists, such as those associated with the so-called new institutional economics, made a serious attempt to analyze the role of fixed capital.[83] Hadley's discussion about this subject clearly anticipated their analysis.

Hadley identified two crucial problems facing the railroads:

1. Where there is a great deal of fixed capital, it can only come in slowly, and withdraw slowly; 2. More important still, the rate at which it pays to come in is very much higher than the rate at which it pays to go out.[84]

Based on his knowledge of the railroads, he concluded that "survival of the fittest is only possible when the unfittest can be physically removed—a thing which is impossible in the case of an unfit trunk line."[85] Where conventional, merchant-oriented economists were concerned to show that markets automatically ensured excellent outcomes, Hadley warned that where fixed capital is extensive, competitive pricing leads to ruin:

if a railroad is threatened with the loss of part of its traffic, it is better to reduce rates almost to the level of operating expenses, even if this leaves nothing for interest and repairs.[86]

Hadley added that "in those [other] lines of industry which involve large capital, under concentrated management, the old theory of free competition is as untenable as it was in the case of railroads."[87]

Hadley was well ahead of the economists of his day in pointing to the growing importance of fixed capital. For the most part, conventional economics remained out of step with the real world. While conventional economists were sweeping fixed capital under their assumed rug of perfect competition, business leaders commonly expressed awareness of the economic realities of the day. For example, the *Commercial and Financial Chronicle* told its readers what they already knew:

The effect of competition in regulating the prices of manufactured articles is not, at best, wholly satisfactory. ...[I]t does not prevent wide fluctuations. ...[After a businessman] has invested his money, he will not be able to withdraw it without loss. This plant, once established, must be kept in operation, even though the returns do not pay interest or fully cover maintenance charges. It then becomes a life-and-death struggle with him to maintain his position in the trade. He will compete all the more actively while prices are below cost, as long as his financial resources will stand the strain.[88]

Competitive pricing was not the only problem facing industry. For Hadley, as for Adams before him, investor irrationality represented a further threat to economic stability. In the case of the railroads, he noted:

In the three years 1880–1882 we built 29,000 miles of railroads, an addition of 34 percent to the railroad mileage of the country. Not more than one third of these were justified by existing business. Another third, perhaps, were likely to be profitable at some future date.[89]

Hadley saw the potential for irrationality to afflict all industries, not just railroads. He observed: "A new permanent investment is almost necessarily speculative. But investors do not look at the matter in that light."[90]

Consequently, irrationality accelerates the rate of fixed capital formation during the boom, while doing nothing to promote the withdrawal of fixed capital during periods when the economy is in decline.

Hadley on the Trust Problem

Despite his extensive training in economics, Hadley strenuously opposed the notion of unrestrained competition. He could not have been more emphatic in shrugging off the shibboleth of laissez faire, writing:

To so great an extent were the economists able to point out the evil results of mistaken legislation, that in the popular mind the teaching of economics has become synonymous with the effort to reduce the activity of government to a minimum. The phrase laissez faire..., which was the motto of the physiocrats, has taken an exaggerated hold on the public imagination, and has been regarded as a fundamental axiom of economic science, when it is in fact only a practical maxim of political wisdom, subject to all the limitations which experience may afford.[91]

Elsewhere, he observed:

All our education and habit of mind make us believe in competition. We have been
taught to regard it as a natural if not necessary condition of a healthful business life.
We look with satisfaction on whatever favors it, and with distrust on whatever hin-
ders it. We accept almost without reserve the theory of Ricardo, that, under open
competition in a free market, the value of different goods will tend to be proportion-
al to the cost of production.[92]

The world that Hadley saw in his study of railroads bore no resemblance to the
simplicity of Ricardo's model of perfect competition in which

the size units of capital is so large that free competition often becomes an impossi-
bility, and theories of economics which are based upon the existence of such competition prove blind guides in dealing with modern price movements.[93]

The railroads produced an entirely different result than the imagined world of
perfect competition:

Railroad competition may exist everywhere, somewhere or nowhere. If it exists
everywhere, rates are reduced to the level of movement charges [variable costs], and
there is nothing to pay fixed charges. ...If there is competition somewhere, the
competitive point will have rates based on movement expenses, and the others will
have to pay fixed charges. This constitutes discrimination. If we have competition
nowhere, this either involves a pool, or amounts to the same thing.[94]

Insofar as railroads and other capital intensive industries were concerned,
Hadley preferred the third alternative. The second alternative created enormous dissatisfaction on the part of shippers on the non-competitive lines who saw huge dis-
crepancies between the prices that they paid and the rates that prevailed on competitive lines. The first alternative, universal competition, is even more unsatisfactory.
When prices fall to near marginal costs in the face of unrestrained competition,
chaos results:

Ricardo's theory...fails, because, far below the point where it pays to do your own
business, it pays to steal business from another man. The influx of new capital will
cease; but the fight will go on, either until the old investment and machinery are
worn out, or until a pool of some sort is arranged.

In order to attract new capital into the business, rates must be high enough to pay not merely operating expenses, but fixed charges on both old and new capital. But, when capital is once invested, it can afford to make rates hardly above the level of operating expenses rather than lose a given piece of business. This "fighting rate" may be only one-half or one-third of a rate which would pay fixed charges. Pig iron in England was three times as high in 1873 as in 1878. Railroad rates, on the other hand, have varied as much as this within a single year.[95]

As a conservative, Hadley did not see much role for the state. He, along with many other leading economists of the time, had come to believe that only trusts, cartels, and monopolies could impose order on the disorderly market around them. He even went so far as to declare that the state was incapable of regulating monopolies. He insisted that legal sanctions would only drive would-be monopolists into secretive arrangements beyond the reach of the state.

Hadley assured the public that private sanctions alone would suffice to prevent any possible abuse of monopoly power. He even preferred to make collusion legal so that public opinion could more easily scrutinize corporate behavior.[96] True, Hadley favored a federal railway commission, but he did not want it to have extensive powers. Instead, Hadley saw the commission mostly as a source of information.

Hadley was correct in realizing the need for far-reaching changes in the organization of society rather than some superficial legal remedies. However, Hadley naively proposed that a combination of the threat of unfavorable publicity together with a presumed sense of corporate responsibility offered the public far more protection than any set of restrictive laws or regulations.[97] Given full public disclosure, Hadley believed that corporations would have no choice but to behave in the public interest. As he explained in 1900 during an address to the Candlelight Club in Denver on the subject "What Shall We Do with the Trusts?":

> This power [of the trusts] is so great that it can only be controlled by public opinion—not by statute. ...There are means enough. Don't let him come to your house. Disqualify him socially. You may say that it is not an operative remedy. This is a mistake. Whenever it is understood that certain practices are so clearly against public need and public necessity that the man who perpetrates them is not allowed to associate on even terms with his fellow men, you have in your hands an all-powerful remedy.[98]

Of course, the threat of being passed over for a dinner invitation from a working-class family might not weigh heavily on the minds of the great robber barons. These magnates did not typically socialize with common folks, but rather with other great robber barons, who might well take offense if one of their peers set a bad example by acting in the public interest.

Hadley's Choice: Neither Socialism nor the Market

Unlike the many distinguished economists during the Great Depression of the 1930s who opted for socialism as an alternative to the failed market, Hadley was still a conservative who wanted to preserve capitalism. Hadley even sounded a bit like a historical materialist, proclaiming, "This large permanent investment necessarily affects the relations of a railroad to its owners, to its users, and to the law."[99] Hadley noted:

> We only call attention to the close relation between the two problems of starvation wages and bankrupt competition. If capitalists and workingmen can but see this analogy, it may help them to an understanding of one another's position. The socialists, in spite of their unpractical proposals, have the merit of seeing the close relation between these two problems.[100]

Hadley's proto-Marxism is not altogether surprising. Although he was conservative to the core, he realized that the socialists were far closer to the truth than those who advocated laissez faire. He wrote to a friend that "while far from agreeing with him [Karl Marx]," he accepted that his work had a "higher scientific aim than almost any work on political economy in the last half century."[101] Elsewhere he observed:

> The socialists are justified in asserting that there is an inconsistency between our political doctrine of equal rights to pursuit of happiness for everybody, and the facts of the industrial world, as we see them about us.[102]

Ironically, the conservative Hadley saw laissez faire as being even more impractical than socialism. Recall that he proposed that unbridled competition would lead to the survival of "the unfittest rather than the fittest."[103] Nonetheless, Hadley concluded that "To enjoy industrial liberty, it will be necessary to resign the claim to industrial lawlessness; the alternative is socialism."[104] Marxists soon learned to appreciate the corporatists' program. Like the corporatists, Marxists recognized the wasteful nature of competition. They welcomed the corporatist consolidation of industry as potentially the first step toward socializing the entire economy. No wonder the reformer Henry Demarest Lloyd wrote to Henry S. Green (14 October 1898) that he regarded Hadley as "by far the most dangerous of all the Bourbon economists"![105]

The Corporatist School of Political Economy

As capital intensity began to increase in other industries, more and more sectors found themselves becoming dependent on expensive, specialized, capital-intensive processes. Just as Hadley had predicted, these industries also felt the impact of what they considered to be excess competition. Many firms reacted to their situation by joining together to form their own trusts, cartels, and monopolies.[106]

Although abstract economic dogma abhors such anticompetitive measures, many economists of the time, including the major theoretician of laissez faire, John Bates Clark, actively supported industry's efforts to blunt the impact of competition. Generalizing what they had learned from the railroads, these economists rejected the market as a means of regulating capital-intensive industries.

Carl Parrini and Martin Sklar identified these dissenters from laissez faire as members of what they termed the corporatist school of political economy.[107] In the words of Sklar:

>...opinion among leaders in business, political, and intellectual spheres began shifting from the old classical economic laws of free competition and supply-and-demand equilibrium to thinking centered on new economic laws of business cycles, crises, and disequilibrium, and on cooperation and administered markets.[108]

The leaders of this corporatist school were all prominent economists. According to Parrini and Sklar:

>Between 1896 and 1901, Arthur Twining Hadley of Yale, Jeremiah W. Jenks of Cornell [President of the American Economic Association in 1907] and Charles A. Conant [a leading authority on banking]...took the lead...in laying the theoretical foundations for the break with the classical model of the competitive market. ...Hadley criticized the classical doctrine as essentially a "commercial theory" that neglected the real conditions of supply in an industrial age. Rising fixed investment in plant and equipment rendered much capital largely immobile. It put a premium on economies of scale. The unintended result was "overproduction."[109]

The corporatists' main tenet was the necessity of an ongoing consolidation of U.S. industry, whether through trusts, cartels, or the formation of monopolies. This consolidation would not just benefit industries that protected themselves by anticompetitive arrangements. The corporatists argued that the economy as a whole would be more efficient if business were free to form trusts, cartels, and monopolies. As Parrini and Sklar noted:

...an administered market...represented the response of a progressive policy to the
instabilities of the competitive market under the conditions of advanced industrial
development and surplus capital.[110]

Hadley, Conant, and Jenks, along with other renowned economists, were convinced that U.S. business had overinvested in the wake of the Civil War boom. In their
eyes, the existing stock of fixed capital acted as an albatross rather than as a strategic
advantage. In short, the corporatists identified competition as a source of inefficiency
rather than a panacea for all social ills.

The corporatists seemed to understand that manufactured goods were becoming
like what the economists call public goods. A public good is something with a zero
marginal cost. Textbooks usually treat public goods as a curiosity, devoting a couple
of brief paragraphs to the subject. The usual example is a lighthouse. Once the lighthouse is operating, providing the warning to another ship is costless. In addition, it
would be difficult to charge the ship for the use of the lighthouse because nobody
could prove that the crew is actually using the signal. The best course is to have the
government pay for the public good through general taxes.

Similarly, modern manufacturing was beginning to produce what are called quasi-
public goods—meaning goods that have high fixed costs and very low marginal costs.
Such goods could not fare well in a competitive market, where prices fell toward marginal costs. Although marginal costs were not zero, as was the case with the lighthouse,
they were small enough that no industry could survive a strong wave of competition.

Even conventional economics should have recognized what the corporatists were
witnessing. The economics of public goods relegated to a few obscure paragraphs in
the textbooks implies that socialization would be the proper solution. The corporatists proposed one form of limited socialization in which the industry would eliminate competition through trusts, cartels, and monopolies. This stunted form of socialization would prevent the destruction of the industry through competition, but it
would also remove the need for further modernization and would penalize the public
by charging monopolistic prices.

The corporatists acknowledged that their own prescription bore some resemblance to that of Marx, but they did not find complete socialization attractive because
they saw the world through the eyes of the great corporations.

Populism, Socialism, and Conventional Economic Theory

Ironically, just as polite public opinion, as well as the corporatist economists, was
beginning to shift to accept the legitimacy of trusts, cartels, and monopolies, groups of
academic economists were forging an elegant, mathematical defense of the market that

remains the core of economics teaching to this day. According to their system of Panglossian proofs, markets supposedly provide the best of all possible worlds. Even many of the corporatists still abstractly approved of conventional economic theory and doggedly taught neoclassical theory to their students.

What could explain the simultaneous rejection of reliance on market forces, on one level of discourse, with the enthusiastic proclamation that the market justly rewards all participants at another level?

To answer this question, consider the mood in the late-nineteenth-century United States. The economy was wallowing in a severe crisis. Both labor and capital were expressing strong dissatisfaction with the state of economic affairs. The Paris Commune of 1871 and the great railroad strike of 1877 demonstrated that labor was capable of asserting itself on a scale that had been previously unimaginable.

Most economists, as well as leaders in business and government, were far from pleased when workers or farmers turned toward either socialism or populism. In this regard, many academic economists worked tirelessly both to reflect and to reinforce the prevailing animus against populism and socialism. Specifically, they attempted to cool the radical ardor of farmers and workers by crafting an abstract theory based on mathematical theorems that claimed to demonstrate that labor could do no better than to trust its fate to the market.

They failed to achieve their ideological goal. After all, few farmers or workers actually read those economics books and articles, but their work did help to stiffen the resolve of government and business leaders to spare no effort to maintain the status quo—at least insofar as the demands from farmers or workers were concerned.

Despite the gaping abyss separating the conditions in the railroad industry from the rarefied assumptions of conventional economic theory, many of those involved in the railroad industry still found comfort in the manner in which conventional economic theory taught workers to accept their lot in life. As Charles Elliott Perkins, president of the Chicago, Burlington & Quincy Railroad, wrote to John Murray Forbes on February 18, 1884, "The spirit of the age is communistic, perhaps because the progress of civilization has developed more rapidly than it has *disciplined* the sympathies of the people. If I were able, I would found a school for the study of political economy in order to harden men's hearts."[111] In truth, the railroaders felt that they had far more to fear at the time from the populists than the socialists. Polite society regarded the populists as both ignorant and misguided, which, in a sense, they were.

Unlike the corporatists, the populists, however, took conventional economic theory seriously. Like conventional economists, the populists contended that market forces would lead to desirable outcomes. Like the conventional economists the populists attributed all the ills in society to departures from perfect competition. Parrini and Sklar explain:

The populist view generally attributed market dislocation to forces external to a just or "natural" market: Illegitimate monopolistic or corrupt political power disrupted market harmonies by imposing credit restrictions, the gold standard, artificial prices, exorbitant rent or interest rates, unfair tariffs and the like. The populist remedy lay in government intervention and regulation [to ensure that nobody took advantage of the market by abusing economic power—Author].[112]

Although some populist groups developed elaborate cooperative enterprises,[113] their underlying vision of capitalism was a community of artisans and small shopkeepers, each of whom earned a fair reward for an honest day's work. Despite the supposedly radical nature of the populist program, for the most part, the populists merely called upon the government to remove the disparity between the market power of the poor farmer and the operators of railroads and grain elevators.

Once the populists failed to win a national consensus for their program, their naive worldview left them susceptible to the call of the silver interests who convinced them that they would accomplish their goal more easily through cheap money. William H. "Coin" Harvey, a hired publicist for the silver interests,[114] struck a responsive chord by proposing, in effect, to abort the emergence of modern, monopolistic capitalism by destroying the value of the capitalists' claims on existing assets and future incomes through inflation.[115] This message was not lost on the financial interests. J. Sterling Morton, President Cleveland's secretary of agriculture, clearly equated the free silver movement with a return to petty proprietorship.[116]

Although the populist literature resonates with grand conspiracies, its underlying logic is at one with contemporary economic thought. For example, in their free silver phase, the populists were perhaps closer to Milton Friedman than Milton Friedman himself.

Both Friedman and the populists focused on the growth of the money supply. Both the populists and Friedman refused to recognize that market forces had revolutionized the economy so thoroughly that it no longer resembled the model of village economy, which Friedman's master, Leon Walras, had assumed when formulating his economic theory.[117]

Although conventional economists had a vision of the economy that was just as idealistic as the populists, the conventional economists were united with the corporatist economists in their opposition to the populist approach. While conventional economists accepted that something like perfect competition was desirable, they were unable to see significant departures from perfect competition in the world around them. They dismissed the populist notion that unfair business practices caused high interest rates or rents.

For the conventional economists, markets—and markets alone—could account for the structure of rents and interest rates. The objective laws of the market sufficed to ensure that rents and interest rates would be both fair and appropriate.

Populists and conventional economists also had divergent visions regarding the gold standard. Where the populists regarded the gold standard as an evil cabal that greedy bankers imposed on the people, most conventional economists looked upon the gold standard as a triumph of rational market principles.

The corporatists looked with equal disdain upon the idealistic visions of a fair market economy promoted respectively by the conventional economists and the populists. This attitude is rather surprising since, as we shall see, some corporatists also doubled as laissez-faire economists, simultaneously achieving prominence in both camps. Unbothered by such inconsistencies, the corporatists, when writing as corporatists, accepted that the theory of free competition may have made some sense back in the early world of merchant capitalism, but they dismissed it as obsolete for an industrial economy with high fixed costs.[118]

The corporatists were certain that the market naturally tends to create disruptive forces in the form of overproduction and the resulting destruction of capital values. In the eyes of the corporatists, capital-intensive industries had no choice but to form trusts and cartels if they were going to survive. Again, in the words of Parrini and Sklar:

> The emergent corporate outlook, in contrast, centered on conceiving "overproduction" and related market disruptions not as exogenously caused but as a chronic tendency endogenous to the market under the conditions of modern capitalist development.[119]

Just as the populists and the conventional economists shared a similar vision of the economy, the corporatists and the socialists had much in common. Certainly, both regarded the market with suspicion. As we noted in our earlier discussion of Hadley, the corporatists generally had more regard for the intellectual analysis of the socialists than that of the populists.

In return, many socialists regarded corporatism as a progressive step toward the socialization of the economy. For instance, Lenin, admittedly more influenced by German than American tendencies, observed that trusts could satisfy people's material needs, but only socialism could accomplish "the free, all-around development of all movements of society."[120] Later, he added that "the development of capitalism, which resulted in the creation of banks, syndicates, railways and so forth, has greatly facilitated and simplified the adoption of measures of really democratic control."[121]

For the corporatists, either the populist or laissez-faire ideal of perfect competition was downright ridiculous. Although the socialists shared many of the populists' sentiments, the socialists had a more industrial view of society than the populists did. According to the populist vision, corporate concentration was a nefarious conspiracy. The socialists held that a capitalist economy naturally evolved into a small number of large industrial firms. Only a small number of individuals could be expected to own an entire industry in a market economy.

The corporatists differed from the socialists in only one fundamental regard: the socialists did not believe that a society in which one group owned the wealth and another worked for wages could ever produce a fair and equitable outcome. In contrast, the corporatists taught that once corporations rather than markets had the right to manage society, the corporations would act responsibly, providing good wages along with a strong economy.

The Strange Case of John Bates Clark

Nowhere was this conflict between the ideological and practical side of economic thought clearer than in the case of John Bates Clark, the most eminent U.S. economist of the late nineteenth century. Today, most economists familiar with Clark would associate his name with his sophisticated elaboration of the mythology of market efficiency, in which perfect competition magically gives everybody exactly what they deserve. In celebration of these contributions to conventional economic theory, the American Economic Association awards the John Bates Clark Medal once every two years to "that American Economist under forty who is adjudged to have made a significant contribution to economic thought and knowledge."

Clark was not only a conventional economist. Few modern economists may be aware that Clark began as a rather enthusiastic populist of a sort, as well as a Christian socialist, although his commitment to either the socialist or the populist camp was rather modest.[122] Still fewer may realize that Clark was one of the most influential corporatists.

Whether in his populist or socialist incarnation, the early Clark was "critical of the injustice that an unregulated capitalist industrial system produced."[123] As Mary Morgan observed:

> Clark…looks both backward with nostalgia to the exchange economies of the earlier age and forward with utopian idealism to that of the future. He regarded his own economy with the eyes of a Christian of socialist leanings and thought that nothing could be worse than the modern predatory behavior of his own society, except perhaps the intertribal trade behavior he reported from the anthropologists.[124]

Like many economists of his day, Clark drew his inspiration for this rejection of laissez faire from the railroads, observing:

Sometimes, as in railroad operations, competition works sluggishly, interrupt-
edly, or not at all; sometimes, as in the transactions of labor and capital, it
works for a time, one-sidedly and cruelly, and then almost ceases to do its
work.[125]

Recall Hadley's similar description of competition that came a decade and a half
later. Like Hadley, Clark recognized that much of modern industry was becoming more
and more like the railroads. In Clark's words, "competition of the individualistic type
is rapidly passing out of existence" and giving way to consolidation and monopoly.
"The principle which is at the basis of Ricardian economics is ceasing to have any general application to the system under which we live."[126]
He continued:

Competition is no longer adequate to account for the phenomena of social industry. Economic science needs modernizing; it was a half-century after the *Wealth of
Nations* that the earlier railroads were built, and it was a century after its publication
that the great railway and telegraph monopolies were effected.[127]

For Clark, "Individual competition, the great regulator of the former era, has, in
important fields, practically disappeared. It ought to disappear; it was, in its later
days, incapable of working justice." Like Hadley, Clark proposed that "The alternative regulator is moral force."[128]

The Evolution of John Bates Clark

In what sense did Clark consider that competition was becoming obsolete? He seems
to have believed that something like perfect competition had existed prior to the rise of
large-scale industry. In that earlier environment, buyers and sellers were more or less
equals.[129]
Over time, huge industrial enterprises arose. The powers of an individual worker
or individual consumer became insignificant compared to the social, political, and
economic forces that the great corporations could muster. He expressed outrage over
these conditions:

Nothing could be wilder or fiercer than an unrestricted struggle of millions of men
for gain, and nothing more irrational than to present unrestricted struggle as a scientific ideal. ...If competition were supreme, it would be supremely immoral; if it
existed otherwise than by sufferance, it would be a demon.[130]

In an earlier time Clark also protested that competition resulted in abominable conditions for workers:

> We do not enslave men now-a-days. …We offer a man a pittance, and tell him to take it…; but we do but coerce him. …We do not eat men precisely —. We consume the product of their labor; and they may have virtually worked body and soul into it; but we do it by such indirect and refined methods that it does not generally occur to us that we are cannibals. We kill men, it is true; but not with cudgels in open fight. We do it slowly, and frequently take the precaution to kill the soul first; and we do it in an orderly and systematic manner.[131]

During that period, Clark maintained that socialism offered a remedy to such inequities. Socialism, as he saw it, could "secure a distribution of wealth founded on justice, instead of one determined by the actual results of the struggle of competition." The transition to socialism seemed to be virtually inevitable. "The beauty of the socialist ideal is enough to captivate the intellect that fairly grasps it."[132] "The way for true socialism has been preparing for a hundred years…as a general development, dictated by the Providence."[133]

Clark Becomes Conventional

Clark's critical eye soon dimmed. Within a few years after he published a series of radical articles, he reworked all but one of them into his book, *The Philosophy of Wealth* (1886). Although most people familiar with Clark take this book as a manifesto of his radical beliefs, John Henry has recently shown how Clark had already begun to dull his radical edges in his editing of the articles.[134]

When Hadley criticized Clark's book as exhibiting the "crudest socialistic fallacies," Clark was quick to defend himself from the charge.[135] Clark continued to shed his remaining vestiges of radicalism.

By 1899, in *The Distribution of Wealth: A Theory of Wages, Interest, and Profits,* Clark had nothing but praise for competitive forces. There he observed, "The indictment that hangs over society is 'exploited labor.' " He set out to prove that this indictment is unwarranted because "the natural effect of competition is to give each producer the amount of wealth that he specifically brings into existence."[136] In making this case, Clark developed the most sophisticated defense of laissez faire yet devised.

In this new incarnation, Clark proclaimed that competition is "a wonderful social mechanism" that rewards each agent according to its productivity.[137] He even went so far as to maintain that competition was "the social guarantor of progress."[138]What caused Clark to reverse his opinion about the competitive process? Furner noted, "as...[he] began to achieve scholarly recognition...[he] also began equating moderateness of opinion with objectivity, and objectivity with scholarly worth."[139] I tend to agree with Furner's evaluation, yet I must take issue with her in one respect.

Furner seems to imply that academic achievement was Clark's focus. However, Clark never confined himself to academic economics. Despite his theoretical advocacy of laissez-faire theory as an effective justification of the existing distribution of income, the mature Clark did not seem to believe that laissez-faire theory had any practical relevance in framing important economic policies. In this regard, Clark stood shoulder to shoulder with the rest of the corporatists. As Martin Sklar pointed out, "Apart from his marginal utility axioms [which were at the core of his defense of laissez faire], Clark's views were...similar to those of Jenks" and the rest of the corporatist school.[140]

The Further Evolution of John Bates Clark

Despite his contradictory beliefs, Clark's thought had a certain degree of continuity. As a mature economist engaged in public affairs, Clark continued to oppose competition, but he was no longer appealing to a socialist future. By this stage in his career, Clark was one of the most influential corporatists.

Yet Clark, the corporatist, expressed a concern with the fate of the worker just as he had before, but with one important exception. The large corporations no longer seemed to be the enemy of the working class; instead, they had become the best hope for working-class egalitarianism:

> America affords the conditions most favorable to the leveling process which is reducing the workman proper to a single social stratum. ...Free education and native versatility elevate the lower substrata, while machine processes depress the higher.[141]

Like the other railroad economists, he was unalterably opposed to the use of antitrust legislation to impede corporate consolidations because of the threat that competition posed to industries with a large investment in long-lived fixed capital. In this vein, he wrote in 1888:

> Combinations have their roots in the nature of social industry and are normal in their origin, their development and their practical working. They are neither to be depreciated by scientists nor suppressed by legislation.[142]

In general, the corporatist Clark looked kindly upon bigness because it fostered socially beneficial technology. He bolstered his argument by asserting that monopolistic practices would be futile. Monopolies could not use their market power to artificially raise prices because the threat of entry of new competition into the market would necessarily eliminate any extra profits that anticompetitive practices could temporarily create.

Although, for Clark, bigness, as such, was not a problem,[143] he still insisted that he did not want to give business a carte blanche:

> There is often a considerable range within which trusts can control prices without calling potential competition into positive activity. The possible competitor does not, by any means, become a real one as promptly as he should. The trouble is, that he has not a fair chance for his life when he actually appears on the scene. He is in very great danger of being crushed by the trust.[144]

Even so, Clark did not seem to take these threats very seriously. He believed that "The investor is at present the most conspicuous of the trusts' victims." Protection of the investor should "stand first in the order of time and of immediate importance."[145] Given his concern with the innocent investor, we should not be surprised that Clark, like Hadley, advocated that the public have access to information about the dealings of the trusts, such as how much the trusts pay for plants.[146] Clark also called for the government to oppose corporate practices that he regarded as unfair competition. However, Clark's concept of unfairness was relatively narrow, restricted to such tactics as threats of violence or such behavior as the creation of false information, price discrimination, and exclusive dealing.[147]

Clark wanted to rely on expert agencies rather than the judiciary to protect the public against such corporate abuses.[148] Along with Jenks, he belonged to a subcommittee of a business group, the National Civic Federation, which proposed legislation to create an agency similar to the Interstate Commerce Commission to prevent monopolistic pricing.[149] However, he must have realized that the Interstate Commerce Commission would typically operate as an arm of the railroad industry.[150]

Clark's Schizophrenic Attitude toward Competition

So here we have John Bates Clark, once sympathetic to both the populist and Christian socialist critiques of competition, eventually defending the trusts and cartels as a corporatist opponent of competition. All the while, the same John Bates Clark, in his role as an academic practitioner of neoclassical economics, was advocating a quasi-religious advocacy of the market based on the unrealistic theory of perfect competition.

While Clark was developing his theory of perfect competition, the railroads, the traditional bane of the populists and the avowed antagonists of competition, were effectively forming powerful alliances that effectively blunted the thrust of competition, upon which Clark's laissez-faire theory depended.[151] By 1914, John Bates Clark, the erstwhile Christian socialist, even rose to the defense of the Colorado National Guard when that agency shot striking workers in Ludlow at the behest of Rockefeller.[152]

In short, Clark offers us two contradictory theories. He implicitly based his ideological theory of perfect competition on the assumption that long-lived fixed capital does not exist. In his more practical theory, long-lived fixed capital was the central fact of life. The only common theme to these theories was his opposition to whatever threatened the status quo.

Today, economists have largely forgotten Clark's perplexing contradictions. His now secure reputation rests on his efforts in "proving" that "free competition tends to give labor what labor creates, to capitalists what capital creates, and to entrepreneurs what the coordinating function creates."[153]

Clark never acknowledged that his strong defense of anticompetitive practices clearly violated the principles of his neoclassical theory. In 1937, the economist Gabriel Hauge asked Clark's son, John Maurice Clark, a distinguished economist in his own right, how his father could embrace such contradictory theories. Clark replied:

> Your inquiry raises the question of a change in my father's attitude in *The Philosophy of Wealth* to a defense of it as a morally justifiable system in *The Distribution of Wealth*.
>
> I do not think my father was conscious of any change in his basic attitude. ...I... recall the earlier book...as a recognition of evils and a plea for moral elements, with hopes of developing cooperative institutions which should themselves make their way by the competitive route, competing with competitive business.[154]

Clark and Johann Karl Rodbertus

Perhaps the closest Clark came to bridging the gap between his contradictory modes of analysis appeared in an introduction that he wrote to an obscure book, Johann Karl Rodbertus's *Overproduction and Crises*.[155] Rodbertus's essay, which appeared in Germany in 1851, argued that overproduction crises plagued capitalism because of the nature of the market.

Although Rodbertus had been a minister of the Prussian government, his work had not exercised much influence on academic economists, even in Germany. His

work did earn a brief notoriety in the 1880s when some of Marx's critics erroneous-
ly claimed that the conservative Rodbertus had anticipated Marx's theory. Then
Rodbertus returned to obscurity again until Clark unearthed his book more than four
decades after its initial publication.

Clark's introduction was surprisingly respectful. He also credited Rodbertus with
anticipating Marx's economic theories,[156] yet Clark still praised the book as a
"work...of great scientific interest."[157] Clark never explained his interest in
Rodbertus's book beyond those words.

Clark seemed to think that Rodbertus was of contemporary relevance, considering the economic crisis of the time. The strength of the socialists and populists worried defenders of the status quo. Presumably, Clark wanted to bring attention to
Rodbertus to calm the troubled waters of the time. The first words of his introduction read:

> The modern world regards business crises much as the ancient Egyptians regard-
> ed the overflowings of the Nile. The phenomenon recurs at intervals; it is of great
> importance to everyone.[158]

Soon afterwards, he noted that the term "overproduction" seemed to satisfy the
popular mind in search of an explanation of crises.[159] Clark felt that overproduction
was central to Rodbertus's thinking, although Rodbertus was probably more inclined
toward the underconsumptionist school. Rodbertus held that crises occurred because
workers were paid too little to be able to purchase their product.

That approach has strong political overtones. Clark had tried to deflect the political
sting of Rodbertus by dismissing the concept of overproduction out of hand. He insisted that overproduction did not cause crises such as the one that the United States was
experiencing at the time. Instead, he claimed that the problem was a misdirection of
investment rather than a fundamental problem with the market itself.

Clark's analogy of the flooding of the Nile suggests that he might not have been
entirely confident in his explanation. According to his Nile analogy, the misdirection of
investment somehow would have had to be periodic. Unfortunately, Clark never
explained what could cause these periodic waves of misdirected investment.

More questions remain. If the consequences of misdirected investment led to
periodic upheavals, what should be done? Would an unemployed worker or a bankrupt owner of a business take much consolation in knowing that they were the victims
of misdirected investment rather than overproduction? Of course not!

Clark's efforts appeared to have failed. He seemed to have intended to make a step
in calming the political storm surrounding the crisis. Yet for this purpose he chose an

obscure work that, if translated into contemporary concerns, could have possibly stirred up political passions.

The corporatists did have an answer to the crisis: trusts, cartels, and monopolies provided the coordination that could prevent overproduction, misdirected investment, or whatever caused the recurrent crises. Rodbertus was an early precursor of the corporatists, although he did not push that part of his analysis in this particular work.

In his introduction to Rodbertus, Clark was silent about his own opinions. What might he have had in mind? Clark, as well as most of the other leading corporatists, enjoyed a German education. The Germans had already carried out most of the policies that the corporatists had envisioned. In Germany, leaders such as Rodbertus could sound socialistic, despite their corporatist objectives. Presumably, Clark would have welcomed a similar outcome in the United States, although he was never open enough to make his intentions clear.

Perhaps Clark was aware of the conflict between his corporatist and academic thinking after all and longed for a German-like situation in which he would not face sanctions for teaching in a manner that went beyond the merchant-oriented school of political economy. In this vein, the founding of the American Economic Association represented an important step toward protecting those who wished to make economics more realistic.

Clark and the Founding of the American Economic Association

The American Economic Association is the largest professional economics organization. Frequently, more than 10,000 economists attend its annual meetings. Now that the American Economic Association has become a secure bastion of neoclassical theory, few contemporary economists may be aware of its corporatist origins. The key figures in founding the American Economic Association—Clark, Hadley, Richard T. Ely, and H. C. Adams—shared much in common besides their identification with the corporatist school. All wrote important books on the trust problem. All were German-educated.[160]

Although the German universities were considered to be the best in the world at the time, some economists held the corporatist association with Germany to be a fault. Unlike the academic economists in the Anglo-Saxon tradition who deduced their economic theories from unrealistic assumptions, German economists eschewed pure theory. They preferred to base their economics on social, cultural, and historical observation.

Alfred Marshall, perhaps the leading British economist of the time, complained that the corporatists in the United States were "much under German influence."[161] Joseph A. Schumpeter, a famous Austrian economist, even mocked Ely as "that excellent German professor in American skin."[162] These corporatist economists were intent

on breaking with the abstract, ahistorical methods that dominated the world of academic economic theory.[163] Like the German economists, most of the key founders of
the American Economic Association rejected the prevailing Anglo-Saxon idea that
economics should be a system of deductions from a few abstract principles. Instead,
they followed their German teachers in attempting to ground economic theory on the
real-life conditions that they observed. In the spirit of his German training, Ely called
for the abandonment of "the dry bones of orthodox English political economy for the
live methods of the German school."[164]

The corporatists watched while strong competition destroyed one railroad firm
after another. We have already seen how they incorporated this experience into their
economic theory.

The corporatists' evaluation of the world around them also led them to reject the
principle of decreasing returns, a key assumption of conventional economics, including Clark's famous proof of the just outcomes of markets. As Ely told the readers of a
popular magazine, "whenever the principle of increasing returns works with any high
degree of intensity, competition can never regulate private business satisfactorily."[165]
Increasing returns meant that two small firms combined together could produce
goods more efficiently than the two separate firms could. As a result, consolidation
rather than competition was the key to efficiency.

Ely and the other founders of the American Economic Association had no institutional incentive to create a rupture with prevailing opinion. On the contrary, they risked
ostracism by orthodox economists. As Ely reminisced much later in life, "If you were
held to be unorthodox, it was a terrible indictment."[166] Francis A. Walker was even more
explicit, recalling, "Here it [laissez faire] was not made the test of economic orthodoxy
merely. It was used to decide if a man were an economist at all."[167]Nonetheless, the organization persisted in its overt challenge of the prevailing orthodoxy. Ely summarized its
principles:

> ...the American Economic Association...represented a protest against the system
> of laissez faire. ...[A] second aspect, and the one on which we were all in complete
> agreement, was the necessity of uniting in order to secure complete freedom of dis-
> cussion. ...It was this second point that came, in final analysis and after much
> debate, to be accepted as the foundation stone of our association.
>
> But the protest against the "laissez faire" philosophy must not be underempha-
> sized in the history of the foundation of the American Economic Association.[168]

The proposed statement of principles of the American Economic Association
read in part:

While we recognize the necessity of individual initiative in industrial life, we hold that the doctrine of laissez-faire is unsafe in politics and unsound in morals; and that it suggests an inadequate explanation of the relations between the state and the citizens. ...We regard the state as an agency whose positive assistance is one of the indispensable conditions of human progress.[169]

Clark, whose name is now synonymous with the laissez-faire ideology of neoclassical economics, was among the rebellious young men who founded the American Economic Association.[170] Although Clark himself suggested weakening the language of the statement, he did not express any reservations about the purpose of the organization, apparently hoping to maintain lines of communication between the two groups. A committee made up of Clark and four other economists rewrote the final statement, which resembled the original except that it no longer treated the rejection of laissez faire as a creed.[171]

This group of heretical economists eventually managed to enlist the majority of economists in the United States. Little more than a decade after Walker noted the strength of the laissez-faire ideology, the major economists of the day had swung over to support the trusts and cartels. One economist who failed to convert to the new way of thought complained:

The socialist who reads some of these arguments must feel that at last many of the criticisms which he has long urged against competition have been accepted by economists of the orthodox types. Certainly, few stronger indictments of the competitive regime have been formulated by socialist critics of the existing order.[172]

The members of the American Economic Association soon forgot the original purpose of the organization. In a relatively short period of time, laissez-faire ideology became the order of the day once again. Many years later, George Stigler reflected on the incident:

It is sobering to reflect on the attitudes of professional economists of the period toward the merger movement. Economists as wise as Taussig, as incisive as Fisher, as fond of competition as Clark and Fetter, insisted upon discussing the movement largely or exclusively in terms of industrial evolution and the economies of scale. They found no difficulty in treating the unregulated corporation as a natural phenomenon, nor were they bothered that the economy of scale should spring forth suddenly and simultaneously in an enormous variety of industries—and yet pass over the minor firms that characteristically persisted and indeed flourished in these industries. One must regretfully record that in this period Ida Tarbell and Henry Demarest Lloyd [muckraking anti-trust journalists] did more than the American Economic Association to foster the policy of competition.[173]

We read nothing about the origins of the American Economic Association in the current pages of its major publication, the *American Economic Review*. Instead, the journal treats its readers to ever more sophisticated displays of technical virtuosity, with barely a nod to the complications created by the existence of long-lived fixed capital.

Lessons from Railroad Economics

The confrontation between railroads and competition illustrates how competitive forces become destructive for industries with low marginal and high fixed costs. Yet, as we shall see, this cost structure becomes typical in a modern economy.

This destructive competition that the roads experienced and that has become common among manufacturing means that the productive potential of higher wages becomes blunted. Presumably, low marginal costs are associated with a relatively small wage bill. As a result, increasing wages would not provide nearly as much of a stimulus for technological development as would be the case in more labor-intensive industries. Firms faced with such conditions certainly do all that they can to gain a slight edge by ruthlessly cutting wages and benefits, but doing so cannot gain them much breathing room. I do not mean that a high-wage strategy would have no impact, but the competitive pressures in the product market would most likely swamp the effect of increasing the wage bill. As late as the 1920s, some economists and more enlightened business leaders still advocated an economy of high wages, but one can never know the extent to which this idea was a response to the economic potential of high wages or a legitimate fear of militant labor movements.

The competitive railroad experience also helps in evaluating the use of economic theory. Traditional economics theory was of no use whatsoever in understanding what was going on in the railroad industry. Even so, the academic economists continue to insist on the correctness of their theory in indoctrinating others. First of all, labor had to learn that exploitation was nonexistent. Second, less sophisticated students might have difficulty in following their analysis of the railroads without taking the next step in adopting Marxist analysis. After all, if the railroads could abrogate competition in order to preserve their profits, why couldn't society as a whole benefit from a more comprehensive organization of production?

4

The Role of Finance

Merchants, Finance, and the Economic Climate

While the corporatist economists did an excellent job of analyzing the dangers of competition, finance represents a serious blind spot in the corporatist analysis. The corporatists in general ignored the crucial role of finance in a modern market economy. Instead, they concentrated on the economy from the standpoint of the productive reorganization of industry. A few of the corporatists were also concerned about banking, but they avoided any reference whatsoever to the motives of the financial agents who were to engineer these changes in industry.

Those who invest in capital goods using borrowed money often need economic policies that rapidly expand the economy. Firms that sell consumer goods also tend to support expansionary economic policies. Those who lend money or who have already invested in long-lived fixed capital generally are more concerned about keeping the value of money stable.

Already in the early years of the United States, we can see signs of the coming struggles between financial and industrial interests in the conflicts between merchants and industrialists, or even in the differences between Alexander Hamilton and Thomas Jefferson. Grossly simplifying their positions, Jefferson wanted to develop an economy based on indigenous agriculture and industry, while Hamilton wanted to keep the U.S. economy more closely integrated with the British economy.

Hamilton's vision demanded a stable money supply. Since the merchants sold largely British goods, they wanted to tie the domestic money supply as closely as possible to gold to facilitate trade with their British counterparts, who demanded payment in gold. To ensure that the wealthy had a vested interest in value of money into the indefinite future, Hamilton even proposed to run a deficit economy to create a

class of bondholders (financial capitalists). Because bonds promise a series of prede-
termined repayments, the bondholders' fate would be tied to the value of the dollar.

We cannot push this Jefferson-Hamilton story too far. After all, Hamilton favored
protectionism to encourage new industrial activity and Jefferson was ambiguous
about the nature of industrial development. In addition, the merchants whom
Hamilton favored were not financial capitalists per se, though they did share a number of traits with financial capitalists.

First and foremost, merchants are usually closer to finance than industry because
their investments in long-lived fixed capital are minimal. Instead, merchants profit
from rapid turnover of their inventories. Although these inventories are real goods,
they probably have more in common with easily tradable financial assets than with
long-lived fixed capital such as railroad track. After all, merchants can turn their
inventories into cash relatively quickly, while railroad track cannot be liquidated easily. Its value depends upon the ability to provide service for decades into the future.

In the early U.S. economy, potential industrialists often lacked adequate credit to
invest in long-lived fixed capital. Even when some merchants did invest in the New
England textile mills, they still maintained the mind-set of merchants rather than
develop an industrial mentality. As a result, they generally failed to develop innovative
methods (see below).

The Role of Financial Intermediaries

With the increasing importance of fixed capital, business became ever more dependent on credit to finance its investments. As a result, much of the investment in long-
lived fixed capital faced an additional obstacle, besides the normal reluctance to invest
in durable investments. Now, such investment also required the assent of lenders.

This assent is not a straightforward assent. The market for business finance is a
very complicated network of borrowers and lenders, many of whom are unaware of
the ultimate source or destination of their funds. For example, banks deal separately
with their depositors and their borrowers. The banks do not consult depositors
before lending their money to other people or to businesses.

Economists refer to agents, such as banks, who interpose themselves between
borrowers and lenders as financial intermediaries. Typically, the financial intermediary rather than the lender must give assent to the business plan.

Economists' interpretation of the role of financial intermediaries has changed considerably over the years. Initially, the ability of banks to channel many minuscule
deposits into large loans struck early economists as the essential function of financial
intermediaries.

Once the importance of risk became more apparent to economists, they changed their focus. Economists observed that banks frequently lent money for relatively long periods, but those who gave the banks disposal over their funds had the right to withdraw them on fairly short notice. Economists frequently characterized this situation by noting that banks lend long and borrow short.

The risks associated with this sort of arrangement came to popular notice in the United States in the 1980s with the savings and loan crisis. The savings and loan industry typically lent money to home buyers for as long as thirty years. Depositors had the legal right to withdraw their funds after giving the savings banks a few weeks notice. In fact, the banks rarely, if ever, exercised their ability to delay withdrawals, allowing depositors to remove their money from the institution whenever they desired.

When interest rates soared, as they did in the 1960s and 1970s, depositors began to remove their funds en masse from the savings and loans. The financial institution lacked the right to call in most of their loans to home buyers. Because of the legal requirements to maintain reserves in the form of cash or deposits with a federal institution, such a run on a bank or savings and loan threatens it with falling into default.

Given this perspective, economists gave banking another interpretation. They argued that banks did more than just channel funds. They specialize in accepting risks. In the words of Hyman Minsky:

> Banking is not money lending; to lend, a money lender must have money. The fundamental banking activity is accepting, that is, guaranteeing that some party [that is, the borrower—Author] is creditworthy.[1]

These economists recognized that most depositors would hesitate to lend their savings to another person for thirty years. Who knows what emergencies might make the depositor need that money somewhere down the line? Besides, banks are better able to collect on debts than modest, individual investors. In return for the right to have immediate access to their deposits, depositors typically forgo any interest and pay the bank for its services in clearing checks and keeping the deposits secure. Even when the bank pays interest on deposits, the bank earns a much larger reward than the depositor, supposedly because it accepts the risk of lending the money for a relatively long period.

According to the newest school of thought, banks are firms that specialize in evaluating risk. In this respect, banks have two advantages over the typical depositor.

In the first place, banks are big enough that they can pool their risks. For example, at any time a fraction of all homes will go into default because of some calamity.

The economic base of the community might collapse or it might have been built on or near a toxic waste dump. If you or I lend enough money to a neighbor to build a house that eventually goes into default, we could lose all, or at least a significant portion, of our net wealth. Because a bank has a broader spectrum of loans, it can bear the brunt of one such disaster because it has other profitable loans to cushion the loss.

More importantly, economists now see banks as firms that specialize in the development of the capacity to evaluate risk. If a friend comes to us with a new business prospect, either friendship or persuasiveness might sway us to invest in it. Supposedly, banks rise above such emotional considerations. Through ongoing business relationships with their customers, banks develop an information base that allows them to make better decisions about their loans that you or I presumably could.[2]

In the words of Ben Bernanke, who later became the chairman of the Federal Reserve Board during the George W. Bush administration:

> The essence of the credit creation process is the gathering and transmission of information. ...[Banks develop a special] expertise in conveying the savings of relatively uninformed depositor to uses...that are information-intensive and particularly hard to evaluate.[3]

The Evolution of Financial Intermediaries

The evolution of banking practices bears a rough similarity to the changing interpretation of financial intermediaries. In the days of early capitalism, banks generally operated under corporate charters. At the time, these charters were not a right which was open to all. Instead, groups had to petition the state for the special privilege of a corporate charter. This arrangement greatly restricted entry into banking, making banks into quasi-monopolistic operations.

In addition, because of the shortage of capital in the early United States, most small communities perceived of a bank as a godsend. As a result, banking was a highly profitable venture, but also a line of business in which unsavory promoters could use their charters to take advantage of naive depositors.

Banks on the whole were rather unstable ventures. Half of the banks formed between 1810 and 1820 failed before 1825; half of those formed between 1830 and 1840 failed by 1845.[4] Much of the discussion of bank risk at the time centered on the risks faced by depositors in unscrupulous banks rather than the lending risks that honest banks encountered.

From the early days of capitalism, banks specialized in supplying funds to merchants. Indeed, bankers seemed to be almost ideally suited to serving merchants. Merchants typically required funds for relatively short periods. As a result, loans to merchants seemed to be less risky than industrial or agricultural loans, which took longer to repay.

In addition, bankers and merchants were familiar with each other's economic environment. In fact, bankers were often indistinguishable from their merchant customers. For example, in New England, businesspeople often organized the region's banks with the intention of lending money to themselves.[5] Amasa Walker, an economist who was once a merchant himself, suggested that this motivation might have been the rule rather than the exception. He noted: "It has come to be a proverb that banks never originate with those who have money to lend, but with those who want to borrow."[6]

Even in the late nineteenth century, a good number of the leading investment banks, including Morgan, the Lehman Brothers, and Kuhn Loeb, evolved from the textile or dry goods merchants.[7] Although banks continued to concentrate their lending to the merchant sector, some industry did develop, because, more often than not, merchants took the lead in developing industry.

For example, the textile industry represented the largest industrial concentration in the early United States. The leading textile owners had been merchants. Following the War of 1812, the United States imposed tariffs. These merchant shipowners experienced falling profits because of the sharp reduction in trade with England. As a result, Almy and Brown of Providence, along with the Lowells, Cabots, Appletons, and Lawrences, shifted their investments from trade into cotton production.[8] Merchant-financed industry was a hybrid between the industrial and merchant world. Like industry, these enterprises produced goods, but like traditional merchant firms, they generally failed to pursue new technologies energetically. Alfred Chandler observed that because the owners of the new textile industry were traditional businessmen who clung to traditional ways, they also had little impact on the development of modern industrial management.[9] Bankers benefited from the restriction of corporate charters to potential competitors. Would-be bankers chafed under the exclusion. In the United States, the Jackson administration called for an end of special corporate privileges and for the right of free incorporation for all businesses.[10] Once Jackson vetoed the Second Bank of the United States, states began to charter banks. As a result, by the mid-1840s banking had begun to become a far more open business.

The French economist Chevelier was shocked to discover a bank in a small Pennsylvania community of thirty houses, with stumps still standing in the streets.[11]

A number of these banks were unscrupulous operations that held their reserves in a chest with a thin layer of gold coins covering a mass of nails or window glass. On the basis of these fictitious reserves, depositors would trust the banks with their savings. The banks, in turn, would print up paper bank notes that would serve as money. Merchants would have to subscribe to the *Bank Note Reporter* to know the relative value of the various issues of bank notes.[12]

With free incorporation allowing for more competition in banking, profits became less assured. Because the state was less likely to exercise any oversight on freely incorporated entities, the risk of corporate mismanagement by bankers increased. Given this situation, we might not be surprised that economists were tardy in recognizing banks as absorbers of risk and providers of information.

Finance Capital and the Gold Standard

Finance capital, a shorthand expression for the most powerful financial interests, generally calls for stringent monetary conditions. Finance capital generally acts as a creditor. Inflation can eat away at creditors' profits. The same policies that benefit finance capital typically harm the economy as a whole. For example, restrictive monetary policies limit the creation of industrial capital, the real investment that actually produces goods. In addition, making money scarce weakens many existing firms that sell to consumers. Finance capital often takes advantage of the turmoil that tight credit unleashes to obtain a greater degree of control over weakened companies.

Monetary policy is not usually a subject of popular controversy. Governments merely announce their intention to refrain from using their powers to manipulate the money supply or interest rates, say, by committing themselves to follow a seemingly abstract rule. In following such a policy, governments generally maintain that they are only following their duty; that their policy favors no class. Their stated goal is not to help a specific industry, such as steel or automobile producers. As Joan Robinson caustically observed:

> There is in some quarters a great affection for credit policy because it seems the least selective and somehow lives up to the ideal of a single overall neutral regulation of the economy. [I]t conceals the problems of political choice under an apparently impersonal mechanism.[13]

In the late nineteenth century, when the United States decided to return to the gold standard, limiting the money supply by demonetizing silver, the government's studied pose of objective neutrality was unpopular.

The extraordinary financial demands of fighting the Civil War had forced the U.S. government to resort to printing paper money and thereby abandoning the gold standard. Even so, the war was not a defeat for finance capital. In fact, the war greatly expanded the reach of finance since the government had to market a huge stock of debt. A single banker, Jay Cooke, employed 2,500 agents selling federal bonds to the public throughout the loyal states and territories.[14] Not long after the war ended, the government had to make a conscious decision to return to the gold standard, tightening the grip of finance capital.

Although merchant and financial interests controlled most of the reins of power, the policies they favored did not go unchallenged. The majority of people in the early United States opposed finance capital. The gold standard promised a relatively high interest regime. Under the gold standard, governments could still affect interest rates through banking legislation, but only to a very limited degree. Although national legislation allowed individual banks various economic options, the gold standard severely restricted what the banking system as a whole could do.

The populist movement insisted that adherence to the gold standard was a highly political act. The populists maintained that under the gold standard, governments had to accept rules of economic behavior that made them act in conformity with the interests of finance capital. If any economy somehow began to defy finance capital and opt for easy money, gold would quickly begin to flow out of the country, creating a financial panic, once creditors began to realize that many people would lack the means to repay their debts.

Of course, governments could abandon gold altogether, turning to silver or paper money, but to do so threatened to cut the economy off from the rest of the world that followed the gold standard. Any future decision to abandon the gold standard would become increasingly costly as the economy became more tightly integrated into the system of international trade based on the gold standard.

Those who favored the gold standard self-righteously pretended that their objective was nothing more than a patriotic concern for sound money. Any violation of the gold standard would be nothing less than an act of supreme immorality. After all, who in their right mind could favor unsound money? Given this cloak of objectivity, finance capital had little reason to articulate its own particular objectives. It could merely join the chorus of leaders advocating the protection of the domestic gold supply without going into details about how finance would benefit.

Throughout the nineteenth century, popular forces in the United States took a keen interest in monetary policy, especially after the return to the gold standard. Not surprisingly, farmers were the leading voice of dissent. True, they also felt victimized by the railroads and grain elevators, but financial concerns were uppermost in their minds. Banks were reluctant to extend the long-term credit that farmers needed. Instead, the bankers preferred to provide short-term credit to merchants, which appeared to be a more profitable type of loan.

These conditions sparked a debate that helped to fuel the populist and silverite movements. Industrial capital, however, even where it might have benefited, never lent significant support to the soft money school.

These popular forces rejected the idea that the gold standard should be inviolable. In fact, in the late nineteenth century United States, concern with monetary policies became so excessive that occasionally almost all other issues seemed to fall from view. During the heyday of populism, the majority of people in the country probably believed that the creation of a new monetary regime would suffice to solve the nation's ills.

Today, the political mood has swung to the opposite extreme. Monetary policy has fallen into popular obscurity, except for some fringe groups that regard the Federal Reserve as part of a dark conspiracy. The media treat monetary policies as a technical matter that only experts are capable of deciphering. Not surprisingly, popular attention focuses on more emotional issues that have only peripheral relevance to our lives.

In the 1970s, the public became irritated with inflation, but, even then, it did not usually connect inflation with monetary policy. Instead, the public has been conditioned to blame inflation on "excessive government spending."

Of course, even though monetary policies are important, we must keep the extent of their importance in perspective and take care to not fall into the one-sided politics of earlier times. Nonetheless, we should not lose sight of the fact that when those who structure economic regimes become overly solicitous of the preferences of the financial leaders, the industrial structure suffers.

In fact, the alarming decline of the U.S. economy reflects to a considerable degree a growth in the influence of finance relative to industry.[15] I will return to this subject later.

The Interests of Industrial Capital

For the most part, industrial interests did not directly confront finance capital in the early United States. This stance should not be surprising. After all, many of the early industrialists themselves began as merchants. Even with the prolonged deflation of the late nineteenth century, industrial capital seemed relatively uninterested in a monetary solution. Instead, major industrial firms welcomed Morgan's efforts to consolidate their markets, to which we will soon turn.

In addition, many industrialists who were not merchants had little reason to take much interest in the general financial climate. Access to sufficient bank credit was often problematical for industrial concerns, especially smaller operations. As a result, their owners could not hope to profit much by shaving a few points from interest rates on loans that they probably could not get anyway.

Rather than putting their energies into challenging the financial structure, many early industrialists focused on obtaining protection from foreign competition. With assured markets and an insufficient domestic industrial base to create a dangerous level of competition, most industrialists could be relatively confident of success with strong protectionist measures—the railroads being an obvious exception. In addition, during the late nineteenth century many industrial interests, along with farmers, placed a good deal of hope in military spending to increase demand and to open up foreign markets.[16]

Fortunately for these industrialists, the government shared their concern, hoping to use foreign policy to overcome the crisis of overproduction. According to a 1898 State Department report:

> It is frequently asserted... that the output of factories working at full capacity is much greater than the domestic market can possible consume, and it seems to be conceded that every year we shall be confronted with an increasing surplus of man-ufactured goods for sale in foreign markets if American operatives and artisans are to be kept employed year round. The enlargement of foreign consumption of the prod-ucts of our mills and workshops has, therefore, become a serious problem of states-manship as well as of commerce.[17]

The government had an even more important interest in protectionism, since tariffs provided the most important source of public revenue. However, protection-ism injured the interests of the merchants, producers who depended on foreign trade for marketing their products (especially farmers), and consumers in general.

Despite the unfavorable financial climate and thanks in part to protection, indus-try did develop in the United States, albeit slowly. By the eve of the Civil War, indus-trialists had become powerful enough that the newly founded Republican Party began to articulate their interests. At the same time, Henry Carey was introducing his vision into the literature of economics, but, of course, not without strong resistance from the dominant school of merchant-oriented economics.

Although industry gained strength relative to the economy as a whole, financial activity developed even faster. In the process, industry grew increasingly dependent on financial markets.

Carnegie and Productionist Management

Although Andrew Carnegie came to the steel industry by way of deal-making and business connections, he symbolizes that bygone time when industrial values rather than financial interests were paramount. Carnegie once declared, "I manufacture steel, not securities."[18] Carnegie avoided becoming dependent on finance capital. He kept large cash reserves on hand to be able to buy other firms that stumbled when the economy faltered.[19] Because Carnegie's costs were lower than his competitors, he profited from the same forces that were driving the railroads into bankruptcy.

Carnegie was contemptuous of those executives who were obsessed with the financial end of business, writing:

> It is surprising how few men appreciate the enormous dividends derivable from investment in their own business. There is scarcely a manufacturer in the world who has not in his works some machinery that should be thrown out and replaced by improved appliances. ...And yet most businessmen whom I have known invest in bank shares and far-away enterprises, while the true gold mine lies right in their own factories.[20]

John Maynard Keynes insightfully observed, concerning this disappearing management ethic that Carnegie represented:

> In former times, when enterprises were mainly owned by those who undertook them or by their friends and associates, investment depended on a sufficient supply of individuals of sanguine temperament and constructive impulses who embarked on business as a way of life, not really relying on a precise calculation of prospective profit.[21]

Keynes did not mean that profits were unimportant to productionist managers, but only that they pursued their profits within the context of a particular way of life.

For example, Carnegie did not just produce for the sake of producing. He paid extremely close attention to the market. In fact, his operation was exceptional in its relentless pursuit of lower costs. He assiduously applied financial controls to almost every aspect of his business. For example, one of his associates wrote:

> A workman building a heating furnace for Carnegie said, "There goes that —— book-keeper. If I use a dozen bricks more than I did last month, he knows it and comes round to ask why!" The minutest details of cost of material and labor in every department appeared from day to day...; and soon every man around the place was made to realize it.[22]

In its zeal to cut costs, the Carnegie operation paid little attention to overhead and capital costs.[23] Chandler went so far as to claim that he was concerned "almost wholly with prime costs."[24] In fact, at the time manufacturers generally saw no difference between acquiring inventories and investing in plant and equipment.[25]

For some reason, the productionist mentality was more pronounced in Carnegie's companies than most others. In particular, he was unusual in his willingness to scrap old and outmoded capital goods.[26] Once when his young assistant, Charles Schwab, reported a superior design for a rolling mill, Carnegie ordered him to raze and reconstruct an existing three-month-old mill.[27] Carnegie's overall strategy was to cut his costs and sales prices ruthlessly during recessions, then raise his prices with the rest of the industry when better times returned.[28] Not surprisingly, this behavior did not endear Carnegie to his competitors. According to Mark Perlman:

> There is some evidence that one of the main motives for the establishment of U.S. Steel Co. was to slow down rates of technological change because Carnegie's aggressiveness on that score served to make all of his competitors nervous about costs.[29]

While Carnegie's efforts were spurring technical change, they were also potentially destabilizing. In effect, this rapid technological change that Carnegie was pursuing was intensifying the same sort of competitive pressures that the railroads were experiencing. To make matters worse, Carnegie was actually preparing to build a railroad line to carry raw materials to his factories. John W. Gates, an official of U.S. Steel, told a congressional committee:

> Mr. Hill and Mr. Morgan dined together. Mr. Morgan had expressed to Mr. Hill the fear that if Congress went into the building of railroads he would demoralize the entire railroad situation, and that if he built a tube works at Ashtabula it would result in a demoralization of the price of tubes. ...He was like a bull in a china shop. He would get a thing into his head once in a while and go and do absurd things. ...Mr. Morgan stated to Mr. Schwab and me—that if Mr. Carnegie should build this tube works at Ashtabula and a railroad from Ashtabula to his works in the Pittsburgh district it would demoralize the whole situation.[30]

Faced with this intense competition, Morgan bought out Carnegie Steel, merging it with a number of other steel companies, forming U.S. Steel, a company that comprised 213 different manufacturing plants, forty-one mines, and almost one thousand miles of railroad.[31]

Of course, Carnegie was never just concerned with production for the sake of production. Profits were extremely important to Carnegie. What separated Carnegie from financial operators was the manner in which he chose to make his money. His chief aim was to make money by producing steel. When he bought new firms, his intention was to integrate them into his business of making steel.

Carnegie never gave any indication that he would ever consider abandoning the steel industry in an effort to earn a slightly higher rate of profit in some other industry. To the end, Carnegie maintained a productionist mentality that was already fast disappearing from corporate America.

J. P. Morgan and the Reorganization of the Market

The most dramatic event in this victory of finance capital over industry was J. P. Morgan's buyout of Carnegie, who epitomized the vigor of industrial capital. Where Carnegie was most prominent representative of the productionist side of the U.S. economy, J.P. Morgan symbolized the financial side of corporate America.

Carnegie was able to escape the fate of the railroads despite his inattention to fixed costs only because he was able to stay far ahead of the technology curve. As a result, Carnegie destroyed the capital values of his competitors far faster than those of his own firm. J. P. Morgan, the preeminent representative of finance capital and the victim of Carnegie's ruthless destruction of capital values, had the money to swallow Carnegie's operation and put an end to rapid technological change in the steel industry.

Like the corporatists, "America's most famous financier was a sworn foe of free markets." "[T]he House of Morgan always favored government planning over private competition, but private planning [meaning corporate planning] over either."[32]

The parallel between Morgan and the corporatists is hardly accidental. The economics profession typically comes to reflect the prevailing thinking among business and financial leaders. Economists might lag behind business for a while, but not for long. For example, once the dominance of industry became apparent, the economists' largely slavish devotion to the merchants' interests evaporated. In addition, the role of Morgan in the U.S. economy resembled that of the great banks in Germany, where many of the most prominent corporatist economists had studied.

The House of Morgan first won prominence as the leading representative of British holders of United States railroad bonds. Typically, bondholders had an unrealistic view of their investments. For them,

> Railway bonds had much resemblance to government securities; the railways did not appear, at first blush, to be dependent on the efforts of individuals, but rather

on the condition of the tributary country, and their income was quite similar to the taxes paid to the government.[33]

Obviously, the Morgan clients were none too pleased about the financial conditions of the railroads once the value of their bonds began to evaporate with the absence of sufficient profits. By the mid-1870s, Morgan's father, Junius, was warning the president of the B&O that rate wars were undermining investors' confidence.[34] Such warnings went unheeded.

In December 1888, J. P. Morgan gathered representatives from the major railroads at his house. He proposed that if the railroads would stop cutting rates, the financiers would refrain from underwriting new railroads. That effort also came to naught. At another meeting in January 1889, the railroads agreed that Morgan would head up a committee to regulate rates, arbitrate disputes, and fine offenders, but the group fell apart because of a renewed outbreak of rate wars in the West.[35]

Morgan tried to stabilize the railroads once again on December 15, 1890. He proposed an association with one director from each railroad. He exulted to a reporter, "Think of it—all the competing traffic of the roads west of Chicago and St. Louis, in the control of about thirty men!"[36]

Alas, none of these plans worked. Despite Morgan's best efforts, by 1893 one-third of the railroads fell into receivership. Morgan tried to reorganize bankrupt roads and transfer control to himself. Eventually, he succeeded in controlling many of the largest roads, including the Erie, Chesapeake and Ohio, Northern Pacific, Great Northern, and New York Central, a total of 63,000 miles of road, equaling one-sixth of the total for the nation as a whole. The combined revenues of these operations equaled one-half of the total receipts of the federal government.[37]

Morgan's railroad consolidation initiated a pattern that Morgan would repeat in many other industries. Wags even spoke of "Morganization" as a synonym for consolidation.

The stakes in these industrial consolidations were enormous. The 1901 merger that created U.S. Steel was capitalized at $1.4 billion, equivalent to about 6.8 percent of the Gross National Product of the United States at the time.[38] U.S. Steel was only a part of a far larger picture:

> Samuel Untermeyer [chief investigator of the Pujo Committee] had argued that Morgan, his partners, and their peers at a handful of smaller banks were directors, voting trustees, or principal shareholders of corporations capitalized at $30 billion—the equivalent, in proportion to the size of the economy, of $7.5 trillion today. Perhaps 40 percent of all industrial, commercial, and financial capital in the United States was in some way under the penumbra of this Morgan-centered Money Trust.[39]

Morgan's business was highly profitable, generally earning him a fee of about 3 percent of the value of a consolidation.[40] Even if his share had been exceedingly modest, given the size of these transactions, his earnings still would have been enormous. A typical railroad merger routinely brought him around $1 million.[41]

Morgan had learned from Cornelius Vanderbilt, one of the most notorious railroad projectors, the trick of valuing the stock that he floated on projected earnings, as well as current assets. As a result, part of Morgan's fees represented the difference between the value of the firms when they competed their profits away and the value investors expected once Morgan succeeded in eliminating much of the competition. As George Stigler observed, Morgan had discovered "a new and lucrative industry: the production of monopolies."[42]

Investors responded enthusiastically, or even overenthusiastically. For example, the Bureau of Corporations valued Morgan's greatest consolidation, U.S. Steel, at only half its $1.4 billion selling price. Even so, the stock opened at 38, rose to 55, then fell to less than 9 during the Panic of 1903. By January 1904, it could not cover its dividends.[43]

Despite the huge sums that Morgan garnered, profits never seemed to be uppermost to him. He could have earned much more from many of his deals, but he never seemed to try to push his profits to the limit. Morgan's behavior led Ron Chernow to conclude that "Morgan's real vice was not money, but power...to take what he saw as a topsy-turvy financial world and set it right."[44]

Morgan's restraint should not mislead us into believing that the House of Morgan was a charitable institution. On the contrary, wealth, power, and morality went hand in hand for Morgan. Although Chernow depicted Morgan as a strict moralist who promoted numerous movements to project his own ethical values,[45] we might well see his seemingly ethical behavior as nothing more than a shrewd business tactic. Investors came to trust Morgan just because he seemed to distinguish himself from lesser business figures by reining in his apparent rapacity. Of course, the watering of the U.S. Steel stock should serve to remind us that the limits on Morgan's greed were relative rather than absolute.

The trust that investors placed in Morgan brought him still more funds that allowed him to negotiate even more deals. Because much of his influence depended upon his reputation, Morgan had good reason to refrain from behaving in a manner that could jeopardize his standing in the financial world.[46] More sophisticated investors realized that interlopers had relatively little to lose from spoiling their not yet solid reputations. As a result, they would prefer to do business with Morgan than with lesser luminaries of the financial world. In this sense, Charles Sabel refers to Morgan's behavior as a "calculating display of honesty."[47]

As far as Morgan's supposed preference for power over money is concerned, here again we may have a distinction without a difference. Morgan frequently deployed his power and influence into profitable rulings from government authorities turning his love of power into a handsome profit.

J. P. Morgan's American *Keiretsu*

Even if Morgan's motives were no more than calculated greed, some economists would still not begrudge him the wealth he amassed. They contend that Morgan performed a valuable service for society by helping the economy to prosper by transcending destructive market forces.[48]

Morgan realized—unlike the more ideologically minded economists of today—that a free-wheeling market results in chaos. He also grasped that the maximization of short-run returns was inconsistent with high, long-run profits. These insights allowed him to comprehend the enormous rewards that could be reaped by imposing order on an otherwise chaotic economy.

With few exceptions, investors who put their money on Morgan generally prospered.[49] Those who put their money in a Morgan institution certainly faced far fewer risks than the earlier investors who found themselves at the mercy of the rapacious financial manipulations of the likes of Jay Gould or Jim Fisk.

Although the monopolistic power that Morgan assembled generated some of Morgan's profits,[50] DeLong is correct in noting that rationalization in Morganized industries also created potential social benefits. Many observers ranging from conservative defenders of the trusts to Thorstein Veblen and even Lenin agreed that consolidations fostered increased efficiency—at least in the short run.[51]

Morganized efficiency, of course, was a restrictive conception of efficiency that took no notice of industrial impacts on workers or the environment. Most observers recognized that consolidations did allow management to eliminate much old and relatively unproductive plant and equipment in a way that a market never could. For example, in 1894 John Searles, chief spokesman for the Havemeyer sugar interests, told the Senate Committee to Investigate Attempts at Bribery:

> Under the old regime, when the consumption was decreased, every refiner, in trying to keep his refinery in operation, rather than close it up, was obliged to cut down his production 25 percent, 40, sometimes 50 percent at an enhanced cost of frequently one-eighth of a cent a pound on the entire product. ...Under the existing arrangement...we close up factories which cost the most per pound to operate, and only run those which can be run with the greatest economy, and run those to their fullest capacity.[52]

In addition, freed from the pressures of intense competition, the great trusts eliminated many of the sales positions that they had inherited from the component firms.[53] Other observers applauded the consolidations for promoting efficiency by facilitating the centralization of managerial authority.[54]

Indeed, Morgan's own right-hand man, George W. Perkins, even argued, in language similar to that of Lenin, that the trusts represented a high order of socialism. After all, Perkins asked, "What is the difference between the U.S. Steel Corporation…and a Department of Steel as it might be organized by the government?"[55] In the early days of corporate consolidations, Frederick Engels had come to a similar conclusion, appending an editorial note to Marx's *Capital*, proclaiming, "the ancient and celebrated freedom of competition is at the end of its road and must itself confess its evident and scandalous bankruptcy."[56]

Of course, not everyone agreed with Engels, Lenin, and Morgan. A few defenders of laissez faire even blamed the inefficiencies that the trusts corrected on the tax structure and other government policies,[57] but they were a distinct minority. For most economists and government leaders, a Morganized economy, although not an ideal economy, seemed to be preferable to the anarchy of the marketplace.

Something similar to the corporatist organization of the economy occurred in Japan, a country that began to emulate Germany about the same time that the corporatist economists from the United States were studying there. The Japanese firms were not organized along Morganized lines, in which one company would take over an entire industry. Instead, large corporations developed a large network of companies across industry lines. Each of these networks, known as *keiretsu*, had a main bank that would assure adequate capital for its associated companies.

Isolated from finance, these Japanese companies prospered mightily during the 1970s, when the oil shock rattled market economies around the world. At the time, many observers believed that the Japanese would take over the world with their magnificent economic organization.

The economic success of the Japanese economy unleashed a wave of speculation so intense that the market value of the land in Tokyo was equal to that of the entire state of California. The resulting bubble soon burst and with it the Japanese economy. The Japanese system of organization was stable enough that the country avoided many—but certainly not all—of the human costs associated with prolonged stagnation.

Both the corporatist system in the United States and *keiretsu* in Japan buffered their economies from some of the worst excesses of a market economy, but neither approach was capable of transcending the deeper contradictions of capitalism.

The Dark Side of Morganization

Although the great consolidations seemed to make remarkable progress, they were less successful in fulfilling their promise in the long run. Once the great consolidated organizations had eliminated the overhang of inefficient capital goods, they had little incentive to follow through with new investments. After all, new plant and equipment could make their surviving capital goods obsolete. Instead, the trusts were content to rake in profits from high prices rather than from superior products or technologies.

Rather than improving their productive capabilities to meet the challenge of any potential competitors that might arise, the great consolidated firms typically would buy out the new entrants. Although this strategy was consistent with short-run profit max-imization, over time it depleted the great consolidated firms while the challengers gained strength.[58]

The history of U.S. Steel is instructive in this respect. Although the trusts prom-ised great efficiencies, U.S. Steel did not deliver much even with respect to short-run efficiencies. One writer charged, "The new monster...the largest corporation in the world was over-capitalized, lacked proper coordination, and functioned poorly."[59]

Despite the corporatist rhetoric of efficiency, the purpose of the steel industry merger had nothing whatsoever to do with potential efficiencies. The merger was intended to prevent competition from breaking out in the industry. Indeed, once Morgan consolidated much of the steel industry into U.S. Steel in 1901, competition for markets in the United States became far less brisk.

Within the consolidated corporation, profits depended more on high prices than on any productive efficiencies. Lacking competition, by 1904 domestic steel prices rose to about 50 percent higher than prices on the export market where competition was stronger.[60]

Freed from competitive pressures, the company did little to modernize its opera-tions.[61] The operation that Carnegie furiously drove to maximize productivity became a technological laggard.

The company never bothered to improve its overall management either. For example, Alfred Chandler pointed out that the company retained a primitive organi-zational structure until the 1930s.[62] Why go through the painful process of corporate reorganization in the absence of competition?

Eventually, competitive forces did take shape. High prices both enticed new firms to enter the market and encouraged existing firms to expand production. Smaller companies, with less capital values to protect and thus less to gain from restricting output, behaved more aggressively. They were more inclined to modern-ize and to expand. These challengers also ran their factories nearer to full capaci-ty.[63] As a result, they grew relative to the industry giant. For example, U.S. Steel's share of ingots and castings fell from 66 percent in 1901 to 41 percent in 1927 to 33 percent in 1933.[64]

U.S. Steel was relatively fortunate in one respect. The high capital costs of steel helped to restrict entry by potential competitors. In other branches of the industry, such as the wire and nail sector, where entry was relatively easy, consolidations quickly exhausted themselves in attempting to buy out all the new firms that entered the market to challenge the industry leaders.[65]

Market forces eventually made themselves felt in the steel industry. U.S. Steel experienced the same fate in slow motion as the nineteenth-century railroads, but only after almost three-quarters of a century had passed since the founding of U.S. Steel. By that time, the large, integrated steel producers in the United States were so backward that their very survival depended upon protection from foreign imports and exemptions from environmental regulations. I will discuss the inglorious fate of this firm in more detail in Chapter 7.

In conclusion, Morganization proved to be only a temporary success; although it provided a healthy flow of profits for a period of time, it also helped to create the Great Depression, exposing the flaw in another recipe for dealing with a modern economy with extensive fixed capital.

Andrew Carnegie's Crystal Ball

Just before the great U.S. Steel merger, Andrew Carnegie published two remarkable essays about the trusts. In the first essay, "The Bugaboo of the Trusts," Carnegie penned one of the most cogent statements of the elementary logic of corporatist economics:

> Political economy says…[g]oods will not be produced at less than cost. This was true when Adam Smith wrote, but it is not quite true today. …As manufacturing is carried on today, in enormous establishments with five or ten millions of dollars invested and with thousands of workers, it costs the manufacturer much less to run at a loss per ton or per yard than to check his production. Stoppage would be serious indeed. The condition of cheap manufacture is running full. …Manufacturers have balanced their books year after year only to find their capital reduced at each successive balance. While continuing to produce may be costly, the manufacturer knows too well that stoppage would be ruin. …The manufacturers are in the position of patients that have tried in vain every doctor of the regular school for years, and are now liable to become the victim of any quack that appears. Combinations, syndicates, trusts—they are willing to try anything.[66]

The second essay described the eventual outcome of the consolidation, foreshadowing the future course of the U.S. Steel, except for one fact. Carnegie seemed to believe that the consolidations would involve weakened firms. Vital organizations like his Carnegie Steel would remain outside of the process. Here is how Carnegie painted the scene:

> ...finally the promoter makes his appearance, and our unfortunate manufacturers fall an easy prey. Enormous sums are offered for antiquated plants which may not have been able to do more than pay their way for years. These are tied together...under the delusion that if a dozen or twenty invalids are tied together vitality will be infused thereby into the mass.[67]

These consolidations promised to go beyond protecting corporate profits since they also held the lure of potential economies of scale. In Carnegie's words: "Now the cheapening of all these good things...is rendered possible only through the operation of the law, which may be stated thus: cheapness is in proportion to the scale of production. ...Every enlargement is an improvement, step by step, of what has preceded."[68]

At first, Carnegie predicted that all would go as planned. "For a short time competition is hindered, but rarely, if ever, completely stifled."[69] New competitors emerge. The trust purchases them, eventually leading to disaster. "Every attempt to monopolize the manufacture of any staple article carries within its bosom the seeds of failure."[70]

The corporatists never went as far as Carnegie in their understanding of the logic of the trusts. They only concerned themselves with the immediate benefits of corporate reorganizations. They failed to take account of the predictable, opportunistic behavior of mammoth organizations that dominated an entire industry.

Although the corporatists favored trusts, cartels, and monopolies, they explained away the inevitable monopolistic behavior that these organizations facilitated. They convinced themselves that monopolies would never act like monopolies, certain that full public disclosure of information would assure that they would not abuse their power through underhanded dealings. Fearing potential competition, even where none existed according to the corporatist doctrine, the monopolies would set prices too low to entice new firms to enter their industry.

Economic forces would take care of everything else. For example, although Clark expressed some concern that an established monopoly "would not need to be forever pulling out its machines and putting in better."[71] the possibility of technological stagnation that U.S. Steel experienced did not seem to be much of a threat to the other corporatists.

In short, the corporatists put their trust in the organized market of consolidated industries rather than in competitive forces. While they correctly identified the deep contradictions of competitive capitalism, they altogether failed to recognize equally serious flaws in a Morganized economy—flaws that were obvious to Carnegie from his years of corporate experience.

Neither alternative—the competitive capitalism that the corporatists opposed or Morganized capitalism that the corporatists supported—was capable of efficiently directing economic activity in an economy that largely depends on long-lived fixed capital.

Corporatist Economics and Financial Manipulations

In expressing their faith in organized markets, the corporatists paid scant attention to the world of finance; yet they had to know that financial interests were blatantly manipulating firms in order to further their own advantage, even when these actions severely injured the health of the firm in the process. Nonetheless, even after Adams published his scathing indictment of the Erie, we hear little more about the role of finance. In any case, as we saw with Clark, the corporatists implicitly assumed that any abuse perpetrated by financiers would harm shareholders rather than the business.

Until the twentieth century, most industry had been relatively immune from the arcane world of finance. Management salaries were surprisingly small compared to today. As late as 1911 salaries of $5,000 to $6,000 ($100,000 to $120,000 in 2005 dollars) were common for presidents of substantial manufacturing concerns[72]—a weekly income for elite CEOs today. In contrast, huge profits awaited clever financial manipulators. The experience of the railroads such as the Erie should have alerted the corporatists to the ability of financial interests to undermine industry.

Although J. P. Morgan became the symbol of high finance, he was hardly typical of that world. Although the long-run benefits of Morganization were questionable, the actions of more unsavory financiers were not open to debate. Seeing the immense profits from the railroad mergers, many unscrupulous financial promoters, unburdened by Morgan-like reputations to protect, began to organize less than solid industrial consolidations.

For these promoters, the risk of besmirching their relatively nonexistent good names seemed a small price to pay for the immense rewards that they could reap by cutting a few corners. Since stocks were displacing real estate as the fashionable speculative arena, many unsuspecting investors provided an enthusiastic market for the watered stocks in these new ventures.[73]

These unscrupulous promoters took full advantage of the opportunities to amass great wealth. Indeed, quite a few great fortunes were made in this way. In 1899, even before the creation of U.S. Steel, promoters organized the Distilling Company of America, popularly known as the "whisky trust," from the stock of four companies with book values of $53.4 million. They valued the new company at $77.5 million, of which $24.1 million went to promoters. The president of the new firm, Samuel Rice, who was not one of the organizers, pleaded ignorance about the finances of the company in testimony before the Industrial Commission, stating in words that still resonate in the courtrooms where a handful of the financial manipulators stood trial, "I have no knowledge of that. ...That is their [the promoters'] business, not mine."[74]

The promoter of the American Tin Plate Company in 1899, Judge William Moore of Chicago (also organizer of Diamond Match and National Biscuit), earned $10 million on the $46 million of stock issued.[75] While most of Morgan's ventures proved to be successful, at least in the short run, the majority of his competitors' consolidations promptly failed to deliver on their promises.[76]

Even if the unscrupulous promoters may have reaped unconscionable profits from their enterprises, could these consolidations have served a positive purpose by clearing the way for future industrial efficiency? The tragic industrial failures of the telecom bubble of the late twentieth century suggest that a negative response to that question may be obvious. However, let us not get ahead of ourselves.

Why were the corporatists so blind to the problems created by financial interests? Perhaps the corporatists intended to distance themselves from the populists who saw financial conspiracies in every corner of the economy. Perhaps the growing dominance of the investment bankers relative to the swindlers and promoters in the railroad industry made them expect a similar movement in other industries. Or, perhaps, the corporatists believed their recommendation that government agencies provide the public with full information about corporate behavior would ensure that financial abuses would become uncommon.

Popular language reflected a healthy opposition to finance. For example, during the heyday of the populists the idea of the working class was far broader than it is today. The notion of workers included farmers and shopkeepers. Industrialists and sometimes even lawyers were considered workers, but never bankers.

With the growth of industrial consolidations, antagonism toward finance grew. Individuals found themselves at a distinct disadvantage in dealing with the huge ventures that finance capital put together. Many were dismayed by the increasing influence of speculative movements. Each time speculative excesses led to crashes, masses of people who had no direct connection with the world of finance suffered the consequences, even though they had reaped none of the rewards.

Conflicting Versions of Laissez Faire

Advocates of both competitive capitalism and Morganized capitalism offered an unambiguous explanation of how the economy would function within their preferred system. Let us begin with the contemporary vision of laissez faire under competitive capitalism.

Protagonists of laissez faire under competitive capitalism contend that without the discipline of the market, management has interests that may not necessarily be consistent with those of society. For example, any firm would like to be able to sell as much as possible at the highest conceivable price.

Laissez-faire economists dismiss any concern that competitive firms might abuse their power at the expense of the public. After all, under competitive capitalism small firms would predominate. No single firm could have enough influence to do much harm, because market forces limit their discretion. The market would penalize any firm that refused to act in the public interest. Only those firms that carefully follow market signals could survive.

True, survival is not assured, even when an efficient firm follows the dictates of the market once long-lived capital goods become important. Carnegie was the exception that proves the rule. The recurrence of periodic depressions shows that the entire system can run itself into bankruptcy. I have been stressing the role of long-lived fixed capital as a destabilizing influence only because that factor has been underappreciated. Despite the fact that any number of factors, such as speculation or lack of demand, can throw a market economy into a crisis, proponents of competitive capitalism never face up to that possibility.

Ignoring that aspect of the nature of competitive capitalism, we must admit that proponents of laissez faire do offer a clear, though unrealistic, vision of the appropriate policy under competitive capitalism: since no single firm is big enough to affect the economy to a significant degree, the best policy is to let the market take care of itself.

The corporatists told a quite different story, but that was equally clear and consistent. Unlike the laissez-faire economists, who suggest that we should leave decision making in the hands of the managers of enterprises because they are small, the corporatists contended that the enormous capital requirements of modern industry preclude business from prospering under competitive conditions. Only the large corporations that could hold competition in check and muster enough resources to perfect modern technologies could operate efficiently. The public would benefit because these huge enterprises, enjoying economies of scale, could reduce prices far below what a large number of small firms could possibly deliver.

The corporatists dismissed the notion of any possible conflict between corporate leadership and the public. They concluded that the likely outcomes of a corporatist economy would benefit both the individual enterprise and the public at large.

As I have already mentioned, one of the greatest failings of the corporatists was their failure to address the financial abuses associated with corporate consolidations. For the corporatists, the decisions of the management of large corporations would be mostly technical in nature. They naively assumed that the threat of either unfavorable publicity or new competitors would suffice to make the large corporations refrain from acting against the public interest. In short, the very size of the giant corporations offers management a scope of vision that allows it to make the best possible decisions.

Although the laissez-faire economists are unrealistic about their economic principles, they do offer a realistic view of the self-seeking behavior of business owners and managers. In contrast, the corporatists, who were far more realistic about the nature of a market economy, altogether unrealistically assumed that business leaders would refrain from taking decisions contrary to the public interest, either because of the technical nature of these decisions or because of thoroughgoing public disclosure.

In this sense, knowing what we do today, the corporatists seem every bit as naive as the laissez-faire economists. We live in an economy in which many corporations are large enough to make decisions that threaten our welfare in obvious ways—spreading toxic substances, selling dangerous products, or putting the health of their workers at risk. Those public agencies that are supposed to protect us from corporate misconduct seem thoroughly beholden to those whom they are supposed to regulate.

5

Industry Takes Command:
The Rise of Welfare Capitalism

The First Stirrings of Corporate Liberalism

As the nineteenth century wore on, the influence of agrarian interests and the associated populist movement waned. The failure of William Jennings Bryan's presidential
campaign, which was largely a haphazard assault on the gold standard, symbolized
this transition. Protests no longer focused on the economic losses associated with the
gold standard. Instead, dissatisfaction largely focused on the abuse of power generally associated with the great nonfinancial corporations.

The enormous industrial consolidations of the early twentieth century created a
Morganized core economy surrounded by a periphery of smaller, generally marginal
companies that operated in more competitive sectors. Ruthless business leaders from
the Morganized core displayed a haughty public-be-damned attitude, running
roughshod over workers, consumers, small business, and the environment. The public was becoming impatient with the arrogant behavior of many business leaders.
Demands that the government take a firmer stand on the trust question were coming
from those who suffered under the heels of big business as well as from those who still
believed in a competitive economy.

In response, in the years from 1910 to 1917, many corporate leaders felt con-
strained to make the case that their actions were in the public interest. To appear more
responsive to public opinion, they took on the posture of being more concerned with
increasing rational economic organization than making quick profits.[1] They put forth
the idea that enlightened members of their community, rather than bureaucrats or
politicians, were ideally suited to serve as disinterested contributors to social policy.

Corporate leaders did not merely want to defuse public antipathy toward their greed. They hoped to change the legal climate to give them even more leeway. By this time, the prevailing public opinion no longer accepted the notion that unregulated markets could provide efficiency. Only a distinct minority called for a return to competitive capitalism, despite what professors were teaching their students. Instead, federal regulation of corporate behavior seemed more likely.

Rather than accede to public demands for regulation, corporate leaders hoped to convince the body politic that the corporatist system was in the public interest. These corporate leaders projected a vision that business could reorganize itself on its own, avoiding the widespread abuses that were infuriating the public. Already in October 1907, the National Civic Federation sponsored the National Conference on Combinations and Trusts, including a supposedly broad spectrum of people from labor, manufacturing, and trade, all of whom were expected to support the call for a redefinition of the Sherman Act.[2]

Many business leaders proposed that government and business, along with a few respectable union leaders, could combine to create standards that would be far superior to any market outcomes. Events turned out to be more persuasive than the theories of economists. As the United States began to build up in preparation for the First World War, the public became more receptive to the idea that corporate power could work to the public benefit.

War Socialism

Suddenly, with the actual outbreak of war, those responsible for military preparations fell in line with the corporatist perspective, acknowledging that the inefficiencies of the market represented a luxury that a society under siege could ill afford. An all-out war effort required planning, not competition. As a result, leaders of the great industrial combines joined with government officials and a select group of union officials to make economic policy like never before. In the words of Ellis Hawley:

> ...[given the obvious deficiencies of the market in the face of a crisis], "[t]he need was for an administrative network with unifying, planning, and directive capabilities...through the creation of a quasi-corporative bureaucracy, part private and part public, yet with its public side substantially distinct from the regular agencies of government. On the public side the characteristic organization was the commodity division, technically a government agency but staffed mostly with people who were on leave from positions in the private sector. On the other side the characteristic organization was the industrial authority or war service committee.[3]

As Robert Sobel remarked, "Men like [Bernard] Baruch [head of the War Industries Board] were brought into government, and were transformed from the sharks of Wall Street to the heroes of Pennsylvania Avenue."[4] Baruch reminisced that the War Industries Board had enabled businessmen to enjoy "the tremendous advantages both to themselves and to the general public, of combination, of cooperation and common action with their natural competitors."[5] To the public, this arrangement seemed so at odds with what they imagined to be the American way that it was sometimes referred to as "war socialism."[6]

The war socialists were perhaps justifiably proud of their accomplishments. Unlike the Civil War period, when business displayed unrestrained greed, during the time of war socialism, business mixed its compulsion for acquisitiveness with a certain degree of public concern.[7] Given the favorable outcome of the war, the war socialists emerged with their reputations largely intact.

With the return of peace, the war socialists were anxious to continue to apply their experience to the postwar economy. Now that the wartime emergency had passed, the same energies that had gone into fighting a war could be profitably turned to develop the civilian economy. Always the master of self-promotion,[8] Bernard Baruch subsidized a book by Grosvernor B. Clarkson, an advertising executive and public relations agent. Baruch also had one of his top aides carefully check the finished manuscript.[9] According to Clarkson:

> The World War was a wonderful school. …It showed us how so many things may be bettered that we are at a loss where to begin with permanent utilization of what we know. The Conservation Division alone showed that merely to strip from trade and industry the lumber of futile custom and the encrustation of useless variety would return a good dividend on the world's capital. …Yet now the world needs to economize as much as in war.[10]

These war socialists gave no indication that they sensed any contradiction whatsoever between the public good associated with a military victory and the private interests that businesses ordinarily pursue. Perhaps they calculated that the public-minded vision that Clarkson proposed would have great appeal in that era.

Ellis Hawley summed up the ideals of the business leaders at the time, observing that they believed their program "would allow liberal societies to overcome social fragmentation and realize their ideals without undergoing either socialist revolutions or some kind of statist regimentation."[11]

Herbert Hoover was the business leader who emerged from the war with the greatest reputation for his success in applying his business acumen for public purposes.

Hoover also became the most prominent proponent of this new economic form. Despite his abiding conservatism, as secretary of commerce he published a book, entitled *American Individualism,* which was not about individualism at all. Instead, he proclaimed that laissez faire had been "dead in America for generations," except in the recalcitrant hearts of some "reactionary souls."[12] He went on to proclaim:

> Today business organization is moving strongly toward cooperation. There are in cooperation great hopes that we can even gain in individuality, equality of opportunity, and at the same time reduce many of the great wastes of overreckless competition in production and distribution.[13]

Seen retrospectively during a time when faith in markets was becoming more common, this call for government and business to cooperate seemed highly unusual. For example, Eric Goldman would later write:

> Many of the dollar-a-year men went back to their fifty-thousand-dollar-a-year jobs with an idea buzzing in their heads. Perhaps their decades-old battle for "free competition" and against "government in business" had not been wise. They had been given striking proof that federal activity need not be anti-business, and they had seen the advantages that could come from joint operations under federal aegis.[14]

Welfare Capitalism: An Introduction

Some of the ideals of war socialism found expression in what came to be known as welfare capitalism, a movement based on the premise that publicly-minded business people could lead society to a general level of prosperity and social justice. The welfare capitalists themselves frequently spoke in the most sincere terms of the depths of their personal concern with the welfare of their workers, giving rise to the phrase, "welfare capitalism."

The heyday of welfare capitalism was a hopeful period. According to the fashion of the day, welfare capitalism was more than just charity; it was supposed to be an excellent business proposition. Many industrial workers, as well as new holders of common stock, expected to share in the generous rewards that capitalism was supposed to bring.

Welfare capitalism had important antecedents. We can trace its origins back at least to the early nineteenth century efforts of Robert Owen to build model villages designed to lure Scottish highlanders into employment. Indeed, although Owen spent so much more on his workers than comparable employers, his partners demanded that he cut back on such expenses to make his dividends even higher. Knowing better, Owen refused and went on to enjoy healthy profits.

Impressed by Owen, textile mill owners in New England developed the Lowell system a few decades thereafter, where young farm girls employed in the Massachusetts textile mills lived in a sheltered, somewhat paternalistic environment. We can see more modern anticipations of welfare capitalism in the town built by George Pullman or in Procter and Gamble's 1886 profit-sharing plan.[15] A number of other large corporations had already begun their own stock purchase and pension plans prior to the First World War.[16] These exceptional early gestures stood out because of the more typical, openly exploitative attitude toward labor.

John D. Rockefeller, Jr., provided the most important precedent for welfare capitalism. Rockefeller was concerned about shedding the violent image he earned after the Ludlow massacre, where the Colorado state militia, defending his corporate interests, attacked a camp of strikers, leaving eleven children and two women dead. In the wake of Ludlow, Rockefeller went to great lengths to portray himself as a devout Christian who immersed himself in Christian charities. In an unpublished 1920 essay entitled "Why Am I a Church Member?" Rockefeller wrote:

> The men in the Colorado coal fields, who some years ago had been on strike for many months and in whose minds the most intense bitterness had grown up, responded to the genuine spirit of brotherhood when it was made manifest among them, while personal contact and the rubbing of elbows soon dispelled hatred and bitterness and established mutual confidence and good will.[17]

To foster this spirit of brotherhood, Rockefeller hired Mackenzie King, who had recently served as labor minister in the Canadian government and who would later serve more than two decades as Canadian prime minister.[18] King designed a grievance system for Rockefeller, involving employee representation.

In light of his reforms, Rockefeller claimed before the Industrial Commission that he supported the principle of the right of labor to organize and engage in collective bargaining, even though he still refused to recognize unions as bargaining agents for his own employees.[19]

Labor-Management Relations before Welfare Capitalism

The rise of welfare capitalism paralleled the changing labor conditions in the United States. Many of the great manufacturing corporations had depended heavily on immigrant labor prior to the First World War. A good number of these immigrant workers were peasants who were untrained in modern industrial techniques. Others were skilled craft workers who could not find employment in their own trades once they reached the United States.

The usually astute Sumner Slichter once observed that because most of these immigrants came from oppressed classes or races, management could easily drive them hard enough to maximize productivity.[20] Presumably, management (and to some extent Slichter himself) had assumed that these foreign-born "beasts" lacked the intelligence to outfox their bosses. We will return to this faulty observation in a moment.

To further their ability to drive their workers, most employers relied on a strategy of segregating their workforce by ethnic group to minimize workers' solidarity. Management would assign specific nationalities to specific tasks. In the midst of strikes, companies would carefully recruit new ethnic groups that would have the most difficulty in communicating with the existing mix of nationalities.

As a result, the staff of each section of a typical factory consisted almost entirely of a single nationality. In 1911, the U.S. Immigration Commission took note of this practice, observing, "in many cases the conscious policy of the employers [is] mixing the races in certain departments and divisions…preventing concert of action on the part of the employees."[21]

Managers were quite clear about the benefits of what later came to be called, "balancing nationalities."[22] Consider what we find in a confidential letter written by Captain Jones, manager of Carnegie's huge Edgar Thomson works in Pittsburgh in 1875. There, Jones explained, "My experience has shown that Germans and Irish, Swedes, and what I denominate Buckwheats (young American country boys), judiciously mixed, make the most effective and tractable force you can find."[23]

Within this arrangement, unions had difficulty organizing so long as employers could easily replenish their labor force with a steady stream of fresh immigrants, especially those speaking unfamiliar languages. Without unions, workers mostly expressed their dissatisfaction to management through high rates of absenteeism and turnover. In 1913–14, 81.3 percent of newly hired factory workers quit or were fired within a year.[24] Turnover was especially high for workers with repetitious jobs. Breaking in new workers for these jobs was particularly expensive.[25]

Nonetheless, most employers seemed satisfied with this arrangement. Business leaders generally believed that, with a virtually unlimited supply of immigrant labor, technology would eliminate the need for more expensive skilled labor.[26]

Other employers, for whom turnover and absenteeism were reaching crisis proportions, began to question the efficacy of "balancing nationalities" to subjugate labor, slightly opening the door to the idea of welfare capitalism.

Ford's $5 Day

Nowhere was the problem of turnover and absenteeism more severe than in the factory of Henry Ford, where workers' dissatisfaction was running dangerously high. Absenteeism in the Ford plant in 1913 had reached 10.5 percent.[27]

Turnover at the Ford plant had soared to 370 percent by 1913. The company had to hire 50,448 men just to maintain the average labor force of 13,623. Company surveys at Ford revealed that more than 7,300 workers left in March 1913 alone. Of these, 18 percent were discharged; 11 percent formally quit; and 71 percent were let go because they missed five days in row a without excuse and so were deemed to have quit. On each day, it was necessary to make use of 1,300 or 1,400 replacement workers without any experience.[28] One observer remarked, "the Ford Motor Co. had reached the point of owning a great factory without having enough workers to keep it humming."[29]

Hiring new workers, even unskilled workers, and offering them a minimum of training turned out to be an expensive proposition. Stephen Meyer estimates that Ford spent $35 to break in each new worker. With 52,000 workers entering the Ford factory in 1913, the company lost $1,820,000 because of turnover.[30] In addition, although conventional union organizing was not much of a threat for most industrialists at the time, the Industrial Workers of the World was threatening to organize Ford's factory.[31]

These conditions prompted Ford to initiate what was perhaps the most dramatic precursor of welfare capitalism: his famous introduction of the $5 a day wage. Although Ford's gesture seemed unexpectedly generous at the time, Ford himself freely admitted that his motives were entirely self-interested:

> There was…no charity involved. …We wanted to pay these wages so that business would be on a lasting foundation. We were building for the future. A low wage business is always insecure. The payment of $5 a day for an eight-hour day was one of the finest cost-cutting moves we ever made.[32]

Although Ford based his policy on sound business principles, the business community was aghast at his behavior, excoriating Ford as a "mad socialist" and a "traitor to his class." The *Wall Street Journal* and other financial papers enthusiastically joined in the attack.

Nonetheless, the $5 wage was a brilliant stroke of capitalist genius. In 1914, the first year after Ford began the $5 wage, turnover fell dramatically to 54 percent. By 1915, it dropped still further to 16 percent.[33] Absenteeism also subsided, falling to 0.4 percent in 1914.[34]

Despite its effectiveness, the $5 plan was not exactly what it seemed to be. It included a basic hourly wage of only 34 cents per hour plus a profit-sharing rate of 28.5 cents. Workers did not automatically receive the profit-sharing rate. Instead, eligibility profit sharing depended on a number of special conditions. To begin with, workers had to perform satisfactory work to participate in profit sharing. In addition, Ford disqualified all women. According to one source, "Women did not work on the assembly line, and were not likely to drink and fail to show up for work. They did not jump from job to job. So there was no reason to include them."[35]

According to a 1914 Ford pamphlet, to qualify for the plan, a worker also had to be at least twenty-two years old, with six months seniority. Ford imposed numerous other conditions for profit sharing that seemed to be unrelated to work. The company established a Sociological Department, initially consisting of 200 inspectors, to investigate the workers to see if they met the company's qualifications. They "visited workers' homes gathering information and giving advice on intimate details of the family budget, diet, living arrangements, recreation, social outlook, and morality."[36]

For example, the company had to be "satisfied that he [the qualified worker] will not debauch the additional money he receives."[37] Toward this end, the Sociological Department had to be certain that the workers maintained a suitable home, refrained from taking in boarders, operated no outside business, made sure that the family did not associate with the wrong people, avoided excessive smoking or drinking, and demonstrated adequate progress in learning English. In addition, wives of qualified workers could not work outside of the home.[38] Furthermore, the inspectors had to determine whether the workers displayed sufficient thrift, cleanliness, "good manhood," and good citizenship.[39] Workers also had to tend gardens that the inspectors deemed to be adequate.[40] Not surprisingly, during the first two years, 28 percent of all male workers were disqualified from profit sharing.

Ford expected more than improved family life in return for his plan. He expected near absolute obedience. One contemporary study of the Ford system concluded that Ford "desires and prefers machine-tool operators who have nothing to unlearn, who have no theories of correct surface speeds for metal finishing, and will simply do what they are told to do, over and over again, from bell-time to bell-time."[41]

Ford also expected that this obedience would translate into greater effort from the workers. A production foreman named W. Klann reported, "[They] called us in and said that since the workers were getting twice the wages, [the management] wanted twice as much work. On the assembly lines, we just simply turned up the speed of the lines."[42]

Balancing Nationalities No More

For most firms, turnover and absenteeism were less extreme than they were for Ford. With the outbreak of war, however, the old system of balancing nationalities crumbled. Labor could no longer easily immigrate to the United States. Given the high demand for labor, turnover became an even more pressing problem,[43] roughly doubling between 1915 and 1917.[44]

Suddenly, the once supposedly docile immigrants became less cooperative. As David Montgomery noted, the First World War gave workers

> ...a new sense of power. ...New styles of organization within the workplace, often energized by radicals, challenged the scientifically managed enterprise on its own turf and threatened the "bona fide" practices of craft unions at the same time.[45]

In the same article where Sumner Slichter reported on the ease of driving immigrant labor, he also noted that, as soon as the brisk wartime demand for labor gave the previously tractable immigrants more confidence, the same immigrants deliberately began to withhold their productivity.[46] In reality, the outbreak of war gave rise to more overt forms of action than the passive withholding of productivity. Slichter himself pointed out that the number of strikes increased from 1,420 in 1915 to 3,517 in 1916 and 4,450 in 1917.[47]

The armistice cleared the way for even more strike activity. In addition, the labor movement emerged from the First World War with enlarged membership, healthy treasuries, and a temporary guarantee of the right of collective bargaining.[48] Claims of national security were no longer a plausible reason to prohibit strikes. As a result, in the words of David Montgomery again:

> Between 1916 and 1922, when levels of strike participation soared far above those of any other period thus far in the country's history, workers' demands became too heady for the AFL or even the Socialist Party to contain and too menacing for business and the state to tolerate.[49]

Business, of course, was largely responsible for this state of affairs. Although the strategy of ethnic separation may have been fairly successful in keeping unions from organizing entire factories, it backfired under wartime conditions. The corporations had unintentionally fostered ethnic solidarity to keep the workers fragmented, but their actions had also created a further gulf between labor and management.[50] These small groups of ethnically homogeneous, immigrant workers were far more inclined to give credence to someone who shared their background than to a management representative. In short, balancing nationalities had left the workers susceptible to the dreaded influence of "foreign agitators."[51]

The Americanization of Labor

In the face of this growing labor militancy, both business and the government counterattacked. Many firms, especially smaller firms, enthusiastically embraced the Open Shop Movement, which was dedicated to the outright elimination of unions from the workplace.

We should not be surprised that xenophobia became common after the outburst of strikes. Business and the government forces whipped up a convenient Red Scare, which gave the government a pretense to deport as many foreign-born union organizers as they could locate. Many business leaders, especially representatives of small business, fanned the fires of xenophobia, lumping both Bolshevism and unionism into the general category of undesirable foreign influences.

Immigration no longer appeared to be a useful weapon to hold down labor's aspirations. Instead, immigration seemed to be a threat to business. Many business leaders feared that a continuing flow of immigrants would infect the United States with the fervid radicalism that they considered to be rampant throughout Europe.[52]

Others questioned the intellectual capacity of immigrants. Eastern and southern European workers were supposed to have an especially limited level of intelligence. For example, the personnel manager at Pittsburgh's Central Tube Company analyzed the "racial adaptability" of thirty-six different ethnic groups for twenty-four different kinds of work under twelve sets of conditions. Lithuanians, for instance, were supposedly good at trucking barrels or cases, but mediocre at shoveling. They were suited to outdoor work, but poor performers under hot and dry conditions and undesirable at night.[53]

In response to such sentiments, the United States passed laws sharply curtailing immigration. The average number of immigrants fell dramatically, from 856,000 in 1910–15 to 356,000 in 1915–30. The decrease in male immigrants was even more extreme, falling from 584,000 to 217,000.[54]

The leaders of a number of larger, more forward-looking firms understood that their strategy of ethnic separation was a failure. They realized that they could not indefinitely rely on the Red Scare and the Open Shop Movement to keep labor in line. Deportation and union-busting alone were incapable of significantly raising productivity. These leaders concluded that management's callous contempt for its workers in the past had seriously undermined economic efficiency. Over the long run, further confrontational policies were likely to damage productivity even more.

These business leaders decided to take positive action to elicit their workers' cooperation. One noted labor economist remarked at the time that casual labor was a "state of mind" that industry had to replace with "thrift, sobriety, adaptability, [and] initiative."[55] Toward this end, business leaders set off to forge new bonds with their employees through the establishment of welfare capitalism.[56]

Managers of many large corporations dedicated themselves to the Americanization of their workforce.[57] Companies attempted to displace ethnic institutions. They organized corporate social and sporting events as alternatives to more traditional ethnic activities. They sponsored stores and credit unions that could replace ethnic firms.[58] Management felt that this tactic would make the workers more resistant to ethnic organizers and possibly even bind the workers to the firm.

The Strategy of Welfare Capitalism

The wartime experience provided some clues about how companies could induce labor to become more productive. To begin with, the war had demonstrated the importance of training workers.[59] Business also came to recognize that patriotic fervor could stimulate production, underscoring the crucial nature of the human element in production.

In addition, the War Labor Board had ordered large companies to install shop committees in which labor and management could collaborate.[60] After the armistice, some large companies voluntarily installed their own committees to use as instruments of welfare capitalism.

This strategy soon bore fruit, suggesting that a more cooperative system of labor relations could be profitable. In many cases, labor committees pointed out new methods for significantly increasing productivity.[61] A chorus of academic writers soon hailed this awakening on the part of business. One of these exclaimed:

> Our immigrant labor supply has been used by American industry much the same way that American farmers have used our land. But just as the disappearance of free land has led farmers to conserve their soil and to put a considerable investment into maintaining and improving it, so the restrictions on immigration…have led employers to conserve the skill and strength of their labor and to put a considerable investment into training and improving it.[62]

George Soule reported that a steel engineer told him during the 1919 steel strike, "We do not intend to improve the condition of unskilled labor; we intend to abolish it." Sumner Slichter also welcomed the end of a "policy of driving the workers rather than by developing their good will and cooperation." Although he admitted that "managers displayed amazing ingenuity in adapting work to unskilled laborers," the time had come to adapt the workers to modern production methods by recruiting and training a better class of workers.[63]

The logic behind welfare capitalism still made excellent sense. To the extent that welfare capitalism could tie workers to the firm, management could reduce the expense of what appeared to them as excessive labor turnover.[64] In fact, by the 1920s, turnover declined substantially despite the shortage of skilled workers.[65] In the words of Slichter:

> [Corporate labor programs] are one of the most ambitious social experiments of the age, because they aim, among other things, to counteract the effect of modern technique upon the mind of the worker, to prevent him from becoming class conscious and from organizing trade unions. ...To the best men promotion thus becomes a more certain and often easier way of gaining higher wages than is trade union action.[66]

Welfare capitalism had another major benefit. It also offered the attractive promise of shielding firms from the muckraker's increasingly frequent attacks.[67] As a result, a number of major corporations came to accept Ford's sharp calculus of profit maximization, although they rarely seemed to credit Ford's pioneering innovations. Nonetheless, like Ford, they concluded that welfare capitalism made good sense as a business proposition.

The Economy of High Wages

The welfare capitalists contended that generosity was the surest route to high profits. According to their logic, business should pay high wages in the expectation that labor would respond with enhanced productivity, making still higher wages possible. As Hoover told an audience on May 12, 1926:

> The very essence of great production is high wages and low prices. ...The acceptance of these ideas is obviously not universal. Not all employers...nor has every union abandoned the fallacy of restricted effort. ...But...for both employer and employee to think in terms of the mutual interest of increased production has gained in strength. It is a long cry from the conception of the old economics.[68]

An anonymous employer echoed Hoover's sentiments during the following year:

An employer wrote in 1927, "In spite of the fact that wages in our factories have more than doubled in the past fifteen years our manufacturing costs are actually lower now than they were at the beginning of that period. High wages, forcibly thrust upon us by the war, and always opposed by those in charge of our business, have lowered our manufacturing costs, by making us apply machinery and power to tasks formerly done by hand.[69]

Welfare capitalists did not originate the idea of the economy of high wages. This notion had precedents that reached back to the earliest days of political economy. Around 1591, John Hales observed, "the workman never prevails but as the master provokes him with good wages."[70]

John Stuart Mill, the preeminent British economist of the mid-nineteenth century, proclaimed that "the cost of labour is frequently at its highest where wages are lowest." This relationship "is proved...by abundant testimony."[71]

Thomas Brassey (1805–70), who ran a highly profitable railway construction company, compiled twenty-four volumes of interviews with employees, managers, and secretaries covering manufacturing, textiles, railway, and building construction in Britain, Ireland, Germany, France, and India concerning the relationship between work and wages. His son published some of these under the title *Work and Wages* (1872).[72] The positive effect of wages on productivity was the main theme of Brassey's work. Over time, such sentiments became more and more common. With the report of Jacob Schoenhof, the idea of an economy of high wages even became enshrined within the halls of government.[73]

High Wages and Labor Militancy

The growing belief in the efficacy of high wages may have been a reflection of the increasing dominance of large-scale industry. In 1911, two years before Henry Ford began his $5-a-day pay scale, Henry Moore concluded that large employers typically had to pay higher wages. Like Ford, most large employers enforced stricter work rules and required more effort. As a result, they had to pay a premium in wages to attract and retain better workers.[74]

George Stigler offered a theoretical explanation for the relationship between firm size and wages. He speculated that large firms would rationally pay better wages. He suggested, "The small employer can directly observe the performance of the new worker and need not resort to expensive and uncertain practices to estimate the worker's performance."[75] Large employers did not have that option. They had to rely on stricter work rules, paying a premium to those workers who would accept these more stringent work rules.

Where Stigler explained the relationship between firm size and wages as the result of rational bargaining among collaborators, others interpreted the same relationship in terms of conflict. Unions have realized for a long time that large-scale operations are easier to organize because of harsher working conditions. In addition, the massing together of large numbers of workers helps to generate a feeling of solidarity.

Seeing the relationship between wages and firm size in terms of conflict helps to explain why the strike wave following the end of the First World War tended to hit hardest at those companies, such as International Harvester, General Electric, and U.S. Steel, which had already begun to initiate some elements of welfare capitalism.[76] Such employers were temporarily able to repress conflict by balancing nationalities under a policy of rapid immigration, but that policy eventually played itself out, as first Henry Ford and later the welfare capitalists learned.

Large firms have still another reason to offer higher wages: strikes are far more costly for them than for smaller firms. For example, a British industrialist, Edmund Ashworth, told an early nineteenth century economist, Nassau Senior, that "when a labourer...lays down his spade, he renders useless, for that period, a capital worth eighteen pence. When one of our people leaves the mill, he renders useless a capital that has cost 100 pounds." Large firms not only pay higher wages; they tend to keep wages steadier than smaller firms do. A study of cotton spinning firms in Lancashire, England between 1822 and 1852 found that large firms with more than 500 employees did not cut wages as much during minor contractions as small firms with less than 150 employees did. Instead, the large firms tended to work shorter hours.[77]

With the rise of large-scale industry in the late nineteenth century United States, we see an economy-wide diminution in the tendency for wages to move with the business cycle. Christopher Hanes attributes this change to growing labor militancy during the period. He found that firms in the industries that experienced the most strikes were the least likely to cut wages.[78] The experience of the McCormick Corporation clearly illustrates the relationship between militancy and wage policy:

> In [the depression of] 1873, the company cut wages promptly and suffered a foundry strike. In 1884, the company delayed seven months before cutting wages. A strike occurred anyway and the company was forced to capitulate by restoring the cut. In the depression of 1893 the company, mindful of the 1884–85 experience, avoided any across-the-board cut. ...The growing reluctance of the Harvester company to cut wages in depressions has stemmed...at times from the threat of unionism and perhaps from the recognition of its disruptive effect on employee morale.[79]

The depression of 1893, coming close on the heels of the terrible labor troubles of 1885 and 1886, brought a dramatic change in the company's wage-cutting tactics even though at the time there were no unions in the plant. Instead of an across-the board cut in 1884, the company maintained its common labor rate through three years of depression, cutting it only at the end of 1896.[80]

The Rhetoric of Welfare Capitalism

Although self-interest motivated the welfare capitalists, they presented themselves as public-spirited citizens who were providing a service for the community. Like the corporatists before them, the welfare capitalists contended that business, left to itself, was the proper custodian of the nation's welfare.

To buttress such claims, welfare capitalism evolved into an attractive ideology of corporate responsibility with breathtaking speed. Their pronouncements seemed to validate the corporatists' promise that management of the large corporations would care for their workers far better than the impersonal forces of competitive capitalism would.

Booming economic conditions made both wages and profits seem as if they could continue to increase forever without a strong government presence. Given this success, the welfare capitalists seemed to make a convincing case in the eyes of much of the public. No one expressed the spirit of welfare capitalism better than Herbert Hoover, then Secretary of Commerce. For Hoover, "The directors and managers of large concerns...reflect a spirit of community."[81] Consider how Swift and Company described its goals in its 1923 yearbook:

> To make employment more secure, to pay fair wages, and to make this possible by avoiding waste and by improving the whole economic machine; to lead, not drive men...; to provide for self-expression on the part of our workers, and to keep the way open for their education and advancement; to bring about a closer cooperation and a better understanding between the workers and the management.[82]

Similarly, Charles M. Schwab, head of Bethlehem Steel, told the American Society of Mechanical Engineers in December 1927, "Our primary job is to make steel, but it is made under a system which must be justified. If...this system does not enable men to live on an increasingly higher plane, then it is natural that the system itself should fail."[83] No wonder that John Maynard Keynes came to believe that large corporations would become indistinguishable from universities and other public institutions![84]

Despite their appealing rhetoric, the corporations that espoused welfare capital-ism were anything but charitable institutions. Nonetheless, they had an obvious inter-est in making the public believe that they were pursuing socially beneficial policies.

In fact, many of them went so far as to hire public relations agents, such as Bruce Barton, to promote an image linking bigness with goodness.[85] The behavior of many owners of small businesses helped to make this pitch more credible. Lacking the power of big business, many had to resort to ruthless methods in order to earn a profit.

Admittedly, many of the early attempts at welfare capitalism were a step in the right direction. Even though they "did little more than put a padded glove over an iron fist,"[86] the welfare capitalists were an improvement on the corporatists, who went no further than merely claiming that large corporations would not act in a ruthless manner. At least some of the welfare capitalists actually behaved at times as if they had some concern for their employees.

Violating the logic of short-run profit maximization, the welfare capitalists seemed to respond to the needs of their employees, rather than concentrating on immediate market forces. This more generous behavior, along with the prosperity of the period, may help to explain why one historian was able to declare that on the eve of the Depression, business "enjoyed a degree of public approval unique in American history."[87] This support for business was far from unconditional. The public had this greater trust in business only because many business people did not seem to behave as business people. The welfare capitalists made laissez faire seem to be more palat-able by seeming to disregard the logic of laissez faire.

The Appealing Logic of Welfare Capitalism

On a larger scale, welfare capitalism presented itself as a system that could overcome the deficiencies of the market, without an enlarged role for the state. Of course, the welfare capitalists did not really desire to cripple the state. Instead, they wanted the state to more or less act as an agent of the welfare capitalist businesses.

Secretary of Commerce Herbert Hoover, reflecting the prevailing corporate atti-tude, offered these encouraging words to the 1924 national meeting of the Chamber of Commerce:

> The vast tide of these regulations that is sweeping onward can be stopped. ...It is vitally necessary that we stem this tide if we would preserve that initiative in men which builds up the character, intelligence and progress of the people. ...The con-science and organization of business [could help to keep the government out].[88]

The antistatist rhetoric of the welfare capitalists was deceptive. The welfare capitalists were anything but unquestioning advocates of an all-encompassing system of laissez faire. True, they opposed inconvenient state interference in their own activities, but they also encouraged the state to enforce the rules of the trade associations that business established.[89] Corporations were less enthusiastic about the rights of others to organize, calling upon the state to suppress labor unions.

Trade associations were supposed to act in the public interest, educating business leaders, assisting in cooperation, devising and implementing waste elimination schemes, and enabling business leaders to fulfill their social obligations.[90] A cynic might think that they had more interest in keeping prices high enough to sustain their profits, but the rhetoric of the welfare capitalists would have you believe that such mundane concerns as profits were the farthest thing from their minds.

The high-wage strategy promised an additional benefit to business. Limiting immigration, as well as raising wages, was expected to make the American worker appreciate the advantages of welfare capitalism, eradicating the appeal of militant unions once and for all. According to the social theorists of the day, the degree of the appeal of the socialist agitator was an excellent indicator of the level of intelligence of the worker. Only the most ignorant would fail to appreciate the benefits of welfare capitalism and fall prey to the foreign ideology of socialism. As a result, business was confident that labor, once purged of its foreign element, would come to the conclusion that its interests were at one with those of business. In this manner, welfare capitalism appeared to have transcended all conflict between labor and capital.

Considering the appealing message of welfare capitalism, the public—at least the better-off, native-born, white members of the public—found good reason to believe the advocates of welfare capitalism. Since undesirable foreigners were supposedly responsible for our ills, the elimination of their immigration to the United States should be able to make this nation a paradise on earth. Thomas Nixon Carver, a famous Harvard economist of the time, found himself caught up in the euphoria of the day, exclaiming:

> To be alive today, in this country, and to remember the years from 1870 to 1920 is to awake from a nightmare. Those were the years when our ideas were all but obscured by floods of cheap laborers upon whose cheap labor great fortunes were made, and by floods of abuse because we were not instantaneously solving all the social and economic problems these newcomers were inflicting upon us. Those were the years of slums and socialist agitators, of blatant demagogues and social legislation.[91]

The election of Herbert Hoover as president of the United States symbolized the ultimate popular approval of welfare capitalism.

The Success of Welfare Capitalism

Alert readers may have already noticed the absence of any discussion of the reluctance to invest in long-lived fixed capital goods in previous discussions of the 1920s. A number of factors combined to create an investment boom during the period. Long-term interest rates had been falling since 1921.[92] Frederick C. Mills, writing in a careful statistical analysis published with the assistance of Hoover's Committee on Recent Economic Changes, observed, "Probably never before in this country had such a volume of funds been available at such low rates for such a long period."[93]

Besides low interest rates, a plethora of emerging new technologies helped to stimulate an investment boom at the time. For example, the use of the electrical motor in manufacturing had become a mature enough technology to allow for rapid improvements in productivity.[94] Finally, the high-wage strategy of welfare capitalism helped lay the groundwork for more investment.

Of course, neither low interest rates nor the availability of new technologies are sufficient to fuel an investment boom by themselves. These factors must work in conjunction with an optimistic view of the future.

The age of welfare capitalism was indeed one of those rare hopeful times in which businesspeople confidently invest in plant and equipment with little thought of the possibility of failure. Low interest rates and the allure of new technologies were the icing on the cake.

This investment boom was so powerful that it overcame the effects of the restrictions on immigration. Historically, business in the United States relied on immigration, together with migration from the farms, to provide it with enough unskilled labor. Standard economic theory suggests that, other things being equal, curtailing immigration should create a shortage of unskilled workers relative to skilled workers. True, the welfare capitalists' desire to reduce their dependence on immigrants should also have reduced the demand for immigrants. However, unless the welfare capitalists constituted the bulk of the demand for immigrant unskilled labor, we should expect the wages of unskilled workers to rise relative to the wages of skilled workers. Standard economic rhetoric also contends that high real wages reduce profits, thus discouraging investment, even threatening to plunge the economy into a morass of stagnation. In fact, nothing of the kind occurred.

Investment increased enormously. As a result, welfare capitalism, which initially began as little more than an exercise in enlightened self-interest, became an immense success in terms of labor productivity. In this sense, we can say that, stripped of their racial and political biases, both Carver and Hoover were at least partially correct about the outcome of cutting back on the supply of low-wage workers.

Indeed, productivity increased so much that between 1920 and 1929 output per hour of work increased by an astounding 48 percent.[95] President Hoover's Committee on Recent Economic Changes reported in 1929 that no past period had "shown such a striking increase in productivity per hour."[96]

In this respect, the system of welfare capitalism bore a strong resemblance to the Japanese economy during its heyday in the late 1970s and early 1980s. Employers promised more or less steady work to skilled labor, stabilizing industrial relations. For example, by 1926 the number of industrial disputes had fallen to less than one quarter of its 1919 level.[97]

Indeed, welfare capitalism seemed to have fulfilled its promise and transcended its narrow base of privilege. Low-interest rates conditions, good labor relations, and emerging new technologies, combined with optimistic expectations, made investment in long-lived capital goods attractive. Under these favorable economic conditions, the welfare capitalists stepped forth and claimed to be the appropriate economic leaders of the United States. We should not be surprised that many people accepted their claim as credible.

The Limits of Welfare Capitalism

I just compared welfare capitalism to the Japanese system that flourished in the 1970s and 1980s. Welfare capitalism differed from the Japanese experience in one important sense. Where the Japanese system was relatively egalitarian, the benefits of welfare capitalism did not reach a large share of the population.

Despite the generous sentiments of the welfare capitalists, labor certainly was not the recipient of the bulk of the "welfare" in welfare capitalism. Productivity rose so much that manufacturing actually required less labor, even though the curtailment in the flow of immigration coincided with a rise in the demand for manufactured goods.[98] Thus, despite the restrictions on immigration, the wages of unskilled labor actually fell 8 percent compared with 3 percent for skilled workers between 1920 and 1929.[99]

In fact, profits actually increased at the expense of wages. For example, the proportion of total personal income received from interest, dividends, and rents was 22.3 percent in 1929, compared to 12.3 percent in 1950.[100] The 5 percent of households with the highest income received 30 percent of all personal income in the United States in 1929. In contrast, the top 5 percent received only 20.4 percent in 1950.[101]

Although industrial wages declined because of the reduction in the quantity of workers, personal consumption expenditures for manufactured goods climbed from $11 billion in 1912–21, measured in 1929 dollars, to $17 billion, 1922–31, again measured in 1929 dollars.[102] In part, the movement of people from the farm increased demand. Even today, farmers tend to produce more for themselves compared to urban dwellers. Self-produced goods do not count as demand.

In addition, the middle class was expanding. Finally, the introduction of consumer credit allowed people to purchase in advance of their income.[103] However, the capacity to produce far outstripped these increases in demand, laying the groundwork for the Great Depression. In short, the economy of the 1920s was closer to the United States in the first decade of the twenty-first century than the earlier Japanese economy.

Although many did remain poor and downtrodden despite substantial economic growth, others escaped from the ranks of the previously excluded. Such people who suddenly move up in the world are prone to forget their roots and often become even more callous than those who had preceded them into the ranks of the comfortable.

From their blissful perspective, the rich or comfortable could easily overlook violence against minorities and dissident groups. To them, welfare capitalism seemed to have truly become the people's capitalism.

Nonetheless, the deep contradictions of capitalism defied the welfare capitalists' attempt to rationalize the system. In the classroom, economic theory largely overlooked the efforts of the welfare capitalists or the contradictions that would soon destroy their hopes.

6

Modern Finance Capital

The Eclipse of Morgan
and the Temporary Decline of Finance Capital

Ironically, although the banks shouldered much of the popular blame for the Great Depression, the power of finance capital was relatively low in the period leading up to the crisis. True, speculative excesses were a significant part of the problem, but industrial capital rather than financial capital held the edge during the 1920s.

Before the First World War, the influence of finance capital was considerable in the United States. At that time, the United States was a debtor nation, heavily dependent on European creditors. A number of factors led to the temporary weakening of the powers of finance capital.

Consider the fate of J.P. Morgan, who owed much of his power to his privileged position as an intermediary between borrowers within the United States and their European creditors before the war. At the time, European financiers relied on investment bankers such as Morgan to evaluate investments in the United States. These investment bankers knew that their reputations depended on their ability to find sound values for their clients. Morgan helped to establish a mystique of financial acumen by refusing to sell to the general public, generally restricting his list of clients within the United States to a select group of financial institutions, such as insurance companies.

Jack Morgan succeeded his father, who died in 1913. By the end of the war, the regal world of finance over which J.P. had once presided became a relic of the past. Morgan was powerful, but the Morgan powers were greatly diminished. During the war, the United States became a creditor nation instead of a debtor. This reversal diminished the importance of Morgan's position as an intermediary between industry in the United States and investors in Europe.

Business conditions after the war eroded Morgan's strategic position even more. A sequence of strict market regulations during the war, followed by the booming economy of the 1920s, eliminated much of the appearance of risk. In this growing state of confidence, fewer people felt the need for Morgan's much vaunted expertise in sorting out good investments from more risky ventures. As a result, Morgan could not as easily distinguish himself from other investment bankers.

During the prosperous 1920s, domestic bank power also eroded. Profits were high enough that corporate dividends as a share of gross national product rose from 4.3 percent in 1920 to 7.2 percent in 1929.[1] As a result of these dividends, wealthy citizens of the United States had more money of their own to invest, making credit still cheaper.

Business did not merely distribute its profits for dividends. Undistributed corporate profits fluctuated between $230 million in 1922 and $203 billion in 1926.[2] Rising profits also meant that many corporations did not need to borrow much from banks.

Business was able to finance much of its investment with these great profits. These high profits also kept interest rates low, further reducing the profits from banking. In short, because finance was so readily available, the grip of the financial interests loosened considerably—at least temporarily.

Institutional changes further altered the financial landscape. During the war, numerous competing financial operations began to tap the growing domestic supply of funds. Reminiscent of Jay Cooke during the Civil War, they realized that small investors were especially susceptible to patriotic appeals.[3] Consequently, the owners of these ventures, unlike Morgan, did not disdain dealing with the general public. Instead, they took full advantage of the opportunity to reap immense profits by selling U.S. government debt directly to the public.

More and more new financial firms emerged in this environment. Some older institutions joined the newcomers in selling stocks and bonds directly to the public rather than to a select group of individuals and financial institutions. For example, Charles Mitchell of National City Bank began dispatching employees to sell bonds door to door, realizing that finance had come to depend on salesmanship rather than statesmanship.[4]

We can see an indication of this greater emphasis on direct sales reflected in the growing number of main offices and branches of the Investment Bankers' Association. There were only 277 in 1912, then 810 in 1921, and finally 1,072 in 1928.[5] Over time, this diffusion of banking further weakened Morgan's control over the supply of capital.[6] No longer could a Morgan meet with a handful of investors to determine the fate of an entire industry.

Finance without the Dominance of Morgan

Given the increasing scale of industry, combined with low interest rates in the 1920s, large businesses began routinely floating $20 million and $30 million issues, which were too large for any individual bank to handle. To manage these transactions, banks formed syndicates.[7] In contrast to Morgan, these bank syndicates had no reputations whatsoever. They were merely temporary arrangements constituted to handle a single issue. No individual bank was responsible for the overall success of any issue. Each was interested only in earning more fees by selling as many securities as possible.[8]

These syndicates generally found a willing market for their products since business had been prospering, except for a brief downturn in 1920–1921. Profits, rather than risks, were uppermost in the minds of many investors in the United States at the time.

Despite the speculative excesses, the ratio of business indebtedness to the value of business capital appears to have been falling during much of the 1920s.[9] This ratio might be deceptive, however, since the value of business capital depends on investors' valuations. With the appearance of the Great Depression, a substantial part of this business investment disappeared.

This new financial environment was ripe for abuse. Wherever people can lay their hands on cheap money, get-rich-quick schemes tend to become commonplace in the absence of some mechanism to keep them in check. In earlier times, when Morgan dominated financial markets in the United States, he attempted to weed out foolish and fraudulent investments. In the postwar period, no agency comparable to Morgan emerged to certify the soundness of financial paper.

Given the absence of an effective monitor of corporate issues, together with an increase in competition among buyers of securities, we should not be surprised that many businesses took advantage of the situation and floated significant quantities of unsound stocks and bonds. This problem became worse over time.

We can see evidence of the progressive deterioration of the quality of financial issues during the course of the boom of the 1920s by looking at the date of issue of bonds that went into default by the end of 1931. George Edwards reported that 31 percent of the bonds issued in 1927, 1928, and 1929 went into default by the end of 1931. In contrast, for bonds issued in 1925 and 1926 only 21.6 percent were in default. The rate for bonds issued in 1923 and 1924 was even lower, at 18.4 percent.[10]

Great profits, together with low interest rates, induced investors to value stocks and bonds at high levels, despite the erosion of the quality of many financial assets. People shocked by the shenanigans of the Enrons, WorldComs, and Tycos revealed in the aftermath of the bubble of the late twentieth century would do well to look back at this period to see how similar the accounting practices were.

The high stock market prices meant that firms could get money much cheaper by floating stocks and bonds than by borrowing from banks. Some of the more profitable industrial operations, such as the Rockefeller interests, even turned the tables on finance capital and used their profits to gain control of financial institutions.[11]

Flush with more funds than they could employ in making commercial loans, many bankers looked to foreign shores, where governments found themselves in need of huge cash infusions to finance their war machines. In effect, they were financing the war that would eventually help the economy recover from the imminent depression.

Many banks turned to the stock market after their market for industrial loans had been decimated. Some bought stock directly. Others lent funds to others to buy stock. We cannot blame this turn of events on the absence of a Morgan-like figure. Objective conditions played an important role. As Eugene White observed, "…banks' new financial services were not begun as a part of a speculative lark…[but] represented a move by these firms to offset the decline in their traditional business."[12]

Because of the enormity of speculation at the time, the stock market soared. In 1921, outstanding corporate bonds and notes were less than $2 billion, and stocks about $1.5 billion. By 1929, the total issue of bonds and notes had grown by about one-third since 1921, while the total issues of the stock market had more than quadrupled.[13]

We should not be surprised that as the value of securities rose many businesses took full advantage of the lax market conditions to raise far more money than they needed to finance productive activities. After all, the demand for stocks became so great that by the end of 1928 large corporations could earn more by lending to speculators than they could by investing in productive activities.

Finance capital was not entirely absent, but it did not behave in the interest of financial capital as a whole. Instead, flush with funds financiers gained control of some firms in order to generate business for themselves, much like what happened at the end of the late twentieth century. For example, Colin Gordon reports:

New capacity in the paper industry after 1926 bore less relation to the market than…to the desire of the bankers in control of the industry to float new securities. Many firms produced at a loss in the hope of recouping at least capital and financial costs, which in turn lowered prices and created more demand for expensive paper products.[14]

The Stock Market Bubble

These were heady times. Companies would lend money to speculators, who would pay interest to the companies, which would increase corporate profits, making speculators clamor to borrow more money to purchase more stocks. For example, during 1929 Standard Oil of New Jersey contributed a daily average of $69 million to the call market—meaning loans that could be recalled at any time—which went largely for loans to purchase stock. Electric Bond and Share averaged over $100 million. Some firms—City Services for one—even sold securities and lent the proceeds in the stock market.[15]

This arrangement contributed to fanciful valuations in the stock market. Soon it seemed that almost everybody was engaged in speculation. In this environment, hawking stocks became easy. In Robert Sobel's words:

> Selling securities to a gullible public required a certain finesse; the buyer had to believe that the salesman knew something about the shares he was retailing. During each year of the decade the Street welcomed increasing numbers of trainees who, after a few weeks of introduction to methods, were given a telephone, a desk, a list of customers, and a pat on the back. What their predecessors had taken years to attain, the salesmen of the 1920s received in weeks.[16]

Masses of people whose parents may have been fervent populists, suspicious of the bankers' every move at the time, now attentively followed the stock quotations and held their ears open for an opportune tip on a new stock. Frederick Lewis Allen captured the spirit of this obsession on the eve of the Great Depression, recalling:

> The rich man's chauffeur drove with his ears laid back to catch news of an impending move in Bethlehem Steel; he himself held fifty shares on a twenty-point margin. The window cleaner at the broker's office paused to watch the ticker, for he was thinking of converting his laboriously accumulated savings into a few shares of Simmons. ...[A] broker's valet...made nearly a quarter million in the market. ...[A] nurse...cleaned up thirty thousand following the tips given by her grateful patients. ...Literary editors whose hopes were wrapped about American Cyanamid B lunched with poets who swore by Cities Service, and as they left the table, they stopped for a moment in the crowd at the broker's branch office. ...The Big Bull Market had become a national mania.[17]

Not all this information served the investors well. Pools and syndicates of insiders manipulated share prices, spreading rumors and tips to extract profits from uninformed investors.[18]

Unfortunately for the economy at large, despite the flurry of stock market activity, this speculative activity contributed little to the productive capacity of the economy. For example, George Eddy found that "new production enterprises were financed via public securities issues in 1928 to the extent of no more than a few hundred million dollars at most."[19] Based on a classification of securities by the *Commercial and Financial Chronicle*, he concluded:

> even after deducting the…investment trust group, a major proportion, roughly two-thirds, of what was classed as new capital in 1919 was not for new real investment but for financial purposes, analogous to those of investment trusts [and that the]…increase in new capital issues after 1924 consisted wholly of "non-productive" issues.[20]

John Maynard Keynes offered what was perhaps the definitive diagnosis of this turn of the role of speculation, writing, "Speculators may do no harm as bubbles on a steady stream of enterprise. But the position is serious when enterprise becomes the bubble on a whirlpool of speculation."[21]

In the early stages of the boom, speculation was relatively harmless. Indeed, the postwar boom, except for a brief downturn in the early 1920s, resembled Keynes's "steady stream of enterprise." Over time, speculative excesses multiplied considerably faster than the growth of the underlying economy. The parallel between the age of welfare capitalism and the experience of the Japanese economy during the 1970s comes to mind again.

Over time, the relatively insignificant speculative bubbles of the early postwar period eventually took on much greater proportions. Although this whirlpool of speculation may not have been *the underlying cause* of the Great Depression, it certainly was the trigger that set the final denouement in motion.

In any case, traditional finance capital had lost its role as a monitor of the financial system.

Storm Clouds

A few people gave warning of looming problems. Harvard professor William Z. Ripley, who became president of the American Economic Association in 1933, repeatedly warned about the deceptions used to create the illusion of financial strength by leading corporations at the time.[22] When President Coolidge invited him to the White House, Ripley detailed for the president the "prestidigitation, double-shuffling, honey-fugling, hornswoggling, and skullduggery" of market manipulation.[23]

After word of the meeting reached the public, the market briefly reacted, then continued with its climb. The public was too giddy from its enormous stock market returns to pay much attention to such gloomy talk. After all, economic conditions for business seemed to be ideal in the 1920s. The booming stock market made capital cheap for business. New technology was reducing the cost of production.

Nonetheless, storm clouds were gathering on the horizon. In fact, many of the looming dangers were intimately related to the same forces that led to the apparent successes of the period. For example, the wonderful technological advances of the period created menacing imbalances. Between 1919 and 1929, manufacturing production rose 22 percent, yet manufacturing employment was virtually constant.[24] As a result, wealth became far more concentrated during the 1920s.

In 1922, the top 1 percent of adults held 32 percent of the wealth in the United States. By 1928, this same group held 38 percent.[25] This concentration of wealth made savings much more available for business, lowering the cost of capital. Concentration of wealth and income also had a dark side, since it limited the demand for consumer goods. Who was going to buy the goods flowing out of the factories?

Declining population growth had slowed the rate at which new households were forming. As a result of this weakening demographic force, together with the rapid expansion of production, many markets were becoming saturated.

For example, in 1923 new cars outsold used cars three to one. In 1925, the market was evenly split. By 1927, new cars represented only one-third of the market. To help to stimulate demand, Chevrolet paid dealers $25 for each used car they destroyed, taking 650,000 cars off the market between 1927 and 1930. Dealers, however, often resold "junked" cars and collected fees as many as six times for the same car.[26]

Business could try to create demand. Already by 1920, automobiles accounted for one-quarter of all national magazine advertising.[27] Since neither wages nor employment were increasing rapidly, much of the increase in consumer demand relied on the growth of credit, which could not expand indefinitely.[28] Business did not anticipate the limits of demand.

In hindsight we can see that the growth of investment sustained the economy during the 1920s. Business built new capacity to supply other workers who were also engaged in the expansion of new capacity.

Once this general expansion slackened, business suddenly realized that the capacity to produce substantially exceeded the capacity to consume. In response, many firms curtailed investment, eliminating the markets for other business, setting off a downward spiral.

Investment in the 1920s was not as chaotic as it had been prior to the great depression of the late nineteenth century. Even so, events proved that investment was not nearly as safe as it was thought to have been, in spite of decades of industrial consolidations and scores of trade associations designed to coordinate industrial activity.

Business discovered, in the colorful expression of Hugh Johnson, head of the National Recovery Administration, that much of the nation's purchasing power during the 1920s had become "congealed in icebergs of unnecessary building and unneeded plants."[29] A 1932 report for Herbert Hoover's Committee on Recent Economic Change resorted to even more dramatic language, observing that excess capacity stood "like masked batteries of machine guns waiting to lay down a new barrage of production whenever buying appears."[30]

The Great Depression created a more open climate for the study of economics. Faith in the free market rapidly evaporated. Economists were less inclined to work on proofs of market efficiency when the economy was disproving much of what the economists were taught to believe. Economists became receptive to what had previously been considered heretical views, much as in the late nineteenth century. Some economists even became open to the prospect of socialism. This opening to new thinking did not last long, but this period was one of the most exciting times for the study of economics.

Summing up, the decade of the 1920s was neither welfare capitalism nor laissez faire, but a combination of both. Despite the appealing façade of welfare capitalism, the welfare of capitalism was skewed in favor of the rich. In the midst of their temporary prosperity of the 1920s, the combination of financial activity disconnected from productive investment, together with the restricted buying power of the working class, accentuated the underlying contradictions of the market.

7

The Great Depression

Holding the Line

With the onset of the Great Depression, some of the leading welfare capitalists attempted to live up to their rhetoric. Some developed social welfare programs to cushion the blows to their unemployed and underemployed workers. Others even provided a modicum of direct aid for their unemployed workers.

One company rose above the rest. In early 1930, Kellogg announced that by the end of the year it would institute a six-hour day, allowing for an additional shift. It also announced that it would raise the minimum daily wage for an adult male to $4.[1]

Unfortunately, Kellogg stands out as the exception that proves the rule. In most cases, the responses of the welfare capitalists were trivial compared to the magnitude of the Great Depression. Even so, the attempt to cushion their workers from the Depression represented a considerable expense. But, as the costs mounted, the vast majority of welfare capitalists quietly abandoned their welfare programs.[2]

Could we have expected more from these companies? Absolutely not. After all, welfare capitalism was hardly a true pact between labor and capital. The welfare capitalists never saw their firms as charitable organizations. Instead, welfare capitalism was merely a tactic to hold workers' militancy in check rather than a true pact between labor and capital.

The one apparent success of the welfare capitalists was their initial willingness to maintain the level of wages in the face of the Great Depression. Again, self-interest rather than charity was uppermost. Even here, as we shall soon see, their success was less than they made it out to be.

In the past, massive wage cuts were considered to be the natural response to an economic crisis. In order to head off a wave of wage-cutting, on November 21, 1929,

President Hoover summoned many of the nation's leading industrialists. According to a participant in the meeting:

> [He] said that he would not have called them were it not that he viewed the crisis more seriously than a mere stock market crash;…that there were two or three million unemployed by the sudden suspension of so many activities;…that there must be much liquidation of inflated values, debts and prices.[3]

To prevent the stock market crash from turning into a catastrophe for society as a whole, Hoover asked that these employers refrain from cutting wages. The meeting seemed to have been a great success. Henry Ford even promised to raise wages.[4] *Business Week* exulted with an article entitled "This Time They Did Not Cut Wages."[5] Business leaders and economists, in unison with popular opinion, supported the policy of maintaining wage rates.[6]

Even with the onset of the Great Depression, a substantial portion of big business refrained from the expected wholesale cutting of wages. Later in life, Hoover recalled, "I felt that a most important part of our recovery in this period rested on the maintenance of wages and the avoidance of strikes."[7] He noted that during the depression in 1921, 92 percent of the firms reporting to the Bureau of Labor Statistics cut wages. In contrast, only 7 percent cut wages in 1930. For the first seven months of 1931, only 12 percent cut wages, compared to 54 percent in 1921.[8]

To maintain steady wages in the face of the depression would be an enormous accomplishment, especially since falling prices meant that a constant wage could buy more goods and services. Indeed, many large corporations seemed to go to great lengths to maintain the wage rate, although they did cut hours back significantly.[9] Economists recognized the uniqueness of this reticence to cut wages. In the words of Jacob Viner:

> …the Hoover administration became apostles of the…doctrine that high wages are a guarantee and an essential [*sic*] of prosperity. At the beginning of the depression, Hoover pledged industry not to cut wages, and for a long time large-scale industry adhered to this pledge.[10]

Or Did They Hold the Line?

Just as was the case with their welfare benefits, the act of holding the wage level constant appeared to be more than it really was. To begin with, the welfare capitalists were selective in their generosity. Their main concern centered on their coterie of skilled workers.

Consider the case of the electrical manufacturing industry. Ronald Schatz characterized the intentions of the industry leaders at the time with the observation:
"Frustrated by the administration, GE and Westinghouse management struggled to
prevent the Depression from decimating the corps of skilled, loyal employees they
had labored so assiduously to build up during the 1910s and 1920s."[11] Schatz continued, "Afraid that wholesale layoffs would demoralize their employees and cause
skilled workers to migrate to other industries,...[they] transferred skilled workers
and foremen not needed in their own occupations to assembly line work."[12]

Despite their interest in keeping their skilled workforce together, General Electric
and Westinghouse still cut wages by 10 percent from 1928 to mid-1931,[13] although,
as Stanley Lebergott notes, average wages in the industry did remain unchanged.[14]

Lebergott explained how, even though the wages of the typical employed worker fell, average wages held steady during the first two years of the Depression. He
used the example of the electrical manufacturing industry to make a more general
point. Throughout the economy, firms that survived the Depression, such as General
Electric and Westinghouse, tended to be the ones that paid higher wages than the
industry in general. The exodus of low-paying firms by itself would suffice to
increase the average wage. So if enough low-wage firms leave the industry, the
remaining high-wage firms could reduce their wages without lowering the industry
average.

In addition, these remaining large firms radically changed the mix of their personnel. A Westinghouse assembly line worker, who had previously worked as a foreman,
might personally experience a wage cut even though the wage paid for his assembly
line job was unchanged or even increased.

Finally, firms replaced their least productive and least skilled workers with new
workers. Even during the depth of the Depression, factories were hiring a million
workers every three or four months.[15]

Lebergott contends that the combination of the changing mix of firms and the
changing mix of workers obscured a tendency for wages to fall with the onset of the
Depression. He makes a convincing case that wages did fall. What is remarkable is
that they did not fall further.

In conclusion, we can say that some of the corporate capitalists behaved relatively humanely in the early stages of the Depression. Given the actions of many of those
who held the reins of business during more recent crises, they certainly deserve some
credit for their actions. As Schatz observed in his study of the electrical manufacturing industry, "Within the confines of the capitalist system, General Electric and
Westinghouse management had done everything in their power to soften the
Depression's blows."[16]

The Depression and the Limits of Welfare Capitalism

During the Depression, business leaders did not have to read economic journals to realize the havoc that deflation created. The major welfare capitalists quickly realized that the collapse was overwhelming their ability to maintain their commitment to their expressed ideals.

As they watched the prices for their products plummet, they could not help but see that their financial obligations were becoming more burdensome. They had no need to consult professional economists to realize that they would have to sell more goods and services to pay off each dollar of debt.

The welfare capitalists hoped to convince the Federal Reserve Board to use its powers to counteract the deflationary forces. They met with stiff opposition from financial interests. The banking sector, especially outside of New York, had good reason to resist expansionary monetary policies. It was earning the bulk of its profits from holding short-term Treasury notes. Measures to lower interest rates on federal debt would cut into their profits. In the end, the bankers prevailed.[17]

Large welfare capitalists also requested that the Hoover administration take aggressive action to return the economy to prosperity. By 1932, Hoover had established the Reconstruction Finance Corporation as a conduit for low-interest, short-term credit, but this action was too little, too late.

The corporate sector was demanding more dramatic policies. For example, in September 1930, the president of General Electric, Gerald Swope, personally called on the White House to ask President Hoover to begin spending $2 billion on public works. His plan was unprecedented in scope. To put the magnitude of this request into perspective, in 1931 federal spending as a whole totaled only $3.5 billion.[18]

The welfare capitalists prodded the government to go even further. For example, Swope also proposed to the National Electric Manufacturers Association on September 16, 1931, that the country adopt a corporatist system that strongly foreshadowed the National Recovery Administration of the New Deal.[19]

Hoover balked at the suggestion, certain that the Swope Plan was a scheme for "price fixing" through the "organization of gigantic trusts." He was convinced that it would mean the protection of "obsolete plants and inferior managements" and a general "decay of American firms from the day this scheme is born."[20]

Hoover was absolutely correct in one sense. Although investment boomed during welfare capitalism, this boom was not uniform. Some of the large corporate consolidations, originally formed to protect their investments in fixed capital, were largely successful in that regard. Rather than adopting modern innovations that could wipe out their existing capital stock, the more concentrated sectors protected their capital. Had Hoover shielded these industries from further competition, he would have guaranteed that the economy would atrophy.

To do nothing, of course, would also cause irreparable harm. Simple solutions to the intractable contradictions of markets do not exist.

U.S. Steel and the Limits of Corporatism

Perhaps no firm could illustrate Hoover's concern better than the US Steel Corporation. In the midst of the Great Depression, the editors of *Fortune* magazine reported:

> Now there are two possible ways to look at a steel plant or an ore mine. One is as an investment that must be protected. The other is as an instrument of production, to be cherished only so long as it cannot be replaced by a more efficient instrument. The first may be called the banker's point of view; the second, the industrialist's.[21]

According to the investigators at *Fortune*, United States Steel "has always been a management with a financial rather than an industrial turn of mind."[22] This perspective reflected the origins of the corporation. "The Steel Corporation was founded by financiers, has been dominated ever since by financially minded men."[23] Similarly, Charles M. Schwab looked back wistfully when he told the Senate committee in 1933: "I was not engaged in making steel. I was making money!"[24]

While many industries used the expansive conditions of the 1920s to develop improved technologies, the management of U.S. Steel chose a different track. As a result:

> the chief energies of the men who guided the Corporation were directed to preventing deterioration in the investment value of the enormous properties confided to their care. To achieve this, they consistently tried to freeze the steel at present, or better yet, past levels. ...Any radical change in steel technology would render worthless millions of dollars of the Corporation's plant investment.[25]

While firms in less concentrated industries felt pressure to rationalize their operations and prune costs, the financially oriented management of U.S. Steel was intent on maintaining the status quo. Perhaps Hoover, the engineer, realized that protecting the corporate sector from competitive forces would allow more firms to emulate U.S. Steel, making an even larger economic disaster inevitable.

Even the Great Depression was insufficient to make this firm change its ways and modernize. The firm's stodgy, hidebound management muddled through until it finally found itself humbled both by foreign competition and aggressive mini-mills in the late 1960s.

These competitive pressures worked at glacial speeds, but by 1986, seventy-five years after its formation, management changed the corporate name to USX and considered retreating from the steel industry altogether. Perhaps, U.S. Steel represented the ultimate verdict on Morgan and the corporatists.

This largely financially oriented organizational form might have smoothed over some of the rough edges of earlier variants of capitalism, but welfare capitalism lost touch with the productive basis of economy.

The Humiliating Capitulation of Welfare Capitalism

Smaller firms, which had never accepted the rhetoric of welfare capitalism, could not withstand the pressures of competition as long as U.S. Steel did. Many of them cut wages early in the Depression, putting enormous pressure on the welfare capitalists to do likewise to remain competitive.

Rebuffed by both President Hoover and the Federal Reserve, the welfare capitalists saw the momentum of the Depression build up. In the face of these pressures, their attempts at carrying out the supposed mandate of welfare capitalism vanished. By the fall of 1931 major corporate employers could no longer refrain from aggressively cutting wages.[26]

When push came to shove, unrelenting market forces compelled major firms to renounce all pretenses to the ideals of welfare capitalism. From the very beginning, welfare capitalism was, at least in part, an illusion based more on public relations than reality. Most of the welfare capitalists were far less generous than they pretended to be.[27] Yet, judged by the cruel standards of contemporary business practice, the welfare capitalists were certainly generous.

Still, when managers had to choose between "welfare" and "capitalism" in their vision of welfare capitalism, they had no doubt which had priority. As Charles Schwab of Bethlehem Steel admitted after the first wage reduction in steel, "None of us can escape the inexorable law of the balance sheet."[28] Once the logic of the balance sheet took hold, the great corporations abandoned all pretense of welfare capitalism.

We might even say that welfare capitalism reverted to a cruder variant of corporatism, where business called for the right to organize against competition without any grandiose promises about serving some higher purpose. At least until the Great Depression, the welfare capitalists had succeeded in blunting the force of competition.

During the 1920s, the profit rate for the nation as a whole declined, but not for the leading sectors of the economy. Economist Jim Devine attributes these higher profit rates to the ability within concentrated industries to produce more output per unit of capital.[29] This difference between concentrated and competitive industries probably reflected two factors.

During the 1920s, industrial firms, which tended to be more concentrated, were modernizing their methods of production. At the time, management was just learning to take advantage of electricity as a power source. Earlier, factories ran from a central power source that transmitted power to various parts of the plant through a series of belts. Electricity allowed them to decentralize their power sources, eliminating the expensive and inefficient system of belts. The cost-saving was so extreme that even industries without strong competition had good reason to adopt this new technology.

In addition, competitive forces compelled less concentrated industries to lower their prices. The consolidated industries felt far less pressure. Thus, they could demand larger profit margins from their customers than other industries could. Since the government measures industrial output data in terms of the value of the output, one cannot distinguish between increases in physical output and the ability to charge higher prices. In other words, if a concentrated industry successfully conspired to double its prices, this behavior would show up in the data as an increase in productivity.

Once the Great Depression hit, the disparity between concentrated and more competitive industries became far starker. For example, between 1929 and 1932, motor vehicle prices fell only 12 percent while production dropped by 74 percent. Other concentrated industries, such as agricultural implements, iron and steel, and cement, demonstrated a pattern that was only slightly less extreme. In contrast, prices of agricultural commodities fell 54 percent, while output decreased by only 1 percent.[30] In fact, agricultural prices might have fallen further except that poor weather conditions limited production.

Collapsing output in the consolidated industries, together with the weeding out of less productive workers, set off a massive wave of unemployment, which eventually struck one-quarter of the labor force. Many of the unemployed remained out of work for a long time. In Buffalo, for example, in 1930, 21 percent of the adult male unemployed had been unemployed for a year or more. In 1931, this figure was 43 percent. It continued to increase. By 1932, it had reached 60 percent. Finally, in 1933, the rate of long-term unemployment peaked at 68 percent.[31]

Hoover's Welfare Capitalism

The vision of welfare capitalism was not uniquely American. A number of its themes paralleled European fascism. Like the fascists, welfare capitalists saw both foreigners and unions as a major source of trouble. Partisans of both groups were convinced that society required a more cooperative relationship between business-es, as well as a tighter association between business and the state. Finally, in purely economic terms, both welfare capitalism and fascism retained power and privilege for those who already held the reins of power.

Welfare capitalism differed from fascism in one major respect. Whereas fascism flourished under depression conditions, welfare capitalism proved unable to live up to its ideals in the brutal environment of the Great Depression. Faced with the chal-lenges of a depression, it withered.

Nonetheless, welfare capitalism had the capacity to transform itself into fascism without too much difficulty. It already contained a heavy measure of nationalism and racism. It was more than willing to cede more power to the state, provided that the state would act in the interest of the welfare capitalists. It could have also have easily shifted the rhetoric from the obligations that corporations owed to workers to the obligations that workers owed to society or the state.

None of the leaders of welfare capitalism was more sensitive to the fine line between the perspective of welfare capitalism and fascism than Herbert Hoover. Indeed, Hoover's racism, especially in his early years as a mining engineer, was leg-endary. For example, he regarded Asians and Negroes as "working labor of a low men-tal order." He estimated that on the average "one white man equals two or three of the colored races, even in the simplest forms of mine work. In the most highly skilled branches…, the average order is as one to seven, or in extreme cases, even eleven."[32]

Nonetheless, Hoover stood apart from the run-of-the-mill welfare capitalist. To begin with, although he objected to direct federal funding of relief for the unem-ployed, he had more experience in relief work than anybody in the world.[33]

Hoover represented one other difference between welfare capitalism and fascism. In Europe, the First World War created an enormous disillusionment that fostered a culture that appealed directly to the irrational. Hoover, like the welfare capitalists, projected a rationalist image. His upbringing as a Quaker, as well as an engineer, seemed to have helped Hoover to develop an enduring faith in human rationality—although he and the welfare capitalists were not above irrational racial and ethnic stereotyping. So Hoover, who relied heavily on public relations, expressed faith in the rational capacity of the general public, but had a less favorable opinion of those of a "low mental order."

Hoover seemed to believe that engineers were the embodiment of human ration-ality. He insisted that engineers occupied a "position of disinterested service," and "want[ed] nothing…from Congress [except] efficiency in government." In his *Memoirs*, he wrote of the engineer as "an economic social force. Every time he discov-ers a new application of science, thereby creating a new industry, providing new jobs, adding to the standards of living, he also disturbs everything that is. ...He is also the person who really corrects monopolies and redistributes national wealth."[34]

Hoover's Disillusionment

The salad days of welfare capitalism came to an unfortunate end under the watch of Herbert Hoover. The Great Depression put Hoover's beliefs to a severe test. The economy was unable to climb out of this depression for more than a decade. Without the economic boost from the Second World War, the recovery might have taken even longer.

For years, Hoover had taken the position that to surrender to the supposed inevitability of the business cycle was to cede too much to irrationality. As secretary of commerce, he organized a major economic conference on the business cycle. In his introduction to the proceedings, he wrote:

> We are constantly reminded by some of the economists and businessmen that the fluctuation of the business cycle is inevitable…and…cannot in the nature of things be regulated. I have grave doubts whether there is a real foundation for this view.[35]

In fact, Hoover believed that the provision of adequate information would suffice for enlightened business leaders to ward off business cycles. In this vein, he began his introduction to a collection of essays in *The Stabilization of Business* with the assertion:

> Broadly, the business cycle is a constant recurrence of irregularly separated booms and slumps. The general conclusion of the Committee is that the slumps are in the main due to the wastes, extravagances, speculation, inflation, over-expansion, and inefficiency in production during the booms. The strategic point of attack, therefore, is the reduction of these evils, mainly through the provision of current economic information as will show the sign of danger.[36]

Hoover also understood that corporate power had the capacity to degenerate into fascism. He had always appealed to the "conscience and organization of business" believing that in the end business would come down on the side of the public interest.

Hoover, the Iowa Quaker, had an abiding faith in the American way, which for him meant that individuals would take initiative on their own when they saw their neighbors fall into misfortune. Hoover's own world-famous actions in providing food aid during the war personified this admirable instinct.

Once the Great Depression struck with such extraordinary ferocity, Hoover expected that business would behave unselfishly. Given the pressing social needs, the Depression should have brought out the best in people. Needless to say, he was sadly disappointed.

Although Hoover enacted what was by the standards of the day far-reaching legislation to combat the Great Depression, it was hopelessly inadequate considering the magnitude of the situation. In the end, Hoover stood by while the welfare capitalists abandoned all pretenses to social responsibility.

Could we have expected more from a person with such a deeply held conviction that individual initiative rather than government was the answer to social problems? William Appleman Williams proposed that once so many business leaders had broken with what Hoover took to be a social contract, he found himself stymied. This shattering of his faith in cooperative behavior by business leaders, as well as the American people at large, left the president ill-equipped to deal with the Great Depression.[37]

After all, Hoover had always been mistrustful of government. Now business had also betrayed the trust that he had placed with it. He no longer displayed the same faith in business initiative. For example, when confronted with the Swope plan, Hoover, to his credit, balked, realizing that his previous hopes for business responsibility were unrealistically idealistic. Again, when the U.S. Chamber of Commerce proposed a referendum to repeal the antitrust laws in December 1931, Hoover reacted unfavorably, suggesting that such a policy would "drive the country into the Fascism of which it was mostly a pattern, or toward Socialism as the result of public exasperation."[38]

Lacking faith in big government, big business, and big labor, Hoover was unable to formulate a decisive plan to attack the country's massive economic problems. As a result, Hoover appeared to be foolish or incompetent.

Today, few people in the United States remember Herbert Hoover, perhaps the greatest advocate of welfare capitalism. For those who do remember Hoover, their image is often a crude caricature. Hoover has become the president who let the Great Depression happen or the indifferent president who passively watched the masses suffering under the ravages of the Depression. In the popular mind, Franklin Delano Roosevelt is remembered as the hero, the man who led us out of the Depression.

Although Roosevelt's performance was only marginally better than that of Hoover, many people still think of him as the dynamic leader who energetically used the power of the state to transcend the chaos left behind by business. Of course, it was the war, not the New Deal, which put an end to the Great Depression—a war that did not come until the Depression was more than a decade old. Precisely what Hoover could have done to ward off the Great Depression still remains a mystery.

The New Deal and the Resuscitation of War Socialism

Roosevelt's New Deal was not as new as we think. In the words of Jonathan Hughes:

> the lessons learned from World War I would not be forgotten. The WIB would reappear in 1933 as the National Recovery Administration (NRA). The United States Grain Corporation would resurface in the 1930s as the Commodity Credit Corporation. The planning activities of the Food Administration would reappear in the two Agricultural Adjustment Acts. The Emergency Fleet Corporation came back as the National Maritime Administration. The Federal Housing Administration of the 1930s was really born first as the wartime United States Housing Corporation.
>
> The War Labor Board would be continued in part as the Railway Labor Board under the Railway Labor Act of 1926, and then finally, permanently, as the National Labor Relations Board under the Wagner Act in 1935. The Fuel Administration under the Lever Act reemerged in the 1930s as the Bituminous Coal Division in the Interior Department. Senator Joseph Guffey (D, PA), who was instrumental in creating the New Deal laws governing coal and oil output and pricing, had been head of the petroleum division of the WIB.[39]

The New Deal differed from war socialism in one important respect. War socialism arose because planning was more efficient than competition. The intellectual foundation of the New Deal went much further. Competition was not just less efficient than planning. Competitive forces had become so strong that they were threatening to tear the fabric of society apart, but not quite in the same way as they did in the crisis of the late nineteenth century.

Assessing Welfare Capitalism

What lessons should we learn from the experience of welfare capitalism? Was the initial success of welfare capitalism nothing more than the result of an illusion—an American Dream in which everybody would share in the benefits of prosperity? The theorists of welfare capitalism argued that higher wages meant ever higher productivity, but wages did not benefit much. Even if welfare capitalism boosted productivity in the 1920s, we might question how long it could have continued to enjoy such gains in the future since income was distributed so unequally.

Proponents of welfare capitalism should have realized that for welfare capitalism to produce an ongoing productivity spiral the welfare capitalists would have to continue to increase wages steadily. More wages would only whet workers' appetite for still more wages or, even worse, for less onerous working conditions. Would produc-tivity gains continue to outpace workers' ever-increasing spiral of demands?

Higher wages can induce workers to put in more effort, but only within certain limits. At some point, wage-induced productivity gains will encounter limits. To effec-tively boost productivity over the long run would require that industry find a way to tap workers' creativity, as well as their physical energy. To do so might be impossible so long as workers remain mere employees. Although workers could demand a greater voice in the company, welfare capitalism held to a paternalistic vision of management in which the company presumed to know what was best for all, including the work-ers. In this sense, management's vision of welfare capitalism was much too limited to have ultimately succeeded.

Some might even question how much credit to give to the welfare capitalists for the burst in productivity at the time. No doubt other causes contributed some-thing to the improvement in productivity. After all, the welfare capitalist boom began during slack economic conditions. W. Arthur Lewis reminds us that because of the war, "all over the world larders, wardrobes, and shops were empty; all over the world, too, purchasing power had accumulated."[40] In addition, some of the technological improvements, such as standardization and the electrification of industrial production, were merely the application of practices that had already begun during the war.

Despite these questions, I remain convinced that the welfare capitalists did make a substantial contribution in terms of productivity and even in terms of the living con-ditions for the more skilled workers. Yes, Charles Schwab was probably correct that each individual welfare capitalist had no choice in the end but to yield to the logic of the balance sheet and retreat from the ideals of welfare capitalism. Yet, by a different balance sheet that took account of the quality of workers' lives, we would have to judge welfare capitalism to be at least a partial success.

Nonetheless, ultimately welfare capitalism was doomed to failure from the very beginning. Business was incapable of overcoming the tendency of markets to careen out of control. Once the Great Depression struck, people realized that the rhetoric of welfare capitalism was hollow. Most people at the time understood that they could not count on business to protect them from harsh market forces—a lesson that has con-tinued to fade over the subsequent decades.

Yet the rhetoric of the welfare capitalists did provide workers with a standard whereby they could judge their situation.[41] Workers had begun to expect that their employers would treat them with dignity and respect, as well as loyalty. The ruthless cost-cutting measures taken after 1931 left workers with a bitter sense of betrayal, paving the way for the great CIO organizing drives.

We might note that this sense of betrayal could cut both ways. In 1937, after the unions organized Kellogg, the founder, W. W. Kellogg, whose vision inspired the six-hour day, withdrew from the day-to-day affairs of the firm. Under new management, the company abandoned the six-hour day.[42]

Workers soon learned that unions were also incapable of caring for all of the needs of people—especially those who were not actively employed. Perhaps by default rather than conviction, many people turned to the government for answers. The success of the wartime economy appeared to vindicate that faith, at least for a few decades.

The Search for Blame

Few economists were prepared to come to grips with the nature of the Great Depression. Their training as economists stood in the way. After all, economies were not supposed to crash; they were supposed to move toward a stable equilibrium.

By the time of the Great Depression, economists had forgotten the lessons of the corporatists. By this time, economists believed that the cause of the Great Depression would have to be something that prevented the market forces from guiding the economy toward a stable equilibrium. Given this mind-set, economists tried to explain the causes of this particular depression by pointing to interference with market forces. With few exceptions, economists refused to accept that recessions and depressions were an inherent tendency of market economies.

What kind of unusual imbalances could cause such a depression? Economists still disagree about what actually caused the Great Depression. Some attributed it a slowdown in population growth. Others pointed to a lopsided distribution of income. They accused the large corporations of increasing profits at the expense of wages, leaving the country with insufficient buying power.

Although welfare capitalism reveled in the rhetoric of high wages, we saw that workers' productivity far outstripped their ability to consume, leaving markets glutted. In the words of an early study of the causes of the Great Depression:

> Our investigation of the distribution of income…revealed a maladjustment of basic significance. Our capacity to produce consumer goods has been chronically in excess of the amount which consumers are able, or willing, to take off the market, and this situation is attributable to the increasing proportion of total income which is diverted to savings channels. The result is a chronic inability…to find market outlets adequate to absorb our full productive capacity.[43]

Some would blame the Federal Reserve Board's move to increase interest rates. Others would blame the international monetary system, holding that the gold standard had a built-in deflationary bias, which made depressions inevitable.[44] Some even go so far as to suggest that the mere foreknowledge of the impending Smoot-Hawley tariff was sufficient to cause the Great Depression. We could expand the wildly differing list of possible causes into an entire book.

Harold Hotelling suggested still another interpretation of the causes of the Great Depression, which relates to our theme of the importance of long-lived capital goods. According to Hotelling, capital-intensive firms need to pay their overhead costs regardless of economic conditions. The enormous technical change in the capital-intensive industries that occurred during the 1920s called for a fall in their prices. Nonetheless, he noted:

> For several years prior to the crash, the prices of manufactured products stuck fast, while the proportion of national expenditure paid for these products continued to increase. This left a shrinking volume of money payments to be made for the remaining products.[45]

Hotelling argued that if the railroad, utility, and manufacturing concerns had reduced their prices proportionally, the prosperity of 1922–8 might have continued, "But such reductions in selling prices were not possible when an increasing volume of overhead charges had to be paid out of earnings."[46] In fact, he complained, railroad freight rates actually increased in 1931.

Perhaps the most popular explanation of the Great Depression concerned labor. Many conservative economists unthinkingly accepted the dogma that an excessive price of labor was necessarily the cause of unemployment. This explanation was usually framed in the context of accusing workers of irrationally setting their wages too high when the depression struck.

Recall that the welfare capitalists had committed themselves to stabilizing wages as part of their implicit contract with their workers. Hoover and the welfare capitalists believed that this policy had solid economic grounds.

Although some of the varied explanations of the Great Depression contradict each other, we could, without too much difficulty, weave the deflationary pressures of the gold standard, the financial excesses of the 1920s, the unequal distribution of income, and speculation to create a fuller explanation of the Great Depression.

Unfortunately, economists tend to shun such complex analyses. Instead, they generally search, albeit in vain, for a single cause of important events—something that they can put into a model. In the case of the Great Depression, the identification of a single cause would ideally allow policy makers to frame an equally simple remedy capable of protecting the system from a recurrence of such a tragedy. Presumably, this analysis could discover what Hoover could have done differently to prevent the depression in the first place

Ultimately, this effort is futile. As we have argued before, periodic depressions are endemic to a market society. Even if we could somehow pin down the proximate cause of the Great Depression, the proposed remedy could very well prove to be the trigger for the next depression.

Wages, Deflation, and the Way Out of the Depression

John Maynard Keynes took strong exception to the notion that cutting wages would end both unemployment and the Great Depression. He made the obvious point that cutting wages diminishes buying power. Rather than diminishing unemployment, the practice of reducing wages would be likely to intensify the Great Depression.[47] Of course, Herbert Hoover and the welfare capitalists had already understood this relationship, even though it appeared novel to most academic economists at the time.

Gradually, Keynes's ideas penetrated academia, albeit in a much tamer version. Even so, many economists resisted Keynes's ideas. Once the Great Depression ended, traditional economists, always on the alert to defend market forces, counterattacked, thinking that they had discovered a flaw in Keynes's argument. They noted that when deflation occurs, those people with savings become wealthier. According to this reasoning, since prices are lower, a given amount of savings can buy more goods and services. This increase in the buying power is supposed to encourage those with savings to step up their purchases so much that the economy will return to prosperity once again.

This theory has a glaring weakness that few economists had noticed at the time. Falling prices might make savers wealthier, but they also make borrowers poorer. To make matters worse, debtors presumably are more inclined to spend than creditors are.[48]

Consider the behavior of commercial enterprises during a deflation. Even more well-off firms are unlikely to invest a great deal during an economic crisis. After all, business is already down. Those firms that are most financially strapped risk becoming insolvent. They are especially inclined to postpone investments.

This lack of investment creates a substantial drag on the economy. Thus, deflation can set off a chain of bankruptcies that can make a depression far more severe than it might otherwise be.[49]

Deflation has other negative effects. Keynes's opponents contended that consumers might expand their purchases because falling prices allows their money to buy more. However, these same consumers will witness a parallel evaporation of the value of assets they own. For example, the value of their homes will shrink without any offsetting decline in their mortgage payments. This effect will more than offset the potential stimulation from falling prices.[50]

Finally, if recent deflation convinces firms and households that more deflation is likely, they will have even more reason not to invest. By waiting to invest, they can take advantage of lower costs in the future.

As a result, we can conclude that to the extent that firms or individuals attempt to get out from under debt by spending less or by selling more, they reinforce the deadly deflationary spiral. In the words of Irving Fisher:

> The very effort of individuals to lessen their burden of debts increases it, because of the mass effect of the stampede to liquidate in swelling each dollar owed. Then we have the great paradox which, I submit, is the chief secret of most, if not all, great depressions. The more debtors pay, the more they owe.[51]

The Reemergence of Financial Hegemony

Given the strong deflationary thrust of the Great Depression, finance became tight. Firms could minimize their need for credit by curtailing investment. Even so, with the accumulation of debt during the boom times, many firms needed to borrow just to keep up their existing financial obligations.

Although credit was tight, banks refrained from charging as much as they could to maximize their profits. This pricing strategy owed nothing to bankers' charitable instincts. As Joseph Stiglitz and Andrew Weiss noted, selling credit differs from selling other goods. When merchants sell shoes, they expect to be paid in full for their merchandise at the point of sale (except when the merchant also acts as a banker in extending credit). In contrast, banks do not receive their payments until a later time once the debt becomes due.

Bankers know that those who are willing to pay the most interest are not often the best credit risks.[52] Adam Smith had made a similar point more than two centuries ago:

> If the...rate of interest...was fixed so high as 8 or 10 per cent...

the greater part of the money which was to be lent, would be lent to prodigals or projectors, who alone would be willing to give this high interest. Sober people, who will
give for the use of money no more than a part of what they are likely to make by the
use of it, would not venture into the competition. A great part of the capital of the
country would thus be kept out of the hands which were most likely to make a profitable and advantageous use of it, and thrown into those which were most likely to
waste and destroy it.[53]

During the Great Depression, bankers had another important consideration.
They had already lent considerable amounts to their customers. Charging too high an
interest rate could drive these customers into bankruptcy. Given the severity of the
Great Depression, bankers often had no choice but to moderate their interest charges
and sometimes even forgive part of the loan in the hope of making their customer solvent enough to repay all, or at least part, of the outstanding debt.

Bankers could not be so generous with all their customers. With so many firms in
distress, the banks did not have enough funds to go around. Instead, they rationed
credit to a relatively select group of predominantly large firms.[54] Those firms—often
smaller firms—that were unable to obtain credit found themselves at a considerable
disadvantage.[55]

When bankers attempted to nurture their favored customers back to financial
health, they were usually able to demand a significant voice in the management of the
indebted firm. Frequently, they placed one or more members of the bank leadership
on the board of directors of the embattled firm.

In short, although the industrial sector won considerable independence from the
financial system during the prosperous 1920s, the Great Depression allowed the
financial system to reassert a substantial degree of control over industrial interests. By
1934, Joseph Schumpeter could justifiably observe, "The money market is...the
headquarters of the capitalist system."[56]

For a while, the sequence of the Great Depression, the New Deal, and postwar
prosperity left many economists skeptical about laissez faire. Over time, the lessons of
the Great Depression, like the lessons of the corporatists, receded into the hazy past
and were eventually largely forgotten within the discipline of economics.

8

The Golden Age

Background to the Golden Age of Industrial Independence

The Second World War proved to be a godsend for industry in the United States. The military provided an almost unlimited demand that more than made up for the demand that consumers had lacked during the Great Depression. Almost anything that could be built could be sold. Yes, rationing was inconvenient, but everything else fell into place during the war.

The war brought much new capital on line. It sparked innovations that gave the United States the lead in much modern technology. It left the economies of the traditional competitors of the United States in ruins. By the end of the war, the United States held a seemingly unchallengeable economic position.

Even so, the impression of a striking dichotomy between the tragedy of the Great Depression and the great prosperity of the postwar period is somewhat misleading. Although the achievements of the postwar prosperity may seem to represent a transcendence of the failures of the Great Depression, the two were closely connected. In reality, the depression also did much to pave the way for the postwar recovery.

To begin with, the morbid economic sentiments of the Great Depression era had persisted for more than a decade. Most economists expected that business would sink into a recession again once the war ended. As Robert J. Gordon observed, "Surely the greatest *economic* surprise of the first postwar decade was the failure of anything resembling a postwar depression to occur."[1] Because the healthy economic conditions of the early postwar period were so unexpected, the economic strength of the early postwar period seemed to be all the more dramatic, especially considering the recent horrors of the Great Depression. As a result, business responded to new economic opportunities even more enthusiastically than might have otherwise been the case.

In addition, the Great Depression had set off a wave of intense competition that forced many firms to scrap a good deal of outmoded plant and equipment. By 1939, U.S. firms had replaced one-half of all their manufacturing equipment that had existed in 1933.[2] Although the total amount of investment during the Great Depression was relatively small, much of that investment was directed toward modernizing existing plant and equipment. Thereafter, U.S. business produced as much output as a decade before with 15 percent less capital and 19 percent less labor.[3] University of Santa Clara economist Alexander Field makes a convincing case that the rate of productivity increase during the Depression years, 1929–41, was higher than any other period of the twentieth century.[4] Depression-era modernization, coupled with the increase in productive capacity during the war, made the capital stock of the postwar United States the envy of the world.

The Great Depression also contributed to the improvement in financial conditions. By unleashing a wave of bankruptcies, it wiped out much of the existing U.S. corporate debt. The subsequent wartime prosperity provided unprecedented corporate liquidity.

The Great Depression frightened financial institutions enough to make them shy away from wild speculations—at least for a while. As a result, major financial institutions concentrated on high-quality investments whenever possible. This policy helped make the financial sector quite liquid. These factors combined to ensure that the financial conditions at the end of the Second World War were almost ideal.

In terms of international finance, the U.S. economy was also in a solid position. By the end of the Second World War about 70 percent of world's monetary gold stock resided in U.S. vaults.[5]

The Great Depression also contributed to the postwar prosperity by preventing many households from buying a wide array of consumer goods for a considerable period of time. Many of these goods continued to be unavailable during the war because many factories converted their assembly lines from civilian to military production. By the time the war ended, many families had accumulated considerable wartime savings. Once the war ended, they were more than ready to spend some of that savings.

The economy was poised for a wild binge in consumption. The United States was about to enter a period that economists later called the "Golden Age."

Finance Capital in the Postwar Period

Despite the changing conditions, banks were still unable to regain the majestic financial powers that they wielded during Morgan's heyday. First, the Glass-Steagall Act and other New Deal legislation limited bank control over industry. In addition, the period of financial stringency was short-lived. Huge flows of profits during both the war and the postwar period allowed industry to reclaim some of the independence it enjoyed during the prosperous 1920s.

In addition, the government's need to finance the war as cheaply as possible led the Federal Reserve to cap interest rates. As a result, during the 1940s, the rate on Moody's AAA-rated corporate bonds averaged 2.71 percent, varying between a low of 2.53 in 1946 to a high of 2.83 in 1942.[6]

Just as the financial stringency of the Great Depression could lead Schumpeter to remark in 1934 that the money market is the headquarters of the capitalist system, the wartime prosperity led his favorite student, Paul Sweezy, to come to the opposite conclusion only a few years later. According to Sweezy:

> The dominance of financial over industrial capital, which for a while was widely interpreted as a more or less permanent state of affairs, is thus seen to have been a temporary stage of capitalist production, a stage which was characterized above all else by the *process* of forming trusts, combinations, and huge corporations. ...[Thus] bank capital, having had its day of glory, falls back to a position subsidiary to industrial capital, thus reestablishing the relation which existed prior to the combination movement.[7]

Banks did not unduly suffer either from their loss of industrial markets or from low interest rates. Instead of lending to industrial markets, in the immediate postwar period, banks held much of their assets in the form of highly liquid and secure U.S. government securities. Although the interest rates were low, the returns were certain.

The Naive Optimism of the Golden Age

Back in the 1920s, the dominant political mood was to trust business (rather than the market) to ensure continuing prosperity. The Hoover administration faithfully represented the temper of the middle class of the time.

Once the Great Depression struck, much of the public experienced a sudden loss of confidence in business, as well as laissez faire, just as it had during the previous great depression of the late nineteenth century. People looked to the government almost instinctually to find a way out of the Great Depression. Certainly, they would be receptive to a government that could convincingly promise to prevent future depressions. The booms and busts of the typical business cycle seemed to be too high a price to pay for laissez faire at the time.

Some economists participated in this great reversal of public opinion during the Great Depression. In the United States many economists, more often than not young economists, began to read John Maynard Keynes with intense interest. Many of them wholeheartedly accepted what they incorrectly believed to be Keynes's essential idea, that government spending was the most effective means of shoring up a weak economy.[8]

In addition, economists of a Keynesian bent won great prestige for their success in organizing the wartime economy. For example, Paul Samuelson, perhaps the most influential of all American Keynesians and the first American to win a Nobel Prize in economics, commented in 1945 "that the last war was the chemist's war...this one [was] the physicist's. It might equally be said that this [was] the economist's war."[9]

Although some business leaders remained hostile to government intervention,[10] many others vigorously lobbied for a tame rendering of the economic policies that seemed to have worked so well during the New Deal.[11] After all, the government supposedly got the economy out of the Great Depression. Why not let it continue to guide the economy?

Indeed, government policies seemed to do quite well in the early postwar period. The economy of the Golden Age seemed to break the typical cyclical pattern. In fact, the postwar period ushered in an unparalleled period of growth and prosperity.

Coming on the heels of the Great Depression, the surge in wartime demand vaulted the economy into what seemed to be an age of almost perpetual prosperity. Indeed, during the Golden Age, everything seemed to be in place for an economy without depressions or recessions.

As the memories of the Great Depression receded into the hazy past, leaders of business and government, as well as economists in the great universities, deluded themselves into believing that we had somehow mastered the art of managing the economy. This supposed newfound economic mastery was thought to have progressed to the point that the government had the means prevent future depressions.

From time to time between the end of the war and the early 1970s, the U.S. economy experienced a few brief recessions, but they were surprisingly mild. In light of the strong economic performance at the time, the fears of a return of a depression gave way to an overarching confidence in the government's ability to control the economy.

When the economy temporarily slackened, as it did during the Eisenhower years, the self-proclaimed followers of John Maynard Keynes assured the world that a renewed regimen of their policies would ensure another burst of prosperity. At the time, Paul Samuelson insisted that with proper fiscal and monetary policy the economy could have full employment and whatever rate of capital formation and growth it wanted.[12]

In the words of Joseph Garbarino, "By 1955, the American economy had experienced ten years of fairly high-level postwar prosperity and had weathered two minor recessions. The basis for concluding that a new economic era based on government's long-term commitment to stability and on industry's rationalized long-range planning was at hand."[13]

Walter Heller, President Kennedy's chief economic advisor, echoed this spirit, writing: "[W]e now take for granted that the government must step in to provide the essential stability at high levels of employment and growth that the market mechanism, left alone, cannot deliver."[14]

Since the government's apparently skillful application of fiscal and monetary policies seemed to be responsible for much of the economic success, people at the time began to see the happy state of the economy at the time as the normal state of affairs. The confidence about the managed economy that leaders in government and academic economics expressed soon filtered into the public consciousness. Depression-age promises of a chicken in every pot gave way to an expectation of two cars in every garage—at least for those who had a good union job.

Who would have guessed that for many of the citizens of the United States the fear of not even having a home, let alone a garage, would become a reality within a couple of decades? Who could have anticipated that we would soon add such hideous words as homelessness, Rust Belt, and deindustrialization to our vocabulary?

The End of the Golden Age

How did the seemingly all-powerful U.S. juggernaut lose its dominant position in the world economy? Some of the decline was unavoidable. After all, the economies of the chief competitors of the United States had laid in ruins immediately after the war. The inevitable rebuilding of their economies would necessarily reduce the gap between their economies and that of the United States.

In many vital sectors of the economy, competition had been too weak to compel industry to renew its capital stock for a considerable period of time. During the war, the government virtually guaranteed markets for many industrial sectors. Later, during the postwar boom, consumers were too quick to part with their money for business to feel much competitive pressure.

In this environment, business began to reward those who would not rock the boat.[15] Management became staid, uncreative, and complacent. For example, many business leaders in the United States let the capital structures in their industries age. As a result, the competitive position of U.S. industry deteriorated.

The steel industry is a case in point. Steel industry management in the United States was notorious for its unwillingness to invest in modernization. For example, basic oxygen furnaces and continuous casting offered substantial cost savings, but the industry refused to invest in these technologies long after they had become standard in steel plants throughout the world.[16]

Naturally, the strength of the domestic industry declined. In the 1950s, the United States accounted for almost 50 percent of world steel production. By the 1960s, less expensive foreign imports were devastating the industry.[17]

Rather than strengthening its productive base, the steel industry concentrated its efforts on gaining assistance from the government. By 1968, it succeeded in getting the government to coerce countries that had been exporting steel into the United States to agree to voluntary restraints on their steel sales to the United States.[18]

In the long run, voluntary restraints were probably detrimental to the giant integrated steel producers, who fell further behind both their competitors abroad and the new domestic mini-mills at home. Within a couple of decades, U.S. Steel, once the dominant producer in the world, changed its name to USX to signal its retreat from the steel industry. By rechristening itself, the crown jewel of Morganization confessed to the world that it could no longer pin its fortunes on its capacity to manufacture and sell steel.

The Return of Finance Capital

New Deal banking legislation was intended to prevent a repeat of the financial excesses of the 1920s by creating barriers between banks and stock market investment, signaling an end to the swashbuckling days of Morganesque banking. Chastened by the Great Depression, bankers, as well as other financial leaders, sought security rather than quick windfall profits. For example, in the early postwar period interest rates were low but steady. In this environment, bonds offered security with a minimal profit. In 1952, commercial banks, mutual savings banks, and insurance companies held over 69 percent of all U.S. corporate bonds outstanding. Life insurance companies alone held 58 percent, compared with only 1.5 percent of U.S. corporate stocks.[19] Accordingly, the popular stereotypical banker became a conservative bloke who wore blue suits and whose greatest priority was his afternoon golf game.

Banks, however, may be among the more benign representatives of finance capital. Certainly, other financial leaders proved to be far more adventurous than the stereotypical banker. And in good times, adventurers tend to prosper the most—at least for a while.

As a result, bank power soon paled next to those of the more speculative forms of finance. By 1960, institutional investors owned 17.2 percent of the value of the shares and accounted for 24.3 percent of the volume of trading on the New York Stock Exchange.[20]

Many of these institutional investors were not particularly interested in well-run companies that promised stable returns over a long period of time. Instead they sought special situations that would bring them quick profits. They scanned the stock market, searching for the highest possible yield.

Soon, a Wall Street perspective began to pervade the industrial sector. By the 1960s, business began to toy with the absurd proposition that new financial arrangements by themselves were capable of improving economic performance, even in the absence of any improvements in new methods of production.

In the spirit of this new Wall Street perspective, some firms put together huge conglomerates—groupings of unrelated companies. Supposedly, when such a group would take a number of unrelated businesses under its wing, it would somehow confer enormous benefits on its subsidiaries. Wall Street attributed the efficiencies of this sort of arrangement to the creation of a synergy—a mysterious special energy that supposedly arose out of these combinations.

In part, new forms of executive compensation encouraged business managers to engage in these practices. In the 1940s, within a sample of fifty Fortune 500 manufacturing companies, the top five executives derived less than 3 percent of their total after-tax compensation from stock-based rewards. In 1953, the share totaled 14 percent. By 1955, it had reached 28 percent. Then, between 1955 and 1963, the share continued its climb to one-third.[21]

As a result, a financial orientation managed to infiltrate more and more parts of the industrial sector. Many business leaders, realizing that they could reap enormous rewards when their company's stock rose, tried to make their firms attractive to these new investors. This process became so thorough that the distinction between finance and industry became almost meaningless.

Renewed Speculative Frenzy

Investors became wildly enthusiastic about those companies that energetically acquired other firms. They paid a substantial premium for stocks in these companies, valuing them many times more than the expected annual earnings of those companies.

Wall Street told the credulous public that these conglomerates were capable of creating more value merely by acquiring new firms. The conglomerate would purchase the company, but would receive a premium as well as the underlying value of the company since the acquired firm would somehow benefit from the synergy conferred by the conglomerate. Even supposedly sophisticated investors accepted the idea that the newly acquired firm would suddenly take on new value merely by virtue of the change in ownership.

More often than not, these supposed benefits were altogether imaginary or, even worse, the concoctions of unscrupulous accounting.[22] Nonetheless, many investors continued to purchase stocks in these conglomerates for many times their earnings.

These optimistic expectations were generally unwarranted. Roughly one-third of the acquisitions during the 1960s and early 1970s were sold off later.[23]

The prospects of a corporate failure need not dash an investor's hopes so long as he can sell out and take his profits before reality sets in. The objective was just to beat the crowd.

The speculative frenzy on Wall Street in the 1960s was the extension of financial power, without any thought of the sort of statesmanship that Morgan had once exercised. No one seemed to take note of the absurdity of the process. After all, huge profits were being made. Almost no one took the trouble to note that little or nothing was done to develop the underlying industries.

For a while, the pace of corporate takeovers slackened. Then, during the 1980s, a new wave of corporate takeovers swept across Wall Street. At first, some of the largest firms remained immune from the pressures of takeovers. Their unimaginative behavior soon made them inviting targets. Lacking confidence to invest in productive projects, they were content to sit on large accumulations of cash, waiting for the right opportunity to come along. For example, the editors of *Business Week*, in commenting on a 1985 story about Exxon's massive cash surplus, worried, "The sight of so many companies sitting on bags of cash they cannot find profitable use for raises some distressing questions about the vitality of the US economy."[24]

Business Week was altogether justified in its concerns. Why, with so many unmet needs in society, could the major corporations not find anything useful to do with their cash hoards?

The editors of *Business Week* were not alone in noticing the cash positions of these firms. Soon, a small group of unscrupulous takeover specialists discovered how to borrow funds to take over these giant corporations in order to get their hands on those inviting cash reserves.

The takeover artist would offer stockholders much more money than their stock was worth on the open market. This offer would be contingent on the firm selling high-yield junk bonds to finance the purchase. Takeover specialists found additional sources of profits whenever they could. They pulled money out of pension plans. They cut wages. They eliminated health care and anything else, so long as it added to their profit.

After the completion of a typical deal, the cash would be gone and the firm would be left with a demoralized labor force and a huge debt.[25] The corporate raiders accumulated fabulous fortunes in the process, but the industrial structure reeled under the pressure.

Takeovers hit some of the largest companies in the United States. Of the 100 largest mergers and acquisitions on record prior to 1984, 65 occurred between 1981 and 1983 compared to only 11 before 1979. During 1981–84, 45 takeovers involved more than $1 billion.[26]

Eventually, the takeover movement reached such proportions that managers of the largest corporations took measures to restructure their corporation internally, in much the same way that the takeover artist would have done—by buying back stock and taking on debt, all to make itself less attractive as a takeover target. The result would be the same. Those who engineered the deal earned enormous profits, while the company would be left significantly weakened.

Financial Capital versus Industrial Capital

As the stock market became a greater concern for executives, money managers began exercising increasing control over corporate policy. Representatives of this new breed of institutional investor are ever on the alert for quick profits. So are their customers, who choose their investments largely on the basis of recent performance.

In this environment, most institutional investors have no choice but to be impatient. They cannot afford to wait for long-lived capital investments to turn a profit. If, at any time, management fails to show a healthy quarterly profit, investors become restless, leaving the company vulnerable to a takeover threat, which is likely to involve the ousting of management. Corporate executives, fearful of this threat, must struggle to keep short-term profits high.

Even when managers realize that longer-term investment projects might be in the best interest of the company, they understand that the stock market will probably only reward those who make the next quarterly earnings report as favorable as possible. Managers who invested for the long term could cause a decline in their company's stock and even perhaps their own dismissal.

Andrew Sigler, Chief Executive Officer of Champion International and chair of the Business Roundtable's Corporate-Responsibility Task Force, lamented that this change in the investment climate affected corporate investment strategy, declaring:

> The problem is deciding who the hell the corporation is responsible to. I can't ask
> my shareholders what they want. 75 percent of Champion is owned by institutions,

and my shareholders change so fast I don't even know who they are. We're owned
by a bunch of index funds. Who votes for an index fund? Some damn mathematical formula votes your stock.[27]

Given the intense pressure for short-term financial gains, managers cannot invest
in the sort of long-run project that could improve the economic health of their company. As a result, profits suffer, intensifying the pressure for short-term profits.

What are the consequences of this concentration on short-term profits? With
major corporations more intent on shuffling around financial assets than in building
a strong financial base, the U.S. economy continued to weaken.

Bureaucratic Management

Joseph Schumpeter believed that management would evolve into bureaucracies and
that these bureaucracies would further technological development. He speculated:

> The capitalist evolution first rationalizes the economic process. It supersedes less
> efficient technologies by increasingly more efficient technologies and more organi-
> zation. The largest scale of control is the consequence, and the largest scale unit of
> control tends to develop into something akin to a department of state, that is it
> becomes bureaucratized and mechanized and the individual in that kind of world
> counts for less than before.[28]

Schumpeter credited these large bureaucracies with much of the technical
progress of modern society.

> As soon as we go into the details and inquire into the individual items in which
> progress was most conspicuous, the trail leads not to the doors of those firms that
> work under conditions of comparatively free competition but precisely to the doors
> of the large concerns…and a shocking suspicion dawns upon us that big business
> may have had more do with creating that standard of life than with keeping it down.[29]

During the boom times of the 1960s, John Kenneth Galbraith cited Schumpeter,
and then offered a conception of the bureaucracy more inclusive than Schumpeter's.
Like Schumpeter, he still associated the bureaucracy with technological dynamism:

> With the rise of the modern corporation…the guiding intelligence—the brain—of
> the enterprise…[has passed to] a collective and imperfectly defined entity…[which

includes] senior officials...white- and blue-collar workers ..[and] embraces all
who bring specialized knowledge, talent, or experience to group decision making. I
propose to call this organization the Technostructure.[30]

Parts of Galbraith's Technostructure had already displayed a marked disinterest in
technology well before he or Schumpeter made their claims about its competence.
Recall how the Morganization of the steel industry transferred management from people whose roots were in the production of steel to a different group whose orientation
was largely financial.

This sort of financial-industrialist had far more in common with conservative
bankers of old than the new breed of aggressive financiers. For example, the managers
of U.S. Steel were content to stand by and watch their business deteriorate, so long as
their lives were comfortable and the government provided them with some protection.

Today, financial markets will no longer allow management to sit still. Now, management must react quickly and decisively. Unfortunately, many of these decisions violate
the interests of workers and consumers, society as a whole, and even the long-term
health of the businesses that these managers control. The dangers of this sort of management might be obvious today, but quite a bit of time passed before people realized
what was happening.

The Holy Gospel of a Return to Productionism

Eventually, even management experts began to warn that the financial perspective
threatened the long-term interests of business. For example, in 1980, just as the U.S.
economy was about to experience its most severe decline since the Great Depression,
Harvard Business Review published "Managing Our Way to Economic Decline" by
Robert Hayes and William Abernathy.[31]

This article struck a responsive chord. The associate editor of the *Harvard
Business Review* later told the *New York Times* that the article generated substantially
more congratulatory correspondence from the business community than any article
that his journal had ever published.[32]

One of key revelations of this article concerned the professional background of
corporate leadership in the United States. After investigating the histories of the corporate presidents of the 100 largest corporations in 1948–52 and 1973–77, the
authors reported that those with financial and legal backgrounds increased by 33 percent; those with technical backgrounds decreased by a like amount.[33]

Hayes and Abernathy cited a European informant, who told them how industry
in the United States appeared on the other side of the Atlantic: "The U.S. companies

in my industry act like banks. All they are interested in is return on investment and getting their money back. Sometimes they are more interested in buying other companies than in selling products to customers."[34]

The source of this complaint, that firms behave as if they were banks, is significant. Harvard and the other leading business schools had long promoted this style of management.

Hayes and Abernathy charged that this finance-oriented perspective implied a radical premise: the ideal manager is "an individual having no special expertise in any particular industry or technology, who nevertheless can step into an unfamiliar company and run it successfully through strict application of financial controls, portfolio concepts, and a market-driven strategy."

These financial-oriented managers are expected to forsake any productionist tendencies. They must be often willing to change the focus of their business at a moment's notice if they believe that higher profits are available elsewhere.

The business world places a high value on these managers. Ever since professional managers gained control, their salaries have been rocketing upward. By the 1920s, some chief executives in the United States already received $1 million. By 1960, chief executive officers received 43 times the pay of an average worker in the United States. By 1990, chief executive officers were collecting more than 100 times as much as the average worker. This gap had become so extreme that by the early 1990s the former president of Harvard University joined in the public protest against the inequity of this distorted pay scale.[35]

Despite the enormous salaries that top management commands, Hayes and Abernathy charge that their talent is misdirected. In the short run, a firm may benefit from their intensive search for maximum short-term profits, but over time, most businesses will suffer from failing to focus on a long-run vision.

The danger of a purely financial, short-run orientation was the central thrust of the Hayes and Abernathy piece. Unfortunately, their article never addressed the reasons for the changing nature of management. Reading their work, one might imagine that someone, somewhere came up with this misguided notion of good management. Somehow, this new management orientation then became commonplace.

By pointing out the folly of finance-oriented management, Hayes and Abernathy might have convinced themselves that their work was done. Business may have ignorantly chosen the wrong sort of management before, but once the *Harvard Business Review* had provided enlightenment, business leaders should be ready to make a conscious decision to get back on the right track.

At first, this position seemed to have some credence. A number of corporate leaders sincerely claimed to have taken the message of Hayes and Abernathy to heart at the time.[36]

Unfortunately, such conversions had little effect. Shortly after the article appeared, industry in the United States found itself swept up in the junk-bond, takeover craze, exposing the Hayes and Abernathy approach to be naively idealistic.

Michael Jensen and the Critique of Managerialism

The same supposedly irrational practices, which Hayes and Abernathy publicly deplored, seemed absolutely rational to a number of influential economists. Rather than faulting modern management for an excessively financial orientation, these economists maintained that modern management suffers from a deficient financial orientation.

Chief among this school of economics was Michael Jensen, also of Harvard University, who had became one of the most prominent academic advocates of the junk-bond movement. For Jensen, management was not the soul of large enterprises. According to Jensen, the highly paid managers who normally run large corporations may even be the enemy of those firms. Certainly, Jensen did not believe that they have their stockholders' interest at heart.

Instead, Jensen saw management as a collection of selfish bureaucrats who used corporate resources for their own personal self-aggrandizement. Given their comfortable situation, entrenched managers naturally fail to take measures that would make the firm efficient with the same vigor that an independent owner would display.[37]

Jensen's critique of management was not without merit. Certainly, corporate management in the United States had a poor record on many counts. Many managers abuse their position, using corporate funds to provide themselves with extravagant personal benefits, such as corporate jets, boats, limousines, elegant offices, and corporate retreats that contribute little to corporate efficiency.

Even those managers who might forgo the perquisites of office do not necessarily act in the best interest of the shareholders. Instead, because corporate growth is an indication of managerial success they typically concentrate on making the firm grow, whether or not that growth is economically warranted.

For Jensen, corporate growth is not necessarily indicative of efficiency. Resources should go to those activities that are most productive. Even in terms of market rationality, if a firm is not productive, management should actually impede the flow of resources to that firm, rather than promote growth of the firm. In this way, the market could free up resources to flow to those activities where they can earn the highest rate of return.

For the most part, managers of less productive firms aspire to maximize the amount of resources within the specific organizations that they control. As evidence of this perverse managerial behavior, Jensen cites the investigations of Gordon Donaldson, who studied twelve of the Fortune 500 corporations. In his study, Donaldson concluded that managers of these firms were not driven by maximization of the value of the firm, but rather by the maximization of "corporate wealth," defined as the "aggregate purchasing power available to management for strategic purposes."[38]

According to Donaldson, "In practical terms it is cash, credit, and other corporate purchasing power by which management commands goods and services."[39] For Jensen, the long-standing managerial commitment to firm growth and the acquisition of managerial power actually weakens the economy. For Jensen, given management's penchant for feathering its own nest rather than promoting the health of the firm, "The problem is how to motivate managers to disgorge the cash rather than investing it at below the cost of capital or wasting it on organizational inefficiencies."

Jensen contended that corporate takeovers are an ideal means to accomplish the goal of transferring cash out of the firm.[40] When one firm takes over another, the acquiring firm transfers significant funds to the shareholders of the acquired firm. Typically, the acquiring firm lacks sufficient funds to complete the purchase. As a result, it has to take on a heavy debt obligation to complete the transaction.

Jensen welcomed the accumulation of corporate debt, believing that it is in the public interest. He argued that "the debt created in a hostile takeover (or takeover defense)" means "that it [the firm] cannot continue to exist in its old form."[41] Once corporate managers no longer control great cash hoards, capital will flow more easily to those activities where it can be most productive.

If the debt pushes the company to the edge of bankruptcy, so much the better. With the firm's very survival in question, managers must rise to the challenge to make the firm competitive. In addition, banks and other providers of corporate finance will monitor the firm more closely, knowing that the acquiring firm has to struggle to earn enough cash to cover its debt payments.[42] This theory presumes that the stockholders will do a better job of using their newfound wealth than corporate managers did when they had control over their cash hoards.

The Unproductive Labor Dissipated in Corporate Takeovers

Michael Jensen's theory had several flaws. To begin with, he never considered the cost of effecting these corporate takeovers. The transformation of corporate ownership did not come cheaply. For example, in 1984, the three investment banking houses involved in the Gulf-Socal merger earned a total of $63 million for their efforts.[43] The *Wall Street Journal* predicted that if Texaco's $9.89 bid for Getty Oil would be successful four investment banking firms could be expected to share a record $47.1 million in fees. The largest single fee was expected to go to Kidder, Peabody, and Company, which was slated to receive $15 million for advising the Sarah C. Getty Trust. Salomon Brothers, which declined to confirm it, was slated to receive a reported $4 million. First Boston was Texaco's advisor. For seventy-nine hours' work, it was to receive $10 million, or $126,582 an hour.[44]

In the takeover of RJR Nabisco, Drexel Burnham earned $227 million in fees; Merrill Lynch pocketed $109 million for helping to arrange a bridge loan; Kohlberg, Kravis, and Roberts earned $75 million for masterminding the acquisition; Morgan Stanley received $25 million for advice; Wasserstein-Perella earned $25 million mostly just to keep them from serving opposing parties.[45]

As time went on, the merger fees grew apace. By 1988, Campeau's $6.6 billion bid for Federated Department Stores produced $200 million in fees. "It's called the Wall Street Fair Employment Act of 1988," said a lawyer involved in the deal.[46] By 2004, the takeover activities of a handful of private equity groups, led by the Carlyle Group and Kohlberg, Kravis, and Roberts generated only one kind of fee—the payment for banking service.

Lawyers have also fared quite well from the boom in corporate takeovers. The *Wall Street Journal* recently reported that one in nine U.S. lawyers was a millionaire in 1986.[47] Of course, not all these lawyers owed their wealth to takeovers, but a good number did. For example, the firm of Wachtell Lipton was paid $20 million in just two weeks for advising Kraft on its $12.9 billion attempt to take over Philip Morris , a sum that works out to about $5,000 an hour, assuming virtual round-the-clock work by a couple of dozen lawyers.[48]

Individuals who handled the finances of takeovers also prospered. In 1987, over and above his normal salary and the millions and millions of dollars that he earned using inside information for trading on his own account, Michael Milken received a bonus from Drexel Burnham Lambert amounting to an astounding $550 million.[49] Some commentators noted that this bonus exceeded the profits that McDonald's, the 65th largest corporation in the United States, earned at the time.[50]

In comparison, J. P. Morgan never paid an executive more than twenty times the earnings of his lowest employees.[51] Such huge merger fees naturally induce modern financial agents to go to great lengths to construct mergers and takeovers, whether or not they have any economic merit.

Young people understood that even lesser figures in the financial world still earned astronomical amounts. For example, a well-placed Wall Street employee could make several hundred thousand dollars within a couple of years after graduating from college. In light of the enormous amounts of money changing hands, highly educated young people directed their energies and ambitions to participating in speculative activities rather than productive activities. Forty percent of the 1986 graduating class of Yale applied for a job at First Boston![52]

Of course, we need to give our youth more constructive incentives. A cross-country analysis indicates that economies with a high share of engineering college majors grow faster than those who train their youth as lawyers and financial experts.[53]

Although the takeover movement proved to be a bonanza for the financial and legal sectors, the Herculean efforts to change the structure of corporate ownership did nothing to enhance the productive capacity of our economy. Instead these financial manipulations dissipated much of the remaining vitality of the productive sectors of the economy.

Certainly, excessive amounts of money went to financial transactions or legal maneuvering rather than productive investment. Texaco's failed takeover of Getty Oil, mentioned above, is a case in point. Penzoil sued Texaco, claiming it had a prior agreement with Getty. Between 1984 and 1988, Texaco and Penzoil waged an intense legal battle. Penzoil eventually won. The court initially awarded it a judgment that was worth more than $10 billion, although the ultimate settlement was a paltry $3 billion. Even so, an enormous amount of resources was dissipated in the process.

Not unexpectedly, the value of Penzoil's stock rose and Texaco's fell, since Texaco had to give so much money to Penzoil. What is noteworthy was the imbalance in the movements of the respective stocks. The fall in Texaco's value exceeded the rise in Penzoil's. The combined value of the stocks in the two firms fell by about $21 billion.

Could the legal fees consumed in this struggle explain this loss? Probably not. Texaco's legal fees accounted for about $250 million, but the after-tax cost would be only $165 million.[54] The combined productive capacity of these two firms shrunk so much because managers squandered inordinate time and energy in legal maneuvers rather than devoting comparable resources to make their firms more efficient.

More on How Jensen's Approach Backfired

Michael Jensen never realized that the corporate restructuring that he desired would be antithetical to productive efficiency in other ways. He often used the petroleum industry as a prime example of the potential benefits of restructuring.[55]

Jensen believed that takeovers or the threat of takeovers would put management under stress. By creating a "crisis to motivate cuts" management could take measures which would otherwise be unthinkable.[56] He never asked if these otherwise unthinkable cuts also be rational. As Amitai Etzioni noted, "A large body of research shows that under stress people's decision-making becomes less rational."[57]

Indeed, when restructuring hit the petroleum industry, the results were not always desirable. Consider the case of Exxon. Recall the concern that the *Business Week* editorial writers expressed about Exxon's huge cash reserves. Once management restructured the company to make it a less attractive target for takeover specialists, the company engaged in cutbacks, but not necessarily of the kind that make for a more efficient company.

According to a writer for the *Wall Street Journal*, Exxon's workers became stretched thin, but not in a manner that was conducive to efficiency. Several fires broke out in the company's largest refinery in Baytown, Texas, because Exxon was too tight-fisted when it came to winterizing pipes against freezing, despite prior warnings about the danger.[58]

Many observers believed that restructuring was ultimately responsible for Exxon's most famous mishap, the tragic oil spill of the *Exxon Valdez*. Alaskan officials alleged that Exxon's systems for training and monitoring employees were ineffectual. The company's own tanker captains complained of heavy crew cutbacks and other unsafe operating procedures. Numerous former Exxon executives claimed that management's cost-cutting system "created an accident prone system."[59]

In fairness, we should note that some of Exxon's negligence predated its restructuring. In New York City, where a pipeline ruptured, local and federal officials charged that Exxon was negligent and irresponsible in ignoring a faulty leak detection system for twelve years.[60] Of course, money managers had been exercising increasing control over corporate policy throughout the economy prior to the *Exxon Valdez* spill. Nonetheless, no one can doubt that this intense wave of corporate restructuring exacerbated the problems.

This new breed of institutional investor that Jensen advocated was too impatient to wait for long-lived capital investments to turn a profit. If, at any time, management fails to show a healthy rate of return, money managers can either directly oust management or threaten to organize a corporate takeover. Corporate executives, fearful of this threat, must struggle to keep profits high.

Within this environment, managers cannot invest in the sort of long-run project that could improve the economic health of the firm. Concerns about maintenance or safety are often put aside in order to shore up the balance sheet for the next quarter. Over time, such policies will cause profits to suffer, intensifying the pressure for more short-term financial gains.

Jensen in the Context of Economic Theory

Despite my reservations about Jensen's theory, I must at least admit that it is consistent with economic theory. Jensen clearly realized that management commitment to a specific firm contradicts a major premise of conventional economics. In terms of economic theory, managers should indeed make their firms indistinguishable from a bank, in the sense that they should be quick to move their assets to activities that can earn more profits.

This idea is mistaken in two respects. In the first place, long-run commitment is often a vital element of corporate viability. Often, a firm's most valuable assets are its knowledge base and its existing relations with established customers and suppliers. Neither of these assets flourishes under a mercenary management intent on boosting the quarterly profit statement at all costs.

In addition, the analogy with banks is misplaced. Many economists are coming to recognize the importance of forging long-term relations for the banking sector as well as for other types of businesses. While money managers may succeed without any loyalty to any particular company or industry, ideally banks thrive, in part, because they are able to establish long-term relationships with creditworthy borrowers.

I do not need to mention that during the telecom/dot-com bubble, banks also flourished by milking fees from companies that were far from creditworthy.[61] As I mentioned earlier, these banks shielded themselves from losses by shifting the risk of these deals to others. While these maneuvers might have been profitable for the banks, they did untold harm to the economy.

In short, Jensen's uncritical faith in the ability of market to provide managers with signals that allow them to costlessly shift their resources at a moment's notice to the most efficient use accords far better with imaginary economic models than with reality.

Unfortunately, although Hayes and Abernathy performed a valuable service in exposing the problems associated with the managerial form that Jensen championed, the business world conformed more and more to Jensen's vision.

To his credit, Michael Jensen also recognized the error of his ways. His original idea was to create a structure that would both reward and punish managers for producing profits. His self-critique centered on the dishonest information that management provided. He recognized that profits could be fictitious; that companies such as Enron, WorldCom, or Tyco could report bountiful profits among real losses; that the shareholders who were supposed to guide the economy had no way to evaluate deceptive information. Even before the Enron bubble exploded, he began writing papers with titles that evoked the mood of a deceived lover: "How Stock Options Reward Managers for Destroying Value,"[62] "Just Say No to Wall Street,"[63] and "Paying People to Lie."[64]

The Spreading Influence of Financial Capital

Even where financial restructuring was not an issue, the need to raise profits enough to satisfy money managers has proved to be another important factor in promoting the continual deindustrialization of the U.S. economy. In this finance-driven environment, when firms attempt to turn their cash to a profitable use, they want to maintain as much flexibility as possible. As a result, more often than not they neglect productive investment, which generally entails large investments of fixed capital. This pattern reinforces the decline of industry.

To make matters worse, rather than attempting to make their plants more productive, managers often took the easy road of shutting them down. Indeed, a good deal of anecdotal evidence suggests that a number of plant closings were related to what seems to be a sharp increase in the expected rate of return on existing plant and equipment, rather than a competitive crisis. For example, during a pre-negotiation meeting between General Electric and the representatives of workers at its Fort Edward capacitor facility in 1982, "local management announced that while heretofore 9 percent profit had been considered satisfactory, GE nationally was then insisting that all of its facilities show at least a 12 percent profit margin in the future."[65]

David Broderick, chairman of the board of U.S. Steel, told a Pittsburgh audience that the huge Dorothy Six operation would not be worth saving unless it were able to earn 18 to 20 percent profit each year.[66] Bluestone and Harrison cite a similar example:

> The Herkimer [New York] plant, producing library furniture, had been acquired by Sperry Rand in 1955. The plant had made a profit every year except one through the next two decades, and yet Sperry Rand decided to close the plant [in part because it] was not yielding a 22 percent profit on invested capital. That was the standard used by this conglomerate management in determining an acceptable rate of return on its investments.[67]

The 1977 annual report of Genesco, Inc., provides further evidence of increased corporate profit requirements: "In all cases, the ultimate consideration was: 'Does this operation have the potential to produce a 25 percent pre-tax return on assets employed?' "[68]

The behavior of Genesco and Sperry Rand might increase measured profits and even productivity. By eliminating all but the most profitable operations, the average performance of the residual divisions may be higher. Indeed, deindustrialization has raised measured productivity. In fact, the 10 percent decline in manufacturing employment accounted for an estimated 36 percent of the recorded improvement in labor productivity in the United States between 1979 and 1986.[69]

BusinessWeek denounced this tendency to increase productivity by shutting down plant and equipment instead of attempting to make existing operations more efficient. It described such behavior as "slash-and-burn cost-cutting," citing Stephen S. Roach of Morgan Stanley and Company, who warned that it is a "really dangerous…recipe for total capitulation of market share."[70]

The Exploding Cost of Financial Capital

One symptom of this pervasiveness of the finance-driven economy is paperwork. Even though everybody hates paperwork, we keep doing more and more of it, believing it is unavoidable.

The corporate sector has an enormous hunger for paperwork. It develops brilliant schemes to profit through unproductive paperwork, all the while shutting down productive factories. These financial manipulations consume an enormous amount of time and energy.

Just consider the quantity of paper that has to be shuffled to complete one of the epidemics of giant corporate takeovers which swept over the United States during the 1970s and 1980s. In the case of DuPont's $7.5 billion takeover of Conoco, First New Jersey National Bank had the responsibility of overseeing the deal. W. E. Buchsbaum, DuPont's vice president for finance, said that First Jersey was beset with "great, great volumes of paperwork" and "a lot of mismatches between what people said they would tender and the stock certificates that have arrived."

The result: the bank worked from 9:00 a.m. till midnight. The work overflowed into the bank cafeteria. On weekends, sixteen branch managers and some people from DuPont had to work on the paperwork for this transaction.[71]

Had some government regulation required a comparable quantity of paperwork, statements of outrage would pepper the business press. Political candidates would campaign with anecdotes about the imposition of excessive paperwork. Instead, such transactions were held up as examples of capitalist efficiency.

The wave of corporate takeovers that occurred during the 1970s and 1980s caused only part of the explosion of financial transactions. Much of the unproductive financial work is unrelated to corporate restructuring. Increasingly fewer people in the United States perform work that results in useful goods and services. Just look at the phone book under the headings of real estate. Compare the number of firms on these pages with the number of places that are employing people who are engaged in the production of useful goods and services.

Fred Moseley lays the bulk of the blame for many of our economic ills on the escalation of unproductive labor and unproductive investment.[72] He estimates that of the workers in the U.S. economy in 1980 little more than one-half were doing productive labor.[73] This estimate is conservative on two counts. First, Moseley based his calculations on old data. All evidence suggests that the share of unproductive labor has been increasing over time.[74]

Moseley's data indicate that the ratio of productive to unproductive labor rose by about 70 percent between 1950 and 1980.[75] The increasing pace of deindustrialization during the 1980s obviously accelerated the trend. By 1987, Moseley calculates that the ratio had almost doubled its 1950 level.[76] I know of no indication that this trend toward an increasing share of unproductive labor is tapering off.

Second, much of the seemingly productive labor is actually used to produce goods and services that are used for activities that are themselves unproductive. For example, even though paper workers are productive, their work is dissipated unproductively when paper is consumed in the course of corporate takeovers. A goodly number of paper workers or people assembling computers, through no fault of their own, end up producing more paperwork rather than contributing to our standard of living.

The increasing burden of deadweight losses from such unproductive labor is likely to continue. Christopher Niggle illustrates the likelihood of this possibility by analyzing the growth of financial services in the U.S. economy. He notes that the ratio of the book value of financial institutions to the gross national product of the United States was 78.4 in 1960. In 1970, it was only still 82.9. By 1984, it reached 107.4.[77]

Niggle suggests a second ratio to demonstrate the enormous growth of the financial sector: the ratio of financial institutions' assets to the assets of nonfinancial institutions. In 1960, this ratio was 0.957, meaning that the financial and the nonfinancial sectors were about equal. By 1970, the financial sector had overtaken the nonfinancial sector, boosting the ratio to 1.094. By 1983, the dominance of the nonfinancial sector had driven the ratio to 1.202.[78]

Niggle's estimates are an understatement. Today, many industrial companies operate more like banks than producers of real goods. For example, U.S. automobile producers have become banks that sell cars, since virtually all their profits come from their credit operations.[79]

Finally, Niggle reports the growing size of the part of the economy known by the acronym FIRE, which stands for Finance, Insurance, and Real Estate. In 1960, the FIRE sector represented 14.3 percent of the gross domestic product of the United States; in 1980, 15.1 percent. The 1983 share of the FIRE sector was 16.4 percent, meaning that within these mere three years the relative importance of the FIRE sector grew by more than it had in the previous twenty years.[80] The FIRE sector continued its growth, reaching 20.9 percent by 2002.[81]

Just consider the explosion in transactions in the stock market. In 1960, 766 million shares were traded on the New York Stock Exchange. In 1987, 900 million shares changed hands in the average week. More shares were traded on the lowest volume day in 1987 than in any month in 1960. More shares were traded in the first fifteen minutes of October 19 and 20, 1987, than in any week in 1960.[82] By early 2005, the typical daily—not weekly—turnover on the New York Stock Exchange was about 1.5 billion shares worth more than $50 billion.

The stock market represents a relatively small share of all financial speculation. Speculators trade many different types of assets. For example, they buy and sell derivative securities, such as stock futures, which provide the rights to buy or sell stocks at a set price for a specified time in the future. Organized markets in such derivative securities did not even exist in 1970. Today, the value of trades in stock futures exceeds that of the trades in stocks themselves.

By April of 2004, the Bank for International Settlements estimated the daily turnover in derivatives markets was $1.9 trillion.[83] The daily turnover in foreign currency transactions was $2.4 trillion.[84] In just a few days, these two types of financial transactions would equal the total value of the annual production of all the economies of the world, which is estimated at about $30 trillion.

The upsurge in this sort of financial transaction is a consequence, as well as a cause, of the economic decline of the U.S. economy. As the decline took hold, people as well as firms, seeing relatively little promise from productive activities, turned to speculation.

Left unchecked, this process will continue to feed upon itself: more speculation causes fewer productive activities, which, in turn, will lead to more speculation. This spiral will probably continue until financial disaster brings it to a halt at an enormous cost to society.

The Legacy of Morgan

Perhaps nothing typifies the perverse association between the financial sector and the decline in manufacturing than the relationship between Burlington Industries and the great investment banking house Morgan Stanley. The story began around early 1987 when Asher Edelman, a famous corporate raider, was threatening to take over Burlington, the largest textile company in the United States. Morgan offered to rescue Burlington, which it then purchased for $2.2 billion.[85]

Morgan itself put up only $46 million of the total cost. Bank loans and later junk-bond offerings provided the rest. In return, Morgan got all the Class A voting stock and control of the company. In the first fifty days of owning the company, Morgan collected $87 million in fees, almost double what it paid to gain control.

Morgan also charged $29 million for "advising" Burlington on how to be bought by Morgan. Morgan got an additional $8.24 million for underwriting $12.5 million of junk bonds in Burlington. Its fees equaled 4 percent of the value of the acquisition, well above the 3.02 percent that was the average charged for floating junk bonds. Of course, Burlington could not complain. After all, Morgan controlled the board of directors.

For the first two years after the buyout, Burlington laid off 900 headquarters workers and sold 20 businesses to help repay its debt. The divestitures generated $1 billion in cash, which Burlington used to pay down debt. The workforce ultimately shrank from 44,000 in 1986 to 27,000. Not surprisingly, the company ceased to be a leader in the textile industry.

Faced with dissatisfaction from Burlington's management, Morgan devised an Employee Stock Ownership Plan (ESOP) to put stock into workers' hands. The plan required that Burlington pay $175.3 million in dividends to its equity holders, chiefly Morgan. In fact, Morgan's dividend of $56 million equaled more than half of the bank's entire 1989 third quarter dividend. Although Morgan profited from this transaction, it added another $212.5 million junk-bond debt on the textile company, making Burlington's total debt reach $1.6 billion.

The ESOP plan purchased $2.9 million worth of total outstanding Class A voting stock, 36 percent of the total outstanding. Wilson Ellis, an Atlanta banker who helped create the ESOP, said that Morgan Stanley insisted that the ESOP pay $50 per share, five times what Morgan had paid for the stock only two years earlier. After a month of "aggressive negotiation" the plan agreed to purchase the stock at $37.80 a share.

Morgan relied on the appraisal firm Houlthan, Lokey, Howard, and Zukin to help it determine a fair value for the stock. This same firm had aided Morgan in appraising Burlington in 1987 when it purchased the company at $10 per share. Presumably, the appraisers felt that Morgan had somehow added substantial value to the firm. Soon after the formation of the ESOP, the same appraisal firm valued the employees' stock at $14.62, less than half the price the employees paid 14 months earlier. Again, one can only assume that Morgan's association was so valuable that, once it distanced itself from the firm, the value of the stock plummeted.

The Morgan affair left Burlington in shambles, but Morgan Stanley profited handsomely. All in all, Morgan Stanley collected $176 million from the captive textile company, including more than $120 million in investment-banking fees and another $56 million in a special dividend. In addition, the company collected an additional windfall on its sale of its stock. Quite a return on its initial investment of $46 million! One can only wonder what J. P. Morgan would have thought.

By the 1990s, this new phase of the finance-driven economy intensified. Even supposedly solid manufacturing companies began to earn substantial portions of their profits from financial operations. By 2005, reported pretax financial profits were almost half as large as domestic nonfinancial profits.[86] Since 1990, the share of total profits supplied by finance has increased almost 50 percent.[87] Even this amount is probably a serious understatement because the government can only track financial profits of nonfinancial firms where those corporations provide the breakdown between their financial and nonfinancial profits.

Ideally, finance can promote industry by funneling money to where it can be more productive, but where hyperactive finance is looking for immediate profits, it is more likely to behave parasitically. Just as the Morganized U.S. Steel cannibalized the firm and Morgan Stanley devoured Burlington Industries, finance will eventually destroy the underlying economy. An economy built increasingly on finance is a disaster waiting to happen.

Conclusion

Beyond Competition

Much of this book concerns the nature of markets and competition. Political leaders today equate markets with freedom and democracy. Modern economists suffer under the delusion that competition is an unmitigated good for society.

Economic orthodoxy precludes an objective evaluation of cooperation. Instead, economists frame their analyses in terms of unrealistic models that obscure more than they reveal about the economy. These ingenious mathematical models supposedly demonstrate the efficiency of markets. Competitive forces work efficiently within the imaginary world of these economic models. To obtain this outcome the model builders construct a world without conflict between workers and employers and where investors have perfect information about the future. Instead of an abstract model, I have tried to use episodes from the economic history of the United States to illustrate how misleading these conventional economics are.

I hope that this history has exposed the irrelevance of conventional economics, showing that it mostly exists as a justification for an unjust and inefficient means of organizing society. At the same time, some economists along with business leaders and political leaders (corporatists, welfare capitalists, government Keynesianists, etc.), thinking more clearly and less ideologically, have pushed for various reforms, which have also proved incapable of preventing capitalism's contradictions from showing themselves.

New reforms might possibly overcome some of these problems and contradictions, but new ones will emerge in their wake. Ultimately, the basic problem is a system of intractable contradictions inherent in the market itself. In this sense, the corporatists were on the right track, but they could not take the next step and repudiate the system itself.

I look forward to the day when we no longer rely on competition for monetary rewards to guide our affairs; when cooperation and social planning replace the haphazard world of the marketplace. In an advanced, high-tech economy, success will ultimately depend upon the education and empowerment of workers rather than their exploitation.

On a superficial level, the economic justification for competition might seem simple enough. Competition supposedly rewards people according to their contribution to society. As a result, competition supposedly offers the best way of encouraging people to exert themselves to benefit the economy.

The claims for competition do not hold up well under close scrutiny. Competitive efforts can also turn counterproductive in many ways that go beyond the scope of this book. We know that both managers and employees often waste enormous effort by maneuvering to gain an advantage relate to others in the firm. Firms, too, can take actions geared more at undermining their competitors than in providing better service.

Modern economics fails to recognize that competition creates a serious threat to society. As Lester Telser, an exceptional economist who has taken the time to analyze the foundations of economic theory, wisely observed, "It is hard for many economists to accept the proposition that competition may be excessive because the received theory regards competition as always good, the more the better."[1]

Just as too little competition in a market economy causes stagnation and economic decline,[2] too much competition leads to deflation and chaos. Especially in capital-intensive industries, what we take to be normal competition can easily turn into cutthroat competition, as we saw in the case of the railroads.

Information and Competition

In our quick overview of the nature of economic theory, we saw that even though many economists identify economic progress with the accumulation of long-lived, fixed capital, modern economic theory generally evades wrestling with the thorny subject of the accumulation of long-lived, fixed capital. We also noted that the difficulties associated with long-lived, fixed capital result from inadequate information about the future.

If investors had perfect information, long-lived, fixed capital would not present a problem either for the economy or for economists. Excessive competition would not occur because investors would realize the actions that their competitors would take and would only purchase those capital goods that would return a respectable profit. In the absence of excessive competition, only the most inefficient firms would need to cut prices so much that they would suffer losses—but, of course, with perfect information such firms would not even exist.

Without sufficient information, investors can only guess where they should invest. Inevitably, many misguided investments occur. In industries where investment outruns demand, we get crises, with prices falling to the level of marginal costs. The economic crises in these industries can easily spill over into other industries, creating a general crisis. Economic theory has never developed an adequate means for addressing these recurrent crises.

We saw that these same forces, which make long-lived capital goods difficult to integrate into economic theory, also make rational investors reluctant to invest their funds in long-lived fixed-capital goods. So far as Keynes was concerned, our economic well-being depends on the irrational investments of ill-informed businesspeople. Of course, both rash and rational investors can sink their funds in long-lived capital goods, but we cannot identify who belongs in which category until their investments have met the test of time.

We have seen that many of the great business leaders of the late nineteenth century agreed with Keynes. They feared that without some sort of monopolistic control irrational investors would build up excessive capacity, throwing industry after industry into chaos.

Although we typically associate dissent from laissez faire in the United States with the discontent of workers, farmers, and radicals, this logic led great corporate leaders, and even the famous corporatist economists, to question the viability of the market in the nineteenth century United States. Finance capital, say in the guise of J. P. Morgan, also shared the perspective of the corporatist economists.

By the 1920s, corporate leaders proposed that cooperation among large business interests could go beyond avoiding the damage that unrestrained competition threatened; these corporate leaders promised to care for the welfare of their workers, as well as society at large. This atmosphere led Keynes to predict an end of laissez faire.

Skepticism about raw market forces was not unique to the corporatists and the welfare economists. When we review the course of history, we find that, in general, much of the society of the United States mistrusted laissez faire in all but a few brief periods.

In the early years of the United States, government leaders turned to protectionism, lest the market turn the republic into an appendage of the British economy. Later, as fixed capital became more important, many leaders feared that markets could make the economy chaotic, as competition forced prices so low that bankruptcy would become common.

Perhaps we could identify the times of the Democratic administrations between Jackson and the Civil War, the later regimes of Cleveland, Coolidge, Reagan, and maybe the two Bushes as favoring laissez faire—assuming that we ignore the military

Keynesianism of the later episodes. When we look beyond the rhetoric of laissez faire, however, we see enormous favoritism and market rigging that defy the rules of laissez faire.

The Myth of Market Rationality

The present mood is unusual in its expressions of blind trust in the market. We cannot rationally credit the accomplishments of the market for the most recent round of enthusiasm for laissez faire. Instead, we should see it as a natural outgrowth of the disillusionment and disappointment that came with the end of the Golden Age. If governments cannot deliver the continual prosperity that people expect, well, maybe market forces can.

A new understanding of markets also swept across the world of finance. Nobody remembered why Morgan had been concerned about the need to curb competition. Instead, a new short-term perspective has taken hold among finance capital. In truth, this perspective was not new at all. It closely resembled the archaic merchant conception of the economy—the same merchant conception that fell into disrepute when the railroads were experiencing their wave of bankruptcies.

This short-term point of view gradually penetrated the general corporate mentality, as business recruited more and more corporate leaders from the world of finance and marketing. In this way, business finally succumbed to the temptation to let short-term profits guide its policies.

We can understand this change as part of the overall postwar economic decline. Over time, as the postwar boom unraveled, healthy profit margins were becoming more scarce. Managers needed immediate profits to satisfy the investment community. As a result, this destructive, short-term perspective gained more and more influence.

While short-termism was flourishing, technical conditions were calling for an entirely new way of thinking.

Cooperation

Where high technology becomes prevalent, fixed costs become dominant and marginal costs become trivial. Market-based, marginal cost pricing will create chaos, as the corporatist economists learned a century ago. One important factor has emerged since the time of the corporatists. Today, more than ever, the modern, information-intensive economy demands cooperation.

Our economic potential will expand to the extent that everybody has access to as much information as possible. The more information becomes public, the better society can take advantage of the new technologies. Unfortunately, competitive forces put a premium on secrecy that allows firms to maintain a competitive advantage. The future will belong to those economies that learn to cooperate rather than compete. In a socialist economy, people will no longer have an incentive to keep technical information private.[9]

Collective organization of society, imposed either by an authoritarian government or by an intolerant society, can be oppressive. Indeed, at the dawn of the industrial revolution, rampant abuses of traditional forms of power made the possibility of market-based relationships appear as a promise of freedom.

Markets did create an environment in which technology blossomed. This new form of economy brought previously unimagined wonders of convenience and comfort to the well-off. Few among us would willingly abandon all the fruits of modern technology and take up the lifestyle of yore.

Even so, when we look around us we have to admit our society could do far better with the resources at its disposal. Why should the vast majority of the world's population be reduced to squalor? Why should society squander massive amounts of wealth on armaments, which are all too often brutally used? Why should society continue to wantonly ravage the environment? I am sure that you could continue this list of questions on your own with hundreds, if not thousands, of your own entries.

Following our list of questions, you might expect to find a proposal for a better world. In fact, we have many library shelves filled with such recommendations, often filed under the subheading "Utopia," a Greek word meaning "nowhere." Utopias are nowhere and go nowhere because they spring from an individual mind.

A utopian author tells us, "Here is the way I want to see the world." Unless the utopian author's vision happens to coincide with the desires of the rest of society, or at least enough of society to challenge the powers that be, the utopian words will soon be confined to a few dusty library shelves.

I am not a utopian. I do not pretend to have a road map that can guide you to the future. I can say that our present economy is inadequate and that changes are afoot that will make it more so. I do know that our present economic thinking precludes us from commencing on the hard and joyous work of building a better world in which the economy will not continue to produce for the narrow interests of those who control capital. In that spirit, I call for the end of economics and the beginning of something better.

Notes

Introduction

1. John Maynard Keynes, "The End of Laissez-Faire" in *Essays in Persuasion, IX, The Collected Works of John Maynard Keynes*, ed. Donald Moggridge (London: Macmillan, 1972), 272–94.

2. Michael Perelman, *Keynes, Investment Theory and the Economic Slowdown: The Role of Replacement Investment and q-Ratios* (London: Macmillan, 1989), ch. 1.

1. The End of Economics

1. H. W. Arndt, "Political Economy," *The Economic Record* 60: 170 (September 1984), 266–73.

2. P. D. Groenewegen, "Professor Arndt on Political Economy: A Comment," *Economic Record* 61: 175 (December 1985), 744–51.

3. Alfred Marshall and Mary Paley Marshall, *Economics of Industry* (London: Macmillan, 1879), 2.

4. Keith Tribe, *Land, Labour and Economic Discourse* (London: Routledge and Kegan Paul, 1978).

5. See K. Rajani Kanth, *Political Economy and Laissez-Faire Economics and Ideology in the Ricardian Age* (Totowa: Rowman and Allanheld, 1986).

6. See Michael Perelman, *The Invention of Capitalism: The Secret History of Primitive Accumulation* (Durham: Duke University Press, 2000).

7. See Karl Marx, *Capital*, Vol. 1 (New York: Vintage, 1977).

8. Michael Perelman, *Marx's Crises Theory: Scarcity, Labor, and Finance* (New York: Praeger, 1987), 89.

9. Groenewegen, "Professor Arndt."

10. Joseph A. Schumpeter, *History of Economic Analysis* (New York: Oxford University Press, 1954), 38.

11. William Stanley Jevons, *The Theory of Political Economy* (Baltimore: Penguin Books, 1970), 48.

12. See the contributions in *What Is Political Economy: Eight Perspectives*, ed. David Whynes (Oxford: Basil Blackwell, 1984).

13. George J. Stigler, "Do Economists Matter?" in *The Economist as Preacher* (Oxford: Basil Blackwell, 1982), 60.

14. John Maynard Keynes, *The General Theory of Employment, Interest and Money* (New York: Macmillan, 1936).

15. Donald N. McCloskey, *The Rhetoric of Economics* (Madison: The University of Wisconsin Press, 1985).

16. Lawrence H. Summers, "The Scientific Illusion in Empirical Economics," *Scandinavian Journal of Economics* 93: 2 (1991), 130.

17. Joshua S. Gans and George B. Shepherd, "How Are the Mighty Fallen: Rejected Classic Articles by Leading Economists," *Journal of Economic Perspectives* 8: 1 (Winter 1994), 177.

18. Munir Quddus and Salim Rashid, "The Over-Use of Mathematics in Economics: Nobel Overuse." *Eastern Economic Journal* 20: 3 (Summer 1994), 251–66.

19. Gerard Debreu, "The Mathematization of Economic Theory," *American Economic Review* 81: 1 (March 1991), 1. See also McCloskey, *Rhetoric of Economics*, 4.

20. Debreu, "Mathematization," 3.

21. Ibid., 6.

22. George J. Stigler, *Economists and Public Policy* (Washington, D.C.: American Enterprise Institute, 1982), 94.

23. Robert M. Solow, "Economic History and Economics," in *American Economic Review, Papers and Proceedings* 75: 2 (May 1985), 330.

24. Robert E. Lucas, Jr., "Methods and Problems in Business Cycle Theory," *Journal of Money, Credit, and Banking* 12 (November 1980): 696–715, reprinted in *Studies in Business Cycle Theory* (Cambridge, Massachusetts: MIT Press, 1985).

25. Robert E. Lucas, Jr., "On Efficiency and Distribution." *Economic Journal* 102: 411 (March 1992), 233.

26. Wassily Leontief, "Theoretical Assumptions and Nonobserved Facts," *American Economic Review* 61: 1 (March 1971), 1–2.

27. Frank Hahn, "Some Adjustment Problems (Presidential Address to the Econometric Society)," *Econometrica* 38: 1 (January 1970), 1–2.

28. Melvin W. Reder, "Chicago Economics: Permanence and Change," *Journal of Economic Literature* 20: 1 (March 1982), 1–38; see also McCloskey, *Rhetoric of Economics.*

29. David Figlio, "Trends in the Publication of Empirical Economics," *Journal of Economic Perspectives* 8: 3 (Summer 1994), 184.

30. Keynes, *The General Theory of Employment,* 158.

31. David C. Colander, *Why Aren't Economists as Important as Garbagemen?* (Armonk: M.E. Sharpe, 1991), 47.

32. Bruno S. Frey, Werner W. Pomerehne, Friedrich Schneider, and Guy Gilbert, "Consensus and Dissension Among Economists: An Empirical Inquiry," *American Economic Review* 74:. 5 (December 1984), 986–94; Stephen L. Jackstadt, Lee Huskey, Don L. Marx, and Pershing J. Hill, "Economics 101 and an Economic Way of Thinking," *American Economist* 34: 2 (Fall 1990), 79–84.

33. Anne Krueger, et al., "Report on the Commission on Graduate Education in Economics," *Journal of Economic Literature* 19: 3 (September 1991), 1039.

34. John Carter and Michael Irons, "Are Economists Different, and If So, Why?," *Journal of Economic Perspectives* 5: 2 (Spring 1991), 171–77; Daniel Kahneman, Jack L. Knethsch, and Richard Thaler, "Fairness as a Constraint on Profit Seeking: Entitlements in the Market," *American Economic Review* 76: 4 (September 1986), 728–41.

35. Robert H. Frank, "If Homo Economicus Could Choose His Own Utility Function, Would He Want One with a Conscience?," *American Economic Review* 77: 4 (September 1987), 593.

36. Daniel Kahneman, Jack L. Knethsch, and Richard Thaler, "Fairness and the Assumption of Economics." *Journal of Business* 59: 4, Part 2, (1986), S286-S300; Alan L. Olmstead and Paul Rhode, "Rationing without Government: The West Coast Gas Famine of 1920," *American Economic Review* 75: 5 (December 1985), 1044–55.

37. Robert J. Shiller, Maxim Boycko, and Vladimir Korobov, "Popular Attitudes toward Free Markets: The Soviet and the United States Compared," *American Economic Review* 81: 3 (June 1991), 385–400.

38. Robert H. Frank, Thomas Gilovich, and Dennis T. Regan, "Does Studying Economics Inhibit Cooperation?" *Journal of Economic Perspectives* 7: 2 (Spring 1993 but text says 1991), 159–72.

39. Robert M. Solow, "What do we know that Francis Amasa Walker didn't?" *History of Political Economy* 19: 2 (Summer 1987), 189.

40. Herbert Stein, *The Fiscal Revolution in America* (Chicago: University of Chicago Press, 1969), 40.

41. Alain C. Enthoven, "Economic Analysis in the Department of Defense," *American Economic Review* 53: 2 (May 1963), 413–23.

42. George J. Stigler, "The Politics of Political Economists," *Quarterly Journal of Economics* 98 (November 1959) reprinted in his *Essays in the History of Economics* (Chicago: University of Chicago Press, 1965), 51–65.

43. Edward S. Herman, "The Politicized 'Science'," *Z Magazine* (February 1993), 43–48; James Smith, "Think Tanks and the Politics of Ideas," in *The Spread of Economic Ideas*, eds. David C. Colander and A.W. Coats (Cambridge: Cambridge University Press, 1989), 175–94.

44. Colander and Coats, *Spread of Economic Ideas.*

45. Peter N. Warren, "Delta Force: Conservatism's Best Young Economists," *Policy Review*, no. 70 (Fall 1994), 72.

46. J. R. Kearl, Clayne L. Pope, Gordon C. Whitting, and Larry T. Wimmer, "A Confusion of Economists?" *American Economic Review Papers and Proceedings* 69: 2 (May 1979), 36.

47. Richard Whitley, "The Organisation and Role of Journals in Economics and Other Fields," *Economic Notes* 20: 1 (1991), 7, 10. J. Scott Armstrong, "Editorial Policies for the Publication of Controversial Findings," *International Journal of Forecasting* 8: 4 (1993), 343–4.

48. Robert E. Lucas, Jr., "The Death of Keynesian Economics," *Issues and Ideas* (Winter 1980).

49. Charles Babbage, *On the Economy of Machinery and Manufactures*, 4th ed. (London: Charles Knight, 1835), 393–4.

50. Adam Smith, *The Nature and Causes of the Wealth of Nations* (Oxford: Oxford University Press, 1976).

51. Babbage, *On the Economy*.

52. Krishna Bharadwaj, "Marshall on Pigou's Wealth and Welfare" *Economica* n.s. 39: 153 (February 1972), 32–46; John K. Whitaker, "Increasing Returns and External Economics: Some Early Developments," *History of Economics Society Meeting*, Duke University, June 1982; Jan Keppler, *Monopolistic Competition Theory: Origins, Results and Implications* (Baltimore: Johns Hopkins University Press, 1994).

53. Joan Robinson, "What Has Become of the Keynesian Revolution?" in *After Keynes*, ed. Joan Robinson (Oxford: Basil Blackwell, 1973).

54. Wesley J. Yordon, "Evidence against Diminishing Returns in Manufacturing and Comments on Short-run Models of Price-output Behavior," *Journal of Post Keynesian Economics* 9: 4 (Summer 1987), 593–602.

55. John M. Blair, *Economic Concentration: Structure, Behavior and Public Policy* (New York: Harcourt, Brace and Jovanovich, 1972), 472.

56. F. M. Scherer, *Industrial Market Structure and Economic Performance*, 2nd. ed. (New York: Houghton Mifflin, 1980), 350–62.

57. Julio Rotemberg and Larry H. Summers, "Labor Hoarding, Inflexible Prices and Procyclical Productivity," MIT, Alfred P. Sloan School of Management Working Paper No. 1998-88 (March 1988).

58. William J. Baumol and Robert D. Willig, "Fixed Costs, Sunk Costs, Entry Barriers and Sustainability of Monopoly," *Quarterly Journal of Economics* 96: 3 (August 1981), 405–31.

59. John R. Hicks, *Theory of Wages* (New York: St. Martin's Press, 1963), 183.

60. George Akerlof, "The Market for 'Lemons': Asymmetrical Information and Market Behavior," *Quarterly Journal of Economics* 83: 3 (August 1970), 488–500.

2. Economic Theory and the Historical Increase of Fixed Capital

1. John R. Hicks, *Theory of Wages* (New York: St. Martin's Press, 1963), 183.

2. Avinash Dixit, "Investment and Hysteresis," *Journal of Economic Perspectives* 6: 1 (Winter 1992), 107–32.

3. John Carswell, *The South Sea Bubble* (Stanford: Stanford University Press, 1960), 131.

4. Adam Smith, *The Nature and Causes of the Wealth of Nations* (Oxford: Oxford University Press, 1976), I.x.b43, 131–2.

5. Ibid., I.x.b.26, 124–5.

6. James Boswell, *Life of Johnson*, 6 vols., ed. G. B. Hill (Oxford: Clarendon Press, 1934).

7. Olivier Compte and Andrew Postlewaite, "Confidence-Enhanced Performance," *American Economic Review* 94: 5 (December 2004), 1536–57.

8. Dixit, "Investment and Hysteresis," 119; Joseph E. Stiglitz, "Incentives, Information and Organizational Design," *Empirica—Austrian Economic Papers* 16: 1 (1989), 3–29.

9. John Maynard Keynes, "Letter to Townshend," in *Collected Works*, *XXVIV*, John Maynard Keynes (London: Macmillan, 1938), 294.

10. John Maynard Keynes, *General Theory of Employment*, 162.

11. John Maynard Keynes, *A Treatise on Money*, vols. v and vi, *The Collected Writings of John Maynard Keynes*, ed. Donald Moggridge (London: Macmillan, 1971), 246.

12. Richard Florida and Martin Kenney, *The Breakthrough Illusion: Corporate America's Failure to Move from Innovation to Mass Production* (New York: Basic Books, 1990), 106, citing William Sahlman and Howard Stevenson, "Capital Market Myopia," *Journal of Business Venturing* 1 (Winter 1985), 7–14.

13. Smith, *The Wealth of Nations*, 127–28.

14. Ibid., 341.

15. Perelman, *Keynes, Investment Theory, and the Economic Slowdown*, chapter 3.

16. Ibid.

17. Ibid.

18. Perelman, *Marx's Crises Theory*.

19. Keynes, *General Theory*, 150.

20. Nomi Prins, *Other People's Money: The Corporate Mugging of America* (New York: New Press, 2004).

21. Max Weber, *General Economic History* (New York: Collier Books, 1961), 207.

22. Hicks, *Theory of Wages*, 310.

23. Phyllis Deane and W. A. Coale, *British Economic Growth, 1688–1959* (Cambridge: Cambridge University Press, 1967); C. H. Feinstein, "Capital Formation in Great Britain," in *The Cambridge Economic History of Europe*, vol. vii, *The Industrial Economies*, Part 1, eds. Peter Mathias and M. M. Postan (Cambridge: Cambridge University Press, 1978), 28–96; David S. Landes, *The Unbound Prometheus: Technological Change and Industrial Development in Western Europe from 1750 to the Present* (Cambridge: Cambridge University Press, 1969), pp. 64 ff.

24. F. Crouzet, "Editor's Introduction," *Capital Formation in the Industrial Revolution* (London: Methuen, 1972).

25. Michael Chatfield, *A History of Accounting Thought* (Huntington, NY: Robert E. Krieger, 1977), 102.

26. Ronald H. Coase, "Business Organisation and the Accountant," in *Studies in Costing*, ed. D. Solomons (London: Sweet and Maxwell, 1938), 124. Cited in Steven Medema, *Ronald H. Coase* (London: Macmillan, 1994), 55.

27. Joseph Schumpeter, *Business Cycles: A Theoretical, Historical and Statistical Analysis of the Capitalist Process*, 2 vols. (New York: McGraw-Hill, 1939), i, p. v.

28. Perelman, *Keynes, Investment Theory*.

29. Perelman, *Marx's Crises Theory*, ch. 4; see Marx to Engels on August 14, 1851, in Karl Marx and Frederick Engels, *Collected Works*, Vol. 39 (New York: International Publishers, 1982), 424; Karl Marx, *Capital* (New York: International Publishers, 1967), 114.

30. Marx to Engels, November 19, 1869 in Marx and Engels, *Selected Correspondence*, ed. Dona Torr (New York: International Publishers, 1942), 270; Karl Marx, *Poverty of Philosophy* (New York: International Publishers, 1963), 65.

31. Marx, *Capital*, Vol. 1 (New York: Vintage, 1977), 528; Babbage, *On the Economy of Machinery*, 286 and 214. See also William J. Baumol and Robert D. Willig, "Intertemporal Failures of the Invisible Hand: Theory and Implications for International Market Dominance," *Indian Economic Review* 16: 1 & 2 (1981); P. Gaskell, *The Manufacturing Population of England* (London: Baldwin and Cradock, 1833), 43. Cited in Jose Alberro and Joseph Persky, "The Dynamics of Fixed Capital Revaluation and Scrapping," *The Review of Radical Political Economy* 13: 2 (Summer 1981), 32–37.

32. Nathan Rosenberg, "On Technological Expectations," *Economic Journal* 86: 343 (September 1976): 523–25, reprinted in his *Inside the Black Box: Technology and Economics* (Cambridge: Cambridge University Press, 1976); Morton Kamien and Nancy Schwartz, "Anticipating Technical Change," *Western Economic Journal* 10: 2 (June 1972), 123–28; Yves Balcer and

Steven A. Lippman, "Expectations and the Adoption of Improved Technology," *Journal of Economic Theory* 34: 2 (December 1984), 292–318.

33. Arthur Cecil Pigou, *The Economics of Welfare* (London: Macmillan, 1932), 189; C. Emery Troxel, "Economic Influences of Depreciation," *American Economic Review* 26, no. 2 (June 1936), 283–90; Rosenberg, "On Technological Expectations"; Victor P. Goldberg, "Regulation and Administered Contracts," *The Bell Journal of Economics* 7: 2 (Autumn 1976), 426–8.

34. R. S. Sawyers, "The Springs of Technical Progress in Britain, 1919–1939," *Economic Journal* 60 (June 1950), 289. Cited in Rosenberg, *Inside the Black Box*, 113.

35. Carlo Cippola, *Before the Industrial Revolution: European Society and Economy, 1000–1700* (London: Methuen, 1981), 31.

3. Railroads and the Increase in Fixed Capital

1. Joseph Edward Hedges, *Commercial Banking and the Stock Market before 1863* (Baltimore: Johns Hopkins University Press, 1938), 37.

2. Robert Sobel, *The Big Board: A History of the New York Stock Market* (New York: The Free Press, 1965), 54.

3. Paul David, "The Mechanization of Reaping in the Antebellum Midwest," in *Industrialization in Two Systems: Essays in Honor of Alexander Gerschenkron*, ed. H. Rosovsky (New York: John Wiley & Sons, 1966), 3–29. Reprinted in *The Economics of Technical Change*, ed. Nathan Rosenberg (London: Penguin, 1971).

4. Harold C. Livesay, *Andrew Carnegie and the Rise of Big Business* (Boston: Little, Brown, 1975), 34.

5. Alfred D. Chandler, Jr., "Introduction: The Beginnings of Modern Corporate Finance," in *The Railroads: The Nation's First Big Business: Sources and Readings*, ed. Alfred D. Chandler, Jr. (New York: Harcourt, Brace and World, 1965), 43.

6. H. M. Boot, "James Wilson and the Commercial Crisis of 1847," *History of Political Economy* 15, no. 4 (Winter 1983), 569.

7. J. D. Chambers, *The Workshop of the World: British Economic History, 1820–1828* (Oxford University Press, 1968), 38–9.

8. Boot, "James Wilson," 569.

9. Paul M. Sweezy, "Review of J. Steindl, *Maturity and Stagnation in American Capitalism*," *Econometrica* 22: 4 (October 1954), 532.

10. United States Department of Commerce, Bureau of the Census, *Historical Statistics of the United States: Colonial Times to 1970* (Washington, D.C.: USGPO, 1975), 684 and 735.

11. Charles Francis Adams, Jr., *Railroads: Their Origin and Problems* (New York: Harper & Row, 1969), 85.

12. John Stuart Mill, *Principles of Political Economy with Some of Their Applications to Social Philosophy, Collected Works*, J.M. Robson, ed. (Toronto: University of Toronto Press, 1965), vol. 2-3, p. 97.

13. Chatfield, *A History of Accounting Thought* (Huntington, NY: Robert E. Krieger, 1977), 94.

14. Alfred D. Chandler, Jr., *The Visible Hand: The Managerial Revolution in American Business* (Cambridge, MA: The Belknap Press, 1977), 111.

15. Chatfield, *A History of Accounting*, 94.

16. H. Thomas Johnson and Robert S. Kaplan, *Relevance Lost: The Rise and Fall of Management Accounting* (Cambridge: Harvard Business School Press, 1987), 87.

17. Chatfield, *A History of Accounting*, 95.

18. Ibid.

19. Ibid.

20. Ibid., 125.

21. Michael J.L. O'Connor, *The Origins of Academic Economics in the United States* (New York: Columbia University Press, 1944).

22. Ibid., ch. 2.

23. Henry C. Carey, *Principles of Social Science* (Philadelphia: J.B. Lippincott; NY: Augustus M. Kelley, 1963) 1, 148-9 and 152.

24. Arnold W. Green, *Henry Charles Carey: Nineteenth-Century Sociologist* (Philadelphia: University of Philadelphia Press, 1951), 180-1.

25. Ibid., 35.

26. Ibid., 175-6.

27. Hans B. Thorelli, *The Federal Antitrust Policy: Origination of an American Tradition* (Baltimore: Johns Hopkins University Press, 1955). 116.

28. Martin J. Sklar, *The Corporate Reconstruction of American Capitalism: 1890–1916* (Cambridge: Cambridge University Press, 1988), 44; Milton Friedman and Anna Jacobson Schwartz, *A Monetary History of the United States, 1867–1960* (Princeton: Princeton University Press, 1963), 92-3.

29. Anthony Patrick O'Brien, "Factory Size, Economies of Scale, and the Great Merger Wave of 1898–1902," *Journal of Economic History* 48: 3 (September 1988), 639–49; Michael C. Jensen, "The Modern Industrial Revolution: Exit and the Failure of Internal Control Systems," *Journal of Finance* 48: 3 (July 1993), 834.

30. Jensen, "The Modern Industrial Revolution," 835.

31. Edward Chase Kirkland, *Dream and Thought in the Business Community, 1860–1900* (Chicago: Quadrangle Press, 1964), 7.

32. Schumpeter, *Business Cycles*, i, p. 337.

33. Carl P. Parrini and Martin J. Sklar, "New Thinking about the Market, 1896–1904: Some American Economists on Investment and the Theory of Surplus Capital," *Journal of Economic History* 43, no. 3 (September 1983), 561.

34. Herbert Ronald Ferleger, *David A. Wells and the American Revenue System, 1865–1870* (Philadelphia: Porcupine Press, 1977), 219.

35. James Livingston, *Origins of the Federal Reserve System: Money, Class, and Corporate Capitalism, 1890–1913* (Ithaca: Cornell University Press, 1986), 75.

36. Thorelli, *The Federal Antitrust Policy*, 111.

37. Committee on Recent Economic Changes, *Recent Economic Changes in the United States: Report of the Committee on Recent Economic Changes of the President's Conference on Unemployment* (New York: McGraw-Hill, 1929), ix.

38. Joseph Dorfman, *The Economic Mind in American Civilization, 1606–1865* (New York: The Viking Press, 1946-9), 2, 808, 969, 975.

39. Ferleger, *David A. Wells*, 5.

40. David A. Wells, *Practical Economics: A Collection of Essays Respecting Certain of the Recent Economic Experiences of the United States* (New York: Greenwood Publishers, 1968), 138.

41. Ibid., 137.

42. Gregory Clark, "Why Isn't the Whole World Developed? Lessons from the Cotton Mills," *Journal of Economic History* 47: 1 (March 1987), 141-73.

43. Ibid., 142.

44. Ibid., 143.

45. Ibid., 150.

46. Jacob Schoenhof, *The Economy of High Wages: An Inquiry into the Cause of High Wages and Their Effects on Methods and Cost of Production* (New York: G.P. Putnam's Sons, 1893), 33-34.

47. Jeremiah Jenks, *The Trust Problem* (New York: McLure, Phillips & Co., 1900), 254, cited in Livingston, *Origins of the Federal Reserve*, 39.

48. Gavin Wright, "The Origins of American Industrial Success, 1870–1940," *American Economic Review* 80, no. 4 (September 1990), 652.

49. David A.Wells, *Recent Economic Changes and Their Effect on the Production and Well-Being of Society* (New York: Da Capo Press, 1970), 73.

50. Ibid, 74.

51. Ibid., 369.

52. Ibid., 369.

53. Ibid., 369.

54. Ibid., 30.

55. Ibid., 31.

56. Wells, *Practical Economics,* 146; see Edward Atkinson, *The Industrial Progress of the Nation: Consumption Limited, Production Unlimited* (New York: Arno Press, 1973).

57. Ron Chernow, *The House of Morgan: An American Banking Dynasty and the Rise of Modern Finance* (New York: Atlantic Monthly Press, 1990), 53–6.

58. Chandler, *The Visible Hand,* 134.

59. Gabriel Kolko, *Railroads and Regulation, 1877–1916* (Princeton: Princeton University Press, 1965), 7.

60. Chatfield, *A History of Accounting,* 95.

61. J. S. Foreman-Peck, "Natural Monopoly and Railway Policy in the Nineteenth Century," *Oxford Economic Papers* 39: 4 (December 1987).

62. Charles Francis Adams, *1835–1915: An Autobiography with a memorial address delivered November 17, 1915, by Henry Cabot Lodge* (New York: Russell & Russell 1968), 190.

63. Ibid., 171.

64. Thomas K. McCraw, *Prophets of Regulation* (Cambridge: Harvard University Press, 1984), 6.

65. Charles Francis Adams, Jr., and Henry Adams, *Chapters of Erie and Other Essays* (Ithaca: Cornell University Press, 1956), 3–4.

66. George W. Edwards, *Evolution of Finance Capitalism* (London: Longmans, Green and Co., 1938), 155–6.

67. Charles Francis Adams, Jr., and Henry Adams, *Chapters of Erie,* 2.

68. Adams, Jr., *1835–1915: An Autobiography,* 172.

69. McCraw, *Prophets of Regulation,* 49.

70. Adams, Jr., *Railroads: Their Origin,* 118.

71. Ibid., 119–20.

72. Ibid., 80.

73. Charles Francis Adams, Jr., "Railroad Commissions," *Journal of Social Science* 2 (1870), 233–6. Cited in McCraw, *Prophets of Regulation,* 9.

74. Chandler, *The Visible Hand,* 204.

75. Morton J. Horwitz, "*Santa Clara* Revisited: The Development of Corporate Theory," in *Corporations and Society: Power and Responsibility,* Warren J. Samuels and Arthur S. Miller, eds. (New York: Greenwood Press, 1987), 27.

76. Adams, Jr., *Railroads: Their Origin,* 121.

77. Horwitz, "*Santa Clara* Revisited," 28.

78. Arthur Twining Hadley, *Railroad Transportation: Its History and Its Laws* (New York: G.P. Putnam and Sons, 1903), 40.

79. O'Brien, "Factory Size, Economies"; see also Jeremy Atack, "Firm Size and Industrial Structure in the United States During the Nineteenth Century," *Journal of Economic History* 46: 2 (June 1986): 463–75.

80. Livingston, *Origins of the Federal Reserve,* 38–9.

81. Allan Meltzer and Saranna Robinson, "Stability Under the Gold Standard in Practice," in *Money, History and International Finance: Essays in Honor of Anna J. Schwartz*, Michael Bordo, ed. (Chicago: University of Chicago Press, 1989), 163–95.

82. John A. James, "Changes in Economic Instability in 19th-Century America," *American Economic Review* 83: 4 (September 1993), 710.

83. Benjamin Klein, Robert Crawford, and Armen Alchian, "Vertical Integration, Appropriable Rents, and the Competitive Contracting Process," *Journal of Law and Economics* 21 (1978): 297–326, reprinted in *The Economic Nature of the Firm: A Reader*, Louis Putterman, ed. (Cambridge: Cambridge University Press, 1986), 230–49.

84. Arthur Twining Hadley, "How Far Have Modern Improvements in Transportation and Production Changed the Principle that Men Should Be Left Free to Make Their Own Bargains? Part I," *Science* 7: 161 (5 March, 1886), 223–5.

85. Hadley, *Railroad Transportation*, 74.

86. Arthur Twining Hadley, "Private Monopolies and Public Rights," *Quarterly Journal of Economics*, 1886, 28–44; reprinted *Monopoly and Competition Policy*, ed. F. M. Scherer (Aldershot, Hants: Edward Elgar, 1993), 35.

87. Ibid., 41.

88. Alfred S. Eichner, *The Emergence of Oligopoly: Sugar Refining as a Case Study* (Baltimore: Johns Hopkins Press, 1969), 101.

89. Hadley, *Railroad Transportation*, 52.

90. Ibid., 51.

91. Arthur Twining Hadley, *Economics: An Account of the Relations between Private Property and Public Welfare* (New York: Arno Press, 1972), 12.

92. Hadley, *Railroad Transportation*, 69.

93. Hadley, *Economics*, iii.

94. Hadley, *Railroad Transportation*, 142–3.

95. Ibid., 70–2.

96. Hadley, "How Far Have Modern," 224.

97. Hadley, *Railroads Transportation*, 136–40; Hadley, "Private Monopolies," 44.

98. Morris Hadley, *Arthur Twining Hadley* (New Haven: Yale University Press, 1948), 82–3.

99. Ibid., 41.

100. Hadley, *Railroad Transportation*, 79.

101. Arthur Twining Hadley, "Letter to E. D. Worcester, July 29, 1879," cited in Morris Hadley, *Arthur Twining Hadley* (New Haven: Yale University Press, 1940), 32.

102. Hadley, *Economics: An Account*, 94.

103. Hadley, "How Far Have Modern," 224.

104. Ibid., 224–5.

105. Sidney Fine, *Laissez Faire and the General-Welfare State: A Study of Conflict in American Thought: 1865–1901* (Ann Arbor: University of Michigan Press, 1964), 48.

106. Naomi Lamoreaux, *The Great Merger Movement in American Business, 1895–1904* (New York: Cambridge University Press, 1985).

107. Carl P. Parrini and Martin J. Sklar, "New Thinking about the Market, 1896–1904: Some American Economists on Investment and the Theory of Surplus Capital," *Journal of Economic History* 43: 3 (September 1983), 559–79.

108. Sklar, *The Corporate Reconstruction*, 4.

109. Parrini and Sklar, "New Thinking about the Market," 561.

110. Ibid., 565.

111. Thomas Childs Cochran, *Railroad Leaders, 1845–1890: The Business Mind in Action*

(Cambridge: Harvard University Press, 1953), 436–7.

112. Parrini and Sklar, "New Thinking about the Market," 560.

113. Lawrence Goodwyn, *The Populist Movement: A Short History of the Agrarian Revolt in America* (New York: Oxford University Press, 1978).

114. Goodwyn, *The Populist Movement*, 217.

115. Livingston, *Origins of the Federal Reserve*, 94.

116. Ibid., 100.

117. Milton Friedman, "Leon Walras and His Economic System," *American Economic Review* 45, no. 5 (December 1955), 900–9.

118. Hadley, *Economics: An Account*, 87–90.

119. Parrini and Sklar, "New Thinking about the Market," 560.

120. V.I. Lenin, "Notes on Plekhanov's Second Draft Programme of the Russian Social-Democratic Workers Party," in *Collected Works, Vol. 6. January 1902–August 1903* (Moscow: Progress Publishers, 1964), 54.

121. V.I. Lenin, "The Threatening Catastrophe and How to Fight It," in *Collected Works, Vol. 25. June–September 1917* (New York: International Publishers, 1964), 321–73.

122. John F. Henry, *John Bates Clark and the Origins of Neo-Classical Economics*, Ph.D. Diss. 1974. Economics Department, McGill University; John F. Henry, "The Transformation of John B. Clark: An Essay in Interpretation," *History of Political Economy* 14: 2 (Summer 1982), 166–77; John F. Henry, "John Bates Clark's Transformation," *Journal of the History of Economic Thought* 16:1 (Spring 1994), 106–25; Joseph Dorfman, *The Economic Mind in American Civilization, 1606–1865*, 3 vols. (New York: The Viking Press, 1946–9), 194; Dorothy Ross, *The Origins of American Social Science* (Cambridge: Cambridge University Press, 1991).

123. Mary O. Furner, *Advocacy and Objectivity: A Crisis in the Professionalization of American Social Science, 1865–1905* (Lexington: University Press of Kentucky, 1975), 91.

124. Mary S. Morgan, "Marketplace Morals and the American Economists: The Case of John Bates Clark," in *Higgling: Transactors and Their Markets in the History of Economics*, eds. Neil DeMarchi and Mary S. Morgan, Annual Supplement to Volume 26, *History of Political Economy* (Durham: Duke University Press, 1994), 230–31.

125. John Bates Clark, *The Philosophy of Wealth*, 2nd ed. (New York: Augustus M. Kelley, 1967), 207.

126. Ibid., 147.

127. Ibid., 202.

128. Ibid., 148.

129. John Bates Clark, "How to Deal with Communism," *The New Englander* 37 (July 1878), 533–42.

130. John Bates Clark, *The Philosophy of Wealth*, 219.

131. John Bates Clark, "How to Deal," 539. Cited in John F. Henry, "John Bates Clark's Transformation," *Journal of the History of Economic Thought* 16:1 (Spring 1994), 122.

132. John Bates Clark, "The Nature and Progress of True Socialism," *New Englander* 38, no. 4 (July 1879), 580.

133. John Bates Clark, "The Nature and Progress," 572. Cited in John F. Henry, "John Bates Clark's Transformation," 112. See also Ross, *The Origins of American Social Science*.

134. John F. Henry, "John Bates Clark's Transformation."

135. Arthur Twining Hadley, "Recent Works on Economic Theory," *Independent*, 10 February 1887; Dorfman, *The Economic Mind*, 195.

136. John Bates Clark, *The Distribution of Wealth: A Theory of Wages, Interest, and Profits* (New York: Augustus M. Kelley, 1965), 4–5.

137. Ibid., 207.

138. John Bates Clark, cited in Fine, *Laissez Faire and the General-Welfare State*, 292.

139. Mary O. Furner, *Advocacy and Objectivity: A Crisis in the Professionalization of American Social Science, 1865–1905* (Lexington: University Press of Kentucky, 1975), 91.

140. Sklar, *The Corporate Reconstruction*, 290.

141. John Bates Clark, "The Limits of Competition," in John B. Clark and Franklin H. Giddings, *The Modern Distributive Process: Studies of Competition and Its Limits* (Boston: Ginn & Company, 1888), 1–17.

142. Ibid., 11.

143. John Bates Clark and John Maurice Clark, *The Control of Trusts* (New York: Augustus M. Kelley, 1971).

144. Ibid., 14.

145. John Bates Clark, "Trusts," *Political Science Quarterly* 15:2 (June 1990), 104. Reprinted in *Monopoly and Competition Policy,* ed. F.M. Scherer, (Aldershot, Hants: Edward Elgar, 1993) 86–100.

146. John Bates Clark, "Trusts"; John Bates Clark and John Maurice Clark, *The Control of Trusts*, 80.

147. John Bates Clark, *Essentials of Economic Theory as Applied to Modern Problems of Industry and Public Policy* (New York: Macmillan, 1968), 393; Philip Williams, "The Attitudes of the Economics Professions in Britain and the United States to the Trusts Movement," in *A Century of Economics*, eds. John D. Hey and Donald N. Winch (Oxford: Blackwell, 1990), 102.

148. Philip Williams, "The Attitudes of the Economics," 103.

149. G. William Domhoff, *The Higher Circles: The Governing Class in America* (New York: Random House, 1970), 204.

150. Kolko, *Railroads and Regulation.*

151. John F. Henry, "The Transformation of John B."; John F. Henry, *John Bates Clark.*

152. John Bates Clark, "The Crisis in Colorado and Its Lessons," *Business America* (June 1914). Cited in Henry, *John Bates Clark.*

153. John Bates Clark, *The Distribution of Wealth*, 3.

154. Letter of 16 December 1937, cited in Dorfman, "Introduction," John Bates Clark and John Maurice Clark, *The Control of Trusts*, 13.

155. John Bates Clark, "Introduction," Johann Karl Rodbertus, *Overproduction and Crises* (New York: A.M. Kelley, 1969).

156. Ibid., 9.

157. Ibid., 17.

158. Ibid., 1.

159. Ibid., 2.

160. Philip Williams, "The Attitudes of the Economics," 93.

161. Alfred Marshall, "Some Aspects of Competition," in *Memorials of Alfred Marshall,* ed. Alfred C. Pigou (New York: Kelley and Millman, 1956; 1st ed., 1925), 275.

162. Schumpeter, *History of Economic Analysis*, fn. p. 874.

163. Richard T. Ely, *Ground Under Our Feet: An Autobiography* (New York: Macmillan, 1938), 140.

164. Richard T. Ely, "The Past and the Present of Political Economy," *Overland Monthly and Out West Magazine* 2: 9 (September 1883?), 235. http://www.hti.umich.edu/cgi/t/text/text-idx?c=moajrnl;idno=ahj1472.2-02.009;node=ahj1472.2-02.009:1> 140; Richard T. Ely, "The Past and the Present of Political Economy," *Johns Hopkins University Studies in the Social Sciences*, Second Series, 64.

165. Richard T. Ely, "The Future of Corporations," *Harper's New Monthly Magazine* 75 (July 1887): 259–66; reprinted in *Monopoly and Competition Policy*, ed. F.M. Scherer (Aldershot, Hants: Edward Elgar, 1993): 47–54.

166. Ely, *Ground Under Our Feet*, 126–7.

167. Francis Amasa Walker, "Recent Progress of Political Economy in the United States," *Publications of the American Economic Association* 4 (1889): 254. Cited in Furner, *Advocacy and Objectivity*, 254; and Fine, *Laissez Faire and the General-Welfare State*, 48.

168. Richard T. Ely, *Ground Under Our Feet*, 132–3.

169. Ibid., 136, 144.

170. See Ely, *Ground Under Our Feet*, 121ff.

171. Ibid., 140.

172. C. J. Bullock, "Trust Literature: A Survey and a Criticism," *Quarterly Journal of Economics*, Vol. 15 (February 1901), 206.

173. George J. Stigler, "Monopoly and Oligopoly by Merger," *American Economic Review* 40: 2 (May 1950), 30.

4. The Role of Finance

1. Hyman P. Minsky, *Unstabilizing an Unstable Economy* (New Haven: Yale University Press, 1986), 229.

2. Charles Calomiris, "Financial Factors in the Great Depression," *Journal of Economic Perspectives* 7: 2 (Spring 1993), 67.

3. Ben Bernanke, "Credit in the Macroeconomy," *Federal Reserve Bank of New York Quarterly Review* 18: 1 (Spring 1993), 50, 51.

4. Paul B. Trescott, *Financing American Enterprise: The Story of Commercial Banking* (New York: Harper and Row, 1963), 19.

5. Naomi Lamoreaux, "Banks, Kinship, and Economic Development: The New England Case," *Journal of Economic History* 46: 3 (September 1986), 647–67.

6. Amasa Walker, *The Nature and Uses of Money and Mixed Currency, with a History of the Wickaboag Bank* (New York: Greenwood Press, 1969), 10. Cited in Paul B. Trescott, *Financing American Enterprise: The Story of Commercial Banking* (New York: Harper and Row, 1963).

7. Vincent P. Carosso, *Investment Banking in America: A History* (Cambridge, MA: Harvard University Press, 1970), 10–20, and Gerald Berk, *Alternative Tracks: The Constitution of American Industrial Order, 1867–1917* (Baltimore: Johns Hopkins Press, 1994), 27–30.

8. John Murray Forbes, *Letters and Reflections of John Murray Forbes*, ed. S. Hughes (Boston: Massachusetts Historical Society, 1900); Stuart Bruchie, *The Wealth of the Nation: An Economic History of the United States* (New York: Harper & Row, 1988), 57; Alfred D. Chandler, Jr., *The Visible Hand: The Managerial Revolution in American Business* (Cambridge, MA: The Belknap Press, 1977), 183.

9. Chandler, *The Visible Hand.* 72.

10. Oscar Handlin and Mary Flug Handlin, *Commonwealth: A Study of the Role of Government in the American Economy: Massachusetts, 1774–1861* (Cambridge, MA: Harvard University Press, 1969), 126–28.

11. Charles P. Kindleberger, "Keynesian vs. Monetarism in Eighteenth- and Nineteenth-Century France," *History of Political Economy* 12: 4 (Winter 1980), 506.

12. John Jay Knox, *A History of Banking in the United States* (New York: Augustus M. Kelley, 1969).

13. Joan Robinson, *Economic Philosophy* (Garden City, NY: Anchor, 1964), 99–100.

14. Henrietta Larsen, *Jay Cooke, Private Banker* (Cambridge, MA: Harvard University Press, 1938), 125.

15. Michael A. Perelman, *The Pathology of the U.S. Economy: The Costs of a Low Wage System* (London: Macmillan, 1993).

16. Ben Baack and Edward Ray, "The Political Economy of the Origins of the Military-Industrial Complex in the United States," *The Journal of Economic History* 45: 2 (June 1985), 369–75, and Bruce G. Brunton,. "Institutional Origins of the Military-Industrial Complex," *Journal of Economic Issues* 22: 2 (June 1988), 599–606.

17. Cited in William Appleton Williams, *The Contours of American History* (New York: World, 1961), 346.

18. G. N. von Tunzelmann, *Technology and Industrial Progress: The Foundations of Economic Growth* (Aldershot, UK: Edward Elgar, 1995), 213.

19.   Joseph F. Wall, *The World of Andrew Carnegie 1865–1901* (New York: Oxford University Press, 1970), 322.

20.   Louis M. Hacker, *The World of Andrew Carnegie: 1865–1901* (New York: Lippincott, 1968), 356.

21.   John Maynard Keynes, *The General Theory of Employment, Interest and Money* (New York: Macmillan, 1936), 150.

22.   James Howard Bridge, *The History of the Carnegie Steel Company: The Inside History of the Carnegie Steel Company: A Romance of Millions* (New York: Arno Press, 1972), 85.

23.   Michael H. Best, *The New Competition: Institutions of Industrial Restructuring* (Cambridge, MA: Harvard University Press, 1990), 63.

24.   Chandler, *The Visible Hand*, 268.

25.   Thomas H. Johnson, "Towards a New Understanding of Nineteenth-Century Cost Accounting," *Accounting Review* 56: 3 (July 1981), 511.

26.   Hacker, *Andrew Carnegie*, 348.

27.   Thomas K. McCraw and Forest Reinhardt. "Losing to Win: U.S. Steel's Pricing, Investment Decisions, and Market Share, 1901–1938," *Journal of Economic History* 49: 3 (September 1989), 595.

28.   Johnson, "Nineteenth-Century Cost Accounting," 515.

29.   Mark Perlman, "Government Intervention and the Socioeconomic Background," in Bela Gold, William S. Peirce, Gerhard Rosegger, and Mark Perlman, eds., *Technological Progress and Industrial Leadership: The Growth of the U.S. Steel Industry, 1900–1970* (Lexington, MA: D. C. Heath, 1984), 611. See also Harold C. Livesay, *Andrew Carnegie and the Rise of Big Business* (Boston: Little, Brown, 1975), 116–117.

30.   62d Cong., 2d Sess. 1911–1912, Committee on Investigation of the United States Steel Corporation Hearings, cited in John M. Blair, *Economic Concentration: Structure, Behavior and Public Policy* (New York: Harcourt, Brace and Jovanovich, 1972), 261. See also William Harrison Spring Stevens, *Industrial Combinations and Trusts* (New York: Macmillan, 1922), 82–85.

31.   Kenneth Warren, *Big Steel: The First Century of the United States Steel Corporation* (Pittsburgh: University of Pittsburgh Press, 2001), 28.

32.   Ron Chernow, *The House of Morgan: An American Banking Dynasty and the Rise of Modern Finance* (New York: Atlantic Monthly Press, 1990), 54, 56.

33.   John Patterson Davis, *The Union Pacific Railway: A Study in Railway Politics* (Chicago: S. C. Griggs and Company, 1894).

34.   Chernow, *The House of Morgan*, 38.

35.   Ibid., 57.

36.   Ibid., 57, citing George Wheeler, *Pierpont Morgan and Friends: The Anatomy of a Myth* (Englewood Cliffs, NJ: Prentice-Hall, 1973), 180.

37.   Ibid., 67.

38.   McCraw and Reinhardt, "Losing to Win," *Journal of Economic History*, 593.

39.   J. Bradford DeLong, "American Finance—From Morgan to Milken," *The Wilson Quarterly* 16: 4 (Fall 1992), 17.

40.   J. Bradford DeLong, "Did J. P. Morgan's Men Add Value? A Historical Perspective on Financial Market Innovation," in Peter Temin, ed., *Getting Inside the Business Enterprise: The Use and Transformation of Information* (Chicago: University of Chicago Press, 1990), 205–236.

41.   Chernow, *The House of Morgan*, 67.

42.   George J. Stigler, "Monopoly and Oligopoly by Merger," *American Economic Review* 40: 2 (May 1950), 30–31.

43.   Chernow, *The House of Morgan*, 86.

44.   Ibid., 58.

45.   Ibid., 38.

46. DeLong, "Financial Market Innovation," *Getting Inside the Business Enterprise*, 205–236.

47. Charles Sabel, "Comments on DeLong," in Peter Temin, ed., *Inside the Business Enterprise: Historical Perspectives on the Use of Information* (Chicago: University of Chicago Press, 1991), 240.

48. DeLong, "Financial Market Innovation," *Getting Inside the Business Enterprise*, 205–236.

49. Ibid.

50. Sabel, "Comments on DeLong," *Inside the Business Enterprise*, 239.

51. Thorstein Veblen, *The Theory of Business Enterprise* (Clifton, NJ: Augustus M. Kelley, 1975), 259 and V. I. Lenin "The Threatening Catastrophe and How to Fight It," in *Collected Works*, Vol. 25 (New York: International Publishers, 1964).

52. Alfred S. Eichner, *The Emergence of Oligopoly: Sugar Refining as a Case Study* (Baltimore: Johns Hopkins Press, 1969), 110.

53. Jeremiah Jenks, *The Trust Problem* (New York: McLure, Phillips & Co, 1900), 24.

54. Chandler, *The Visible Hand*. See also Martin J. Sklar, *The Corporate Reconstruction of American Capitalism: 1890–1916* (Cambridge: Cambridge University Press, 1988), 163.

55. Cited in John A. Garraty, *Right-Hand Man: The Life of George W. Perkins* (New York: Harper and Brothers, 1957), 219.

56. Karl Marx, *Capital* (New York: International Publishers, 1967), 568–69.

57. C. J. Bullock, "Trust Literature: A Survey and a Criticism," *Quarterly Journal of Economics* 15 (February 1901), 167–217.

58. Naomi Lamoreaux, *The Great Merger Movement in American Business, 1895–1904* (New York: Cambridge University Press, 1985), and George Stigler, "The Dominant Firm and the Inverted Umbrella," in *The Organization of Industry* (Homewood, Ill.: Richard D. Irwin, 1968), 108–12.

59. Thomas Childs Cochran, *200 Years of American Business* (New York: Basic Books, 1977), 67 cited in Richard B. DuBoff and Edward S. Herman, "Alfred Chandler's New Business History: A Review," *Politics and Society*, 10:4, 100, reprinted in Barry E. Supple, ed., *The Rise of Big Business* (Aldershot, Hants: Edward Elgar, 1980), 300–26.

60. Donald O. Parsons and Edward John Ray, "The United States Steel Consolidation: The Creation of Market Control," *Journal of Law and Economics* 18: 1 (April 1975), 193.

61. McCraw and Reinhardt, "Losing to Win," 607, 595.

62. Chandler, *The Visible Hand*, 361.

63. Parsons and Ray, "The United States Steel Consolidation," *Journal of Law and Economics* 215.

64. McCraw and Reinhardt, "Losing to Win," 596–97.

65. Lamoreaux, *The Great Merger Movement*, 69 ff.

66. Andrew Carnegie, "The Bugaboo of the Trusts," *North American Review* 148:387 (1889), 142.

67. Andrew Carnegie, "Popular Illusions about the Trusts," *Century Magazine* 60 (1900), 88.

68. Ibid., 81–82.

69. Ibid., 89.

70. Ibid., 90.

71. Cited in Bullock, "Trust Literature," 199–200.

72. Derek Bok, *The Cost of Talent: How Executives and Professionals Are Paid and How It Affects America* (New York: Free Press, 1993), 33.

73. DuBoff and Herman, "Alfred Chandler's New Business History."

74. Ibid., 112.

75. Ibid., 112.

76. Ibid., 112, and Walter Adams and James W. Brock, *The Bigness Complex: Industry, Labor, and Government in the American Economy* (New York: Pantheon, 1986), 26.

5. Industry Takes Command: The Rise of Welfare Capitalism

1.   Ellis W. Hawley, "Three Facets of Hooverian Associationism: Lumber, Aviation, and Movies, 1921–1930," in Thomas K. McCraw, ed., *Regulation in Perspective: Historical Essays* (Cambridge, MA: Harvard University Press, 1981), 96–7.

2.   Martin J. Sklar, *The Corporate Reconstruction of American Capitalism: 1890–1916* (Cambridge, MA: Cambridge University Press, 1988).

3.   Hawley, "Hooverian Associationism," 98. See also Murray N. Rothbard, "War Collectivism in World War I," in Ronald Radosh and Murray N. Rothbard, eds., *A New History of Leviathan: Essays on the Rise of the American Corporate State* (New York: E. P. Dutton, 1972).

4.   Robert Sobel, *The Big Board: A History of the New York Stock Market* (New York: The Free Press, 1965).

5.   Bernard M. Baruch, *American Industry in the War: A Report of the War Industries Board* (New York: Prentice-Hall, 1941), 105.

6.   Hawley, "Hooverian Associationanism," 99.

7.   Rothbard, "War Collectivism."

8.   John Kenneth Galbraith, *A Life in Our Times* (Boston: Houghton Mifflin, 1981), 30.

9.   Rothbard, "War Collectivism," 70.

10. Grosvernor B. Clarkson, *Industrial America in the World War* (Boston: Houghton Mifflin, 1923). Cited in Rothbard, "War Collectivism," 75–6.

11. Hawley, "Hooverian Associationism," 99.

12. Cited in Joan Hoff Wilson, *Herbert Hoover, Forgotten Progressive* (Boston: Little, Brown, 1975), 43.

13. Herbert Hoover, *American Individualism* (Garden City: Doubleday, Page & Company, 1922), 44.

14. Eric Goldman, *Rendezvous with Destiny: A History of Modern American Reform* (New York: Knopf, 1955), 237.

15. David Brody, *Workers in Industrial America: Essays on the Twentieth Century Struggle* (New York: Oxford University Press, 1993), 49.

16. Richard Edwards, *Contested Terrain: The Transformation of the Workplace in the Twentieth Century* (New York: Basic Books, 1979), 90–5.

17. Charles E. Harvey, "John D. Rockefeller, Jr., Herbert Hoover, and President Wilson's Industrial Conferences of 1919–1920," in Jerold E. Brown and Patrick D. Reagen, eds., *Volunteerism, Planning, and the State: The American Planning Experience, 1914–1946* (Westport, CT: Greenwood Press, 1988), 35.

18. Ibid.

19. Ibid.

20. Sumner H. Slichter, "The Current Labor Policies of American Industries," *Quarterly Journal of Economics* 42 (May 1929), 420.

21. David M. Gordon, Richard Edwards, and Michael Reich, *Segmented Work, Divided Workers: The Historical Transformation of Labor in the United States* (Cambridge: Cambridge University Press, 1982), 141, citing United States Immigration Commission, *Abstracts of Reports of the Immigration Commission* Vol. 1 (Washington, D.C.: U.S.G.P.O, 1911), 531.

22. William Morris Leiserson, *Adjusting Immigrant and Industry* (Montclair, N.J.: Patterson Smith, 1971), 92.

23. James Howard Bridge, *The History of the Carnegie Steel Company: The Inside History of the Carnegie Steel Company: A Romance of Millions* (New York: Arno Press, 1972), 81.

24. Arthur Ross, "Do We Have a New Industrial Feudalism?" *American Economic Review* 48: 5 (December 1958), 913–4.

25. David Montgomery, *The Fall of the House of Labor: The Workplace, the State, and American Labor Activism, 1865–1925* (Cambridge: Cambridge University Press, 1987).

26. Leiserson, *Adjusting Immigrant and Industry*, 106.

27. Sumner H. Slichter, *The Turnover of Factory Labor* (New York: D. Appleton, 1919), 266.

28. Daniel M. G. Raff and Lawrence H. Summers, "Did Henry Ford Pay Efficiency Wages?" *Journal of Labor Economics* 5: 4 (October 1987), S63–4.

29. Keith Sward, *The Legend of Henry Ford* (New York: Atheneum, 1972), 48–9.

30. Stephen Meyer, *The Five Dollar Day: Labor Management and Social Control in the Ford Motor Company, 1908–1921* (Albany: State University of New York Press, 1981).

31. Sward, *The Legend of Henry Ford*, 51.

32. Henry Ford, *My Life and Work* (New York, 1922), 126–7 and 147. Cited in Raff and Summers, "Did Henry Ford Pay Efficiency Wages?" S59.

33. Slichter, *Turnover of Factory Labor*, 243–4.

34. Ibid., 266.

35. R. Conot, *American Odyssey* (New York: Morrow, 1974), 175.

36. James J. Flink, *The Car Culture* (Cambridge, MA: MIT Press, 1975), 89. See also Sward, *The Legend of Henry Ford*, 228–9, and Harvey, "Rockefeller, Hoover and Wilson's Industrial Conference," 277.

37. Raff and Summers, "Did Henry Ford Pay Efficiency Wages?" S69.

38. Conot, *American Odyssey*, 175–6.

39. Ibid., 175.

40. Sward, *Legend of Henry Ford*, 228–9.

41. Horace L. Arnold and Fay L. Faurote, *Ford Methods and Ford Shops* (New York: The Engineering Magazine Company, 1919). Cited in Montgomery, *The Fall of the House of Labor*, 234.

42. Raff and Summers, "Did Henry Ford Pay Efficiency Wages?" S81.

43. Brody, *Workers in Industrial America*, 52–3; Ross, "New Industrial Feudalism?" 903.

44. Slichter, "The Current Labor Policies," 395.

45. Montgomery, *Fall of the House of Labor*, 6.

46. Slichter, "The Current Labor Policies," 420.

47. Ibid., 395.

48. George Soule, *Prosperity Decade: From War to Depression 1917–1929* (New York: Rinehart, 1947), 187.

49. Montgomery, *Fall of the House of Labor*, 6.

50. Slichter, "The Current Labor Policies," 394.

51. Lizabeth Cohen, *Making a New Deal: Industrial Workers in Chicago, 1919–1939* (Cambridge: Cambridge University Press, 1990), 163.

52. Soule, *Prosperity Decade*, 209.

53. Montgomery, *Fall of the House of Labor*, 243.

54. H. T. Oshima, "The Growth of U.S. Factor Productivity: The Significance of New Technologies in the Early Decades of the Twentieth Century," *Journal of Economic History* 44: 1 (March 1984), 163.

55. Don Divance Lescohier, *The Labor Market* (New York: Macmillan, 1919). Cited in Montgomery, *Fall of the House of Labor*, 236.

56. Cohen, *Making a New Deal*, 12 and 160.

57. Ibid., 165.

58. Ibid.

59. Leiserson, *Adjusting Immigrant and Industry*, 106.

60. Ibid., 55.

61. Slichter, "The Current Labor Policies," 401.

62. Leiserson, *Adjusting Immigrant and Industry*, 105.

63. Slichter, "The Current Labor Policies," 393.

64. Cohen, *Making a New Deal*, 160.

65. Ross, "New Industrial Feudalism?"

66. Slichter, "The Current Labor Policies," 432–3.

67. Brody, *Workers in Industrial America*, 51.

68. Cited in William J. Barber, *From New Era to New Deal: Herbert Hoover, the Economists, and American Economic Policy, 1921–1933* (Cambridge: Cambridge University Press, 1985), 30.

69. Irving Bernstein, *The Lean Years: A History of the American Worker, 1920–1933* (Boston: Houghton Mifflin, 1966), 51–2.

70. Cited in Michael Hudson, *Economics and Technology in 19th Century American Thought: The Neglected American Economists* (New York: Garland, 1975), 275.

71. John Stuart Mill, *Principles of Political Economy with Some of Their Applications to Social Philosophy* (Toronto: University of Toronto Press, 1965), 415 f.

72. Ray Petrides, "Brassey's Law and the Economy of High Wages in 19th Century Economics," *Murdoch University (Australia) Working Paper* No. 94 (June 1993).

73. Michael A. Perelman, *The Natural Instability of Markets: Expectations, Increasing Returns and the Collapse of Markets* (New York: St. Martin's Press, 1999), 129–31.

74. Henry Ludwell Moore, *Laws of Wages: An Essay in Statistical Economics* (New York: Augustus M. Kelley, 1967).

75. George J. Stigler, "Information in the Labor Market," *Journal of Political Economy* 70: 3 (October 1962), 94–105.

76. Edwards, *Contested Terrain*, 96.

77. Michael Huberman, "How Did Labor Markets Work in Lancashire: More Evidence on Prices and Quantities in Cotton Spinning, 1822–1852," *Explorations in Economic History* 28: 1 (January 1991), 87–120.

78. Christopher Hanes, "The Development of Nominal Wage Rigidity in the Late 19th Century," *American Economic Review* 83: 4 (September 1993), 751.

79. Ibid., 746, citing Robert Ozanne, *Wages in Practice and Theory: McCormick and International Harvester* (Madison: University of Wisconsin Press, 1968), 92–3.

80. Hanes, "Nominal Wage Rigidity," 746, citing Ozanne, *Wages in Practice and Theory*, 239.

81. Herbert Hoover, *American Individualism* (Garden City: Doubleday, Page & Company, 1922), 40.

82. Cohen, *Making a New Deal*, 161.

83. Brody, *Workers in Industrial America*, 48.

84. John Maynard Keynes, "The End of Laissez-Faire," in *Essays in Persuasion: The Collected Works of John Maynard Keynes*, ed. Donald Moggridge (London: Macmillan, 1972).

85. Roland Marchand, "The Corporation Nobody Knew: Bruce Barton, Alfred Sloan, and the Founding of the General Motors 'Family'," *Business History Review* 65: 4 (Winter 1991), 825–75.

86. Cohen, *Making a New Deal*, 160.

87. Thomas Childs Cochran, *The American Business System: A Historical Perspective, 1900–1955* (Cambridge: Cambridge University Press 1957), 140. Cited in Elizabeth A. Fones-Wolf, *Selling Free Enterprise: The Business Assault on Labor and Liberalism, 1945–1960* (Urbana: University of Illinois Press, 1994), 17.

88. Cohen, *Making a New Deal*, 181, citing "Business Trends toward Self-Government; Secretary Hoover Addresses National Chamber on Signs of Capacity of Commerce and Industry to Correct Own Abuses," *Chicago Commerce* 21 (10 May 1924), 19–20.

89. Hawley, "Hooverian Associationism" and Ellis W. Hawley, "Herbert Hoover and the Sherman Act: 1921–1933: An Early Phase of a Continuing Issue," *Iowa Law Review* Vol. 74 (1989), 1067–1103.

90. Hawley, "Herbert Hoover and the Sherman Act," 1072.

91. Thomas Nixon Carver, *The Present Economic Revolution in the United States* (Boston: Little, Brown, 1925), 261–2. Cited in Barber, *From New Era to New Deal*, 30.

92. Slichter, "The Current Labor Policies," 426.

93. Frederick C. Mills, *Economic Tendencies in the United States: Aspects of Pre-War and Post-War Changes* (New York: National Bureau of Economic Research Publications, 1932), 461.

94. Paul David, "Computer and Dynamo: The Modern Productivity Paradox in a Not-Too-Distant Mirror," *American Economic Review* 80: 2 (May 1990), 355–61.

95. David Weintraub, "The Displacement of Workers through Increase in Efficiency and Their Absorption by Industry, 1920–31," *Journal of the American Statistical Association* (December 1932), 383–400. Harry Jerome, *Mechanization in Industry* (New York: National Bureau of Economic Research, 1934), 5. See also Gerard Dumenil, Mark Glick, and Jose Rangel, "Theories of the Great Depression: Why Did Profitability Matter?" *Review of Radical Political Economy* 19: 2 (Summer 1987), 16–42.

96. Committee on Recent Economic Changes, *Recent Economic Changes in the United States: Report of the Committee on Recent Economic Changes of the President's Conference on Unemployment* (New York: McGraw-Hill, 1929), xv.

97. Slichter, "The Current Labor Policies," 428.

98. Oshima, "Growth of U.S. Factor Productivity," 186.

99. Ibid., 164.

100. Selma Goldsmith, George Jaszi, Hyman Kaitz, and Maurice Liebenberg, "Size Distribution of Income since the Mid-Thirties," *Review of Economics and Statistics* 36: 1 (February 1954), 16.

101. Ibid., 17.

102. Oshima, "Growth of U.S. Factor Productivity," 163.

103. Martha L. Olney, "Demand for Consumer Durable Goods in 20th Century America," *Explorations in Economic History* 27: 3 (July 1990), 322–49.

6. Modern Finance Capital

1. George Soule, *Prosperity Decade: From War to Depression 1917–1929* (New York: Rinehart, 1947), 284.

2. Ibid., 284.

3. Henrietta Larsen, *Jay Cooke, Private Banker* (Cambridge, MA: Harvard University Press, 1938), 120.

4. J. Bradford DeLong, "Did J. P. Morgan's Men Add Value? An Historical Perspective on Financial Market Innovation," in Peter Temin, ed., *Getting Inside the Business Enterprise: The Use and Transformation of Information* (Chicago: University of Chicago Press, 1991), 231.

5. George W. Edwards, *Evolution of Finance Capitalism* (London: Longmans, Green and Co, 1938), 288.

6. Ibid., 288.

7. Robert Sobel, *The Big Board: A History of the New York Stock Market* (New York: The Free Press, 1965), 237.

8. Ibid., 237.

9. Harold James, "Financial Flows across Frontiers during the Interwar Depression," *Economic History Review* 45: 3 (August 1992), 598.

10. Edwards, *Evolution of Finance Capitalism*, 231.

11. David Kotz, *Bank Control of Large Corporations in the United States* (Berkeley: University of California Press, 1978), 42.

12. Eugene White, "Banking Innovation in the 1920's: The Growth of National Banks' Financial Services," *Business and Economic History*, Vol. 13 (1984), 102. Cited in Randall Kroszner and Raghuram G. Rajan, "Is the Glass-Steagall Act Justified? A Study of the U.S. Experience with Universal Banking Before 1933," *American Economic Review* 84: 4 (September 1994), 812.

13. Vincent P. Carosso, *Investment Banking in America: A History* (Cambridge, MA: Harvard University Press, 1970), 243.

14. Colin Gordon, *New Deals: Business, Labor, and Politics in America* (Cambridge: Cambridge University Press, 1994), 74.

15. John Kenneth Galbraith, *The Great Crash* (Boston: Houghton Mifflin, 1961), 36.

16. Sobel, *The Big Board*, 240.

17. Frederick Lewis Allen, *Only Yesterday: An Informal History of the Nineteen-Twenties* (New York: Blue Ribbon Books, 1931), 315–16.

18. Soule, *Prosperity Decade*, 300.

19. George Eddy, "Security Issues and Real Investment in 1929," *Review of Economics and Statistics* 19: 2 (May 1937), 86.

20. Ibid., 79, 84.

21. John Maynard Keynes, *The General Theory of Employment, Interest and Money* (New York: Macmillan, 1936), 159.

22. See William Zebina Ripley, *Main Street and Wall Street* (Boston: Little, Brown, and Company, 1932).

23. William Allen White, *A Puritan in Babylon: The Story of Calvin Coolidge* (New York: Macmillan, 1940), 337–8.

24. Robert Aaron Gordon, *Economic Instability and Growth: The American Record* (New York: Harper & Row, 1974), 25–7.

25. Robert J. Lampman, *The Share of Top Wealth-holders in National Wealth, 1922–56* (Princeton: Princeton University Press, 1962), 228.

26. Gordon, *New Deals*, 43.

27. Ibid., 42.

28. See Martha L. Olney, "Demand for Consumer Durable Goods in 20th Century America," *Explorations in Economic History* 27: 3 (July 1990), 322–49.

29. Hugh Johnson, *The Blue Eagle from Egg to Earth* (Garden City, 1935), 159. Cited in Gordon, *New Deals*, 36.

30. Cited in Gordon, *New Deals*, 36.

7. The Great Depression

1. Benjamin Kline Hunnicutt, "Kellogg's Six Hour Day: A Capitalist Vision of Liberation through Managed Leisure," *Business History Review* 66: 3 (Fall 1992), 479.

2. Lizabeth Cohen, *Making a New Deal: Industrial Workers in Chicago, 1919–1939* (Cambridge: Cambridge University Press, 1990), 238–40; David Brody, *Workers in Industrial America: Essays on the Twentieth-Century Struggle* (New York: Oxford University Press, 1993), 69; Ronald W. Schatz, *The Electrical Workers: A History of Labor at General Electric and Westinghouse, 1923–1960* (Urbana: University of Illinois Press, 1983), 60.

3. William Starr Myers and Walter H. Newton, *The Hoover Administration: A Documented Narrative* (New York: Charles Scribner, 1936), 26–7.

4. Richard K. Vedder and Lowell E. Galloway, *Out of Work: Unemployment and Government in 20th Century America* (New York: Holmes and Meier, 1993), 92.

5. "This Time They Did Not Cut Wages," *Business Week* (31 December 1929), 23–4.

6.   Vedder and Galloway, *Out of Work*, 92–4.

7.   Herbert Hoover, *The Memoirs of Herbert Hoover, The Great Depression, 1929–1941* (New York: Macmillan, 1952), 43.

8.   Ibid., 46.

9.   Richard J. Jensen, "The Causes and Cures of Unemployment in the Great Depression," *Journal of Interdisciplinary History* 19:4 (Spring 1989), 553–84; Anthony Patrick O'Brien, "A Behavioral Explanation for Nominal Wage Rigidity during the Great Depression," *Quarterly Journal of Economics* 104: 4 (November 1989), 719–36.

10. Jacob Viner, *Balanced Deflation, Inflation or More Depression* (Minneapolis: University of Minneapolis Press, 1933), 12. Cited in O'Brien, "Behavioral Explanation for Nominal Wage Rigidity," 724–5.

11. Schatz, *Electrical Workers,* 58.

12. Ibid., 59.

13. Ibid., 61.

14. Stanley Lebergott, " 'Wage Rigidity' in the Depression: Concept or Phrase?" photocopy (March 16, 1990).

15. Jensen, "Causes and Cures of Unemployment," 564.

16. Schatz, *Electrical Workers,* 59.

17. Gerald Epstein and Thomas Ferguson, "Monetary Policy, Loan Liquidation, and Industrial Conflict: The Federal Reserve and the Open Market Operations of 1932," *Journal of Economic History* 44: 4 (December 1984), 969.

18. Schatz, *Electrical Workers,* 53.

19. Brody, *Workers in Industrial America,* 70–1.

20. Ellis W. Hawley, "Herbert Hoover and the Sherman Act, 1921–1933," *Iowa Law Review*, vol. 74 (1989), 1092.

21. "U.S. Steel: The Corporation. Part 1," *Fortune* (March 1936), 170.

22. Ibid., 63.

23. Ibid., 170.

24. William Allen White, *A Puritan in Babylon: The Story of Calvin Coolidge* (New York: Macmillan, 1940), 335.

25. "U.S. Steel: The Corporation," 170, 173.

26. O'Brien, *Behavioral Explanation for Nominal Wage Rigidity.*

27. Cohen, *Making a New Deal,* 193–216.

28. Brody, *Workers in Industrial America,* 73.

29. James Devine, "Falling Profit Rates and the Causes of the 1929–33 Collapse: Toward a Synthesis," *Review of Radical Political Economics* 20: 2 & 3 (Summer and Fall 1988), 87–93.

30. Gardiner C. Means, "Simultaneous Inflation and Unemployment: A Challenge to Theory and Policy," *Challenge* 18:4 (September/October 1975). Reprinted from Gardiner Means et al., *The Roots of Inflation: The International Crisis* (New York: Burt Franklin, 1975), 10.

31. Jensen, "Causes and Cures of Unemployment," 564.

32. Herbert Clark Hoover, *Principles of Mining; Valuation, Organization, and Administration; Gold, Lead, Silver, Tin, and Zinc* (New York: McGraw-Hill, 1909).

33. Broadus Mitchell, *Depression Decade: From the New Era through the New Deal, 1929–1941* (New York: Rinehart, 1947), 86.

34. Cited in Joan Hoff Wilson, *Herbert Hoover, Forgotten Progressive* (Boston: Little, Brown, 1975), 37.

35. Lionel Danforth Edie, "Introduction" in Herbert Hoover, *The Stabilization of Business* (New York: Macmillan, 1973), v.

36. Herbert Hoover, "Foreword," Committee on Unemployment and Business Cycles, *Business Cycles and Unemployment* (New York: Arno Press, 1975), vi.

37. William Appleton Williams, *Some Presidents from Wilson to Nixon* (New York: Vintage, 1972).

38. Hoover, *Memoirs of Herbert Hoover*, 335.

39. Jonathan R. T. Hughes, *American Economic History* (Glenview, Ill.: Scott Foresman, 1987) 441.

40. W. Arthur Lewis, *Economic Survey, 1919-39* (London: Allen and Unwin, 1949), 19. Cited in Derek Aldcroft, *From Versailles to Wall Street, 1919-1929* (Berkeley: University of California Press, 1977), 66.

41. Cohen, *Making a New Deal*, 209.

42. Hunnicutt, "Kellogg's Six Hour Day," 496.

43. Harold G. Moulton, *Income and Economic Progress* (Washington, D.C.: The Brookings Institution, 1935), 45-6.

44. Gottfried Haberler, *Prosperity and Depression: A Theoretical Analysis* (Lake Success, NY: United Nations, 1946), 441.

45. Harold Hotelling, "The General Welfare in Relation to Problems of Taxation and of Railway and Utility Rates," *Econometrica* 6: 3 (July 1938), 266.

46. Ibid.

47. John Maynard Keynes, *The General Theory of Employment, Interest and Money* (New York: Macmillan, 1936).

48. James Tobin, *Asset Accumulation and Economic Activity: Reflections on Contemporary Economic Macroeconomic Theory* (Chicago: University of Chicago Press, 1980), 9 ff.

49. Ben S. Bernanke, "'Bankruptcy, Liquidity, and Recession'," *American Economic Review* 71: 2 (May 1981), 155-9; Ben S. Bernanke, "Nonmonetary Effects of the Financial Crisis in the Propagation of the Great Depression," *American Economic Review* 73: 3 (June 1983), 257-76; John Maynard Keynes, *A Treatise on Money*, in *The Collected Writings of John Maynard Keynes*, ed. Donald Moggridge (London: Macmillan, 1971), vol. vi, 344.

50. F. S. Mishkin, "What Depressed the Consumer? The Household Balance Sheet and the 1973-1975 Recession," *Brookings Papers on Economic Activity*, No. 1, 1977, 123-64; F. S. Mishkin, "The Household Balance Sheet and the Great Depression," *Journal of Economic History* 38: 4 (December 1978), 918-37. See also William P. Gramm, "The Real Balance Effect in the Great Depression," *Journal of Economic History* Vol. 32 (June-September 1972), 499-519.

51. Irving Fisher, "The Debt Deflation Theory of Great Depressions," *Econometrica* 1: 4 (October 1933), 337-57.

52. Joseph E. Stiglitz and Andrew Weiss, "Credit Rationing and Markets with Imperfect Information," *American Economic Review* 71: 3 (June 1981), 393-411.

53. Adam Smith, *The Nature and Causes of the Wealth of Nations* (Oxford: Oxford University Press, 1976), 357.

54. Helen Manning Hunter, "The Role of Business Liquidity During the Great Depression and Afterwards: Differences Between Large and Small Firms," *Journal of Economic History* 42: 4 (December 1982), 884.

55. Ibid.

56. Joseph A. Schumpeter, *The Theory of Economic Development* (Cambridge, MA: Harvard University Press, 1934), 126.

8. The Golden Age

1. Robert J. Gordon, "Postwar Macroeconomics: The Evolution of Events and Ideas," in Martin Feldstein, ed., *The American Economy in Transition: A Sixtieth Anniversary Conference* (Chicago: University of Chicago Press, 1980), 115.

2. Hans Staehle, "Technology, Utilization and Production," *Bulletin de l'Institut Internationale de Statistique* 34: 4 (1955), 27.

3. Ibid., 133.

4. Alexander J. Field, "The Most Technologically Progressive Decade of the Century," *American Economic Review* 93: 4 (September, 2003), 1399–413.

5. Harry Magdoff and Paul Sweezy, "International Finance and National Power," *Monthly Review* 35: 5 (October 1983), 9.

6. William Lazonick, "Controlling the Market for Corporate Control: The Historical Significance of Managerial Capitalism," *Industrial and Corporate Change* 1: 3 (1992), 458.

7. Paul M. Sweezy, "The Decline of the Investment Banker," *Antioch Review* 1: 1 (Spring 1941), 67; Paul M. Sweezy, *The Theory of Capitalist Development* (New York: Monthly Review, 1942).

8. Michael A. Perelman, *Keynes, Investment Theory and the Economic Slowdown: The Role of Replacement Investment and q-Ratios* (London: Macmillan, 1989).

9. Michael A. Bernstein, "American Economics and the National Security State, 1941–1953," *Radical History Review* 63 (Fall 1995), 8–26.

10. Robert Collins, *Business Response to Keynes, 1929–1964* (New York: Columbia University Press, 1981).

11. Herbert Stein, *The Fiscal Revolution in America* (Chicago: University of Chicago Press, 1969); Alfred C. Neal, *Business Power and Public Policy* (New York: Praeger, 1981), 15–22.

12. Stein, *Fiscal Revolution*, 363.

13. Joseph Garbarino, *Wage Policy and Long Term Contracts* (Washington, DC: The Brookings Institution, 1962), 415.

14. Walter Heller, *The New Dimensions of Political Economy* (New York: W. W. Norton, 1966), 9.

15. William Hollingsworth Whyte, *The Organization Man* (New York: Simon and Schuster, 1956).

16. Walter Adams and Joel B. Dirlin, "Steel Imports and Vertical Oligopoly Power," *American Economic Review* 54: 4 (September, 1964), 626–55; Walter Adams and Joel B. Dirlin, "Big Steel, Invention, and Innovation," *Quarterly Journal of Economics* 63: 2 (May 1966), 167–89; Sharon Oster, "The Diffusion of Innovation among Steel Firms: The Basic Oxygen Furnace," *The Bell Journal of Economics* 13: 1 (Spring 1982), 45–56; Donald F. Barnett and Louis Schorsch, *Steel: Upheaval in a Basic Industry* (Cambridge, MA: Ballinger, 1983).

17. Ira C. Magaziner and Robert B. Reich, *Minding America's Business: The Decline and Rise of the American Economy* (New York: Harcourt, Brace, Jovanovich, 1982), 155.

18. Ibid., 162.

19. Lazonick, "Controlling the Market," 453, citing Raymond W. Goldsmith, *Financial Intermediaries in the American Economy since 1900* (Princeton: Princeton University Press, 1958), 224–5.

20. Lazonick, "Controlling the Market," 474.

21. Lazonick, "Controlling the Market," citing Wilbur Lewellen, *Executive Compensation in Large Industrial Corporations* (New York: National Bureau of Economic Research, 1968), 172–3.

22. Abraham J. Briloff, *More Debits than Credits: The Burnt Investor's Guide to Financial Statements* (New York: Harper & Row, 1976); Abraham J. Briloff, *The Truth about Corporate Accounting* (New York: Harper & Row, 1978).

23. David Ravenscraft and F. M. Scherer, *Mergers, Sell-Offs and Economic Efficiency* (Washington, D.C.: Brookings Institution, 1987), 190.

24. Cited in Harry Magdoff and Paul Sweezy, "The Strange Recovery of 1983–1984," *Monthly Review* 37: 5 (October 1985), 11.

25. Connie Bruck, *The Predators' Ball: The Inside Story of Drexel Burnham and the Rise of the Junk Bond Traders* (New York: Penguin, 1989).

26. Hal R. Varian, "Symposium on Takeovers," *Journal of Economic Perspectives* 2: 1 (Winter 1988), 3.

27. Allan Sloan, "Why Is No One Safe?" *Forbes* (11 March 1985).

28. Joseph A. Schumpeter, "The Economic Interpretation of Our Time," in *The Economics and Sociology of Capitalism*, ed. Richard Swedberg (Princeton: Princeton University Press, 1991), 339–400.

29. Schumpeter, *Capitalism, Socialism and Democracy*, 82.

30. John Kenneth Galbraith, *The Great Crash* (Boston: Houghton Mifflin, 1961), 73–4.

31. Robert H. Hayes and William J. Abernathy, "Managing Our Way to Economic Decline," *Harvard Business Review* (July/August 1980), 66–77.

32. Leslie Wayne, "Management Gospel Gone Wrong," *New York Times* (30 May 1982), 1.

33. Hayes and Abernathy, "Managing Our Way," 75.

34. Ibid., 68.

35. Derek Bok, *The Cost of Talent: How Executives and Professionals Are Paid and How It Affects America* (New York: Free Press, 1993), 33, 102.

36. Wayne, "Management Gospel Gone Wrong."

37. Michael Jensen and William Meckling, "Theory of the Firm: Managerial Behavior, Agency Costs, and Ownership Structure," *The Journal of Financial Economics* 3 (1976), 305–66.

38. Michael C. Jensen, "Agency Costs of Free Cash Flow, Corporate Finance, and Takeovers," *American Economic Review* 76: 2 (May 1986), 323, citing Gordon Donaldson, *Managing Corporate Wealth* (New York: Praeger), 3.

39. Donaldson, *Managing Corporate Wealth*, 27.

40. Michael Jensen and Richard S. Ruback, "The Market for Corporate Control," *Journal of Financial Economics* Vol. 11 (April 1983), 5–50.

41. Michael C. Jensen, "Takeovers: Their Causes and Consequences," *Journal of Economic Perspectives* 2: 1 (Winter 1988), 30.

42. Jensen, *Agency Costs*, 323.

43. Richard B. DuBoff and Edward S. Herman, "The Promotional-Dynamic of Merger Movement: A Historical Perspective," *Journal of Economic Issues* 23: 1 (March 1989), 123.

44. "For 4 Days' Work, $126,582 an Hour," *Wall Street Journal,* 17 January 1983.

45. Bryan Burrough and John Helyar, *Barbarians at the Gate: The Fall of RJR Nabisco* (New York: Harper and Row, 1990), 510. Cited in Bok, *The Cost of Talent*, 99.

46. DuBoff and Herman, "Promotional-Dynamic of Merger Movement," 123, citing Stephen Labaton, "200 Million in Wall St. Fees Seen from Federated Deal," *New York Times*, 5 April 1988.

47. Patricia Bellew Gray, "Parties, Polls and Pejoratives: Lawyers Meet," *Wall Street Journal*, 13 August 1986.

48. Stephen J. Adler and Laurie P. Cohen, "Even Lawyers Gasp Over the Stiff Fees of Wachtell Lipton: Firm's $20 Million Bill to Kraft for Two Weeks of Work Sets New Legal Standard," *Wall Street Journal*, 2 November 1988.

49. James B. Stewart, *Den of Thieves* (New York: Simon and Schuster, 1991), 208.

50. Alan Abelson, "The Rise and Fall of the King of Junk," *Barrons*, 3 April 1989.

51. Bok, *The Cost of Talent*, 33.

52. Michael Lewis, *Liar's Poker: Rising through the Wreckage on Wall Street* (New York: W. W. Norton, 1989), 24.

53. Kevin M. Murphy, Andrei Shleifer, and Robert Vishny, "The Allocations of Talent: Implications for Growth," *Quarterly Journal of Economic* 106: 2 (May 1991), 503–30.

54. David M. Cutler and Lawrence H. Summers, "The Costs of Conflict Resolution and Financial Distress: Evidence from the Texaco-Penzoil Litigation," *Rand Journal of Economics* 19: 2 (Summer 1988), 157–72.

55. Jensen, "Takeovers: Their Causes and Consequences," 33.

56. Ibid., 30.

57. Amitai Etzioni, *The Moral Dimension: Toward a New Economics* (New York: The Free Press, 1988), 73.

58. Allanna Sullivan, "Stretched Thin: Exxon's Restructuring in the Past Is Blamed for Recent Accidents," *Wall Street Journal*, 16 March 1990.

59. Chris Welles, "Exxon's Future: What Has Larry Rawl Wrought," *Business Week*, 2 April 1990.

60. Ibid.

61. Nomi Prins, *Other People's Money: The Corporate Mugging of America* (New York: New Press, 204).

62. Michael C. Jensen, "How Stock Options Reward Managers for Destroying Value and What to Do About It," *Harvard NOM Working Paper* No. 04-27, 2001. http://papers. ssrn.com/sol3/papers. cfm?abstract_id=480401#PaperDownload.

63. Joseph Fuller and Michael C. Jensen, "Just Say No to Wall Street," *Journal of Applied Corporate Finance* 14: 4 (Winter 2002), 41–46.

64. Michael C. Jensen, "Paying People to Lie: The Truth about the Budgeting Process," *European Financial Management*, Vol. 9 (September 2003), 379–46. See also fuller discussion in Roger Lowenstein, *Origins of the Crash: The Great Bubble and Its Undoing* (New York: Penguin, 2005), 69, 198.

65. Ed Bloch, "Trade and Unemployment: Global Bread-and-Butter Issues," *Monthly Review* 35: 5 (October 1983), 30.

66. David Morse, "The Campaign to Save Dorothy Six," *The Nation* (7 September 1985), 175.

67. Barry Bluestone and Bennett Harrison, *The Deindustrialization of America: Plant Closings, Community Abandonment, and the Dismantling of Basic Industry* (New York: Basic Books, 1982), 151.

68. Ibid., 151.

69. Michael L. Dertouzos, Richard K. Lester, Robert M. Solow, and the MIT Commission on Industrial Productivity, *Made in America: Regaining the Productive Edge* (Cambridge, MA: The MIT Press, 1989), 31.

70. Karen Pennar, "Slash-and-Burn Cost-Cutting Could Singe the Recovery," *Business Week*, 6 May 1991.

71. George Anders, "DuPont Deal Puts a Strain on Agent Bank," *Wall Street Journal*, 25 August 1981.

72. Fred Moseley, *The Falling Rate of Profit in the Postwar United States Economy* (New York: St. Martin's Press, 1991).

73. Fred Moseley, "The Increase of Unproductive Labor in the Postwar U.S. Economy," *Review of Radical Political Economics* 20: 2 & 3 (Summer and Fall 1988), 100–6. See also Edward N. Wolff, *Growth, Accumulation, and Unproductive Activity: An Analysis of the Postwar U.S. Economy* (Cambridge: Cambridge University Press, 1987).

74. Michael Dawson and John Bellamy Foster, "The Tendency for the Surplus to Rise, 1963–88," *Monthly Review* 43: 4 (September 1991), 37–50.

75. Moseley, "Increase of Unproductive Labor." See also Moseley, *The Falling Rate of Profit*, 113.

76. Moseley, *The Falling Rate of Profit*, 121.

77. Christopher J. Niggle, "The Increasing Importance of Financial Capital in the U.S. Economy," *Journal of Economic Issues* 22: 2 (June 1988), 585.

78. Ibid.

79. Prins, *Other People's Money*.

80. Niggle, "Increasing Importance of Financial Capital."

81. President of the United States, *Economic Report of the President* (Washington, D.C.: U.S. Government Printing Office, 2004), 300, Table B-12.

82. Lawrence H. Summers and Victoria P. Summers, "When Financial Markets Work too Well: A Cautious Case for a Securities Transactions Tax," *Journal of Financial Services Research* 3: 2 and 3 (December 1989), 261–86.

83. Bank for International Settlements, *Triennial Central Bank Survey* (March 2005), 1. http://www.bis.org/publ/rpfx02t.pdf.

84. Ibid., 5.

85. George Anders, "Captive Client: Morgan Stanley Found a Gold Mine of Fees by Buying Burlington," *Wall Street Journal*, 14 December 1990.

86. Board of Governors of the Federal Reserve System, *Flow of Funds Accounts of the United States — Z.1.* (2005), 13, Table F7. http://www.federalreserve.gov/releases/z1.

87. David Henry, "Corporate America's New Achilles' Heel," *Business Week*, 28 March 2005.

9. Conclusion

1. Lester G. Telser, *A Theory of Efficient Cooperation and Competition* (Cambridge: Cambridge University Press, 1987), 6–7.

2. Michael A. Perelman, *Keynes, Investment Theory and the Economic Slowdown: The Role of Replacement Investment and q-Ratios* (London: Macmillan, 1989).

3. Michael A. Perelman, *The Invention of Capitalism: The Secret History of Primitive Accumulation* (Durham: Duke University Press, 2000).

Index